Manly Leaders in Nine___
British Literature

SUNY series, Studies in the Long Nineteenth Century
Pamela K. Gilbert, editor

Manly Leaders in Nineteenth-Century British Literature

Daniela Garofalo

State University of New York Press

Cover image: *Napoleon on Board the Bellerophon* by Sir William Orchardson (1880). Oil on canvas. © Tate Gallery, London/Art Resources NY.

Published by
State University of New York Press, Albany

© 2008 State University of New York

For information, contact State University of New York Press, Albany, NY
www.sunypress.edu

Production by Judith Block and Eileen Meehan
Marketing by Fran Keneston

Library of Congress Cataloging-in-Publication Data

Garofalo, Daniela, 1968 –
    Manly leaders in nineteenth-century British literature / Daniela Garofalo.
        p. cm. — (SUNY series, studies in the long nineteenth century)
    Includes bibliographical references and index.
    ISBN 978–0–7914–7357–3 (hardcover : alk. paper)

    1. English literature—19th century—History and criticism. 2. Masculinity in literature. 3. Men in literature. 4. Leadership in literature. 5. Sex role in literature. I. Title.

    PR468.M38G37 2007
    820.9′353—dc22

                                                            2007024994

10 9 8 7 6 5 4 3 2 1

Contents

Acknowledgments

This book could not have come together without the support, wisdom, and generosity of many teachers, colleagues, and friends. My greatest thanks to Orrin Wang whose insightful reading and theoretical sophistication provided invaluable guidance from the inception of *Manly Leaders*. I wish to thank my other teachers at the University of Maryland, Neil Fraistat, William Cohen, and Marshall Grossman who helped make this a better book. Geoffrey Schramm has been a constant source of encouragement and critical insight. I also owe Joel Faflak a debt of gratitude for supporting this book. The anonymous readers for SUNY Press, who offered wonderful responses, helped clarify and tighten the arguments in *Manly Leaders*.

My colleagues at the University of Oklahoma offered great intellectual support. A special thanks to Daniel Cottom and Ronald Schleifer who helped see me through the process of turning a dissertation into a book. I am grateful also for the insights and kindness of my colleagues Chris Carter, Yianna Liatsos, Kenneth Hodges, and Su Fang Ng. I completed the book with the help of two junior faculty fellowships at the University of Oklahoma.

Finally, thanks to my family, to whom I owe more than I can say, my partner, Riad Hajjnajeeb; my mother and best friend, Fern Garofalo; and my friends, fellow scholars, and siblings, David Garofalo and Micaela Garofalo-Saffire.

An earlier version of chapter 3 appeared as "Political Seductions: The Show of War in Byron's *Sardanapalus*" in *Criticism* 44:1, © 2002, reprinted with the permission of Wayne State University Press. Chapter 5 first appeared as "Communities in Mourning: Making Capital out of Loss in Carlyle' *Past and Present* and *Heroes*," in *Texas Studies in Literature and Language* 45:3, © 2003 by the University of Texas Press; all rights reserved. A part of chapter 2 appeared as "'A Left-Handed Way': Modern Masters in William Godwin's *Caleb Williams*" in *European Romantic Review* 17:2, © 2006.

Chapter 1

Introduction

Fantasies of National Virility and William Wordsworth's Poet Leader

Violent Warriors and Benevolent Leaders: Masculinity in the Early Nineteenth-Century

*I*n 1822 British women committed a public act against propriety. They commissioned a statue in honor of Lord Wellington, whose prowess was represented by Achilles, shield held aloft, nude in full muscular glory. Known as the "Ladies' 'Fancy Man,'" however, the statue shocked men on the statue committee who demanded a fig leaf to protect the public's outraged sensibilities.[1] Linda Colley points to this comical moment in postwar British history as a sign of "the often blatantly sexual fantasies that gathered around warriors such as Nelson and Wellington."[2]

However, the statue in its imitation of a classical aesthetic necessarily recalled not only the thrilling glory of Great Britain's military might, but also the appeal of the defeated but still fascinating Napoleon. After all, the classical aesthetic was central to the public representation of the Revolutionary and Napoleonic regimes. If a classical statue was supposed to apotheosize Wellington, it also inevitably spoke to a revolutionary and martial manhood associated with the recently defeated enemy. Napoleon himself had commissioned a nude classical statue from Canova that Marie Busco speculates "would have been known" to Sir Richard Westmacott, who cast the bronze Achilles. In fact Canova's *Napoleon* was conveniently located in the stairwell of Apsley House after Louis XVIII presented it to the Duke of Wellington.[3]

These associations with Napoleon might simply have underscored the British superiority the Wellington statue suggested. However, the problem of public representation was a delicate business. The subscription committee, run by elite women such as the Duchess of York, intended the statue to be "symbolic of 'the Triumph of Skill and Valour over Force'" (920). The point from the beginning, then, was not to suggest that the British were better than the French at their own game. Rather, the French, associated with war and violence, were different from the English, whose skill and valor were the opposite of French brutality. However, the incorporation of French brass (the statue "was composed primarily of twelve twenty-four pound French cannons captured during Wellington's victorious campaigns," [921]) the use of the classical model (for which the British public was unprepared,) and the choice of Achilles, the martial figure par excellence, suggest a confusion about representational intentions and effects.

The cartoon "Making Decent" by George Cruikshank (see Figure 1) underscores the impropriety of the statue. It represents an outraged William Wilberforce. Known for his abolitionist campaign, he was also the founder of the Society for the Reformation of Manners (923). In this role, he is drawn standing by the statue, covering its fig leaf with his hat. The actual stone inscription under the statue reproduced in the cartoon reads, "To Arthur Duke of Wellington and his Brave companions in arms. This Statue of Achilles cast in French Brass is inscribed by their Countrywomen!! June 18th 1822." The inscription speaks to the double nature of the statue. As it commemorates British victory, the statue cast in French brass suggests that it is also made of Greek form and Gallic stuff and, consequently, may not be as wholly British as patriots might wish. The caption in the cartoon reads, "Making Decent__!! __ This Print Commemorative of Anglo French Brass & True British *Chastity* is inscribed with veneration to that worthy man Mr. Wilberforce who with saintlike regard for the morals of the country has undertaken to make the above fig Decent from 10 in the M.g till Dusk." Implying that brass is the phallic stuff of both nations but chastity is specifically British, the cartoon suggests a certain British shame about exposure that speaks not only to sexual shame, but also to an embarrassment about the overtly masculine and martial power of the statue.

During the extended war with France, as Colley and others have made clear, Britons attempted to define themselves in difference from martial France to propose a specifically British culture of moderation and freedom. Violence and aggression were French characteristics. Britons often imagined themselves as a peaceful, commercial people, slow to anger but resolute and prepared for defense when threatened. However, because the statue suggested certain similarities between the two nations, it spoke to an embarrassing British pleasure in martial aggression. The reference to Achilles, the most arrogant and aggressive of Homeric heroes, the colonizing aggressor of a besieged city, underscores the Napoleonlike qualities of

To ARTHUR DUKE of WELLINGTON
And his Brave companions in arms
This Statue of Achilles
cast in French Brass
Is inscribed by their Countrywomen!!
June 18th 1822
Making Decent—!!
Pub^d by G Humphrey 27 St James's St London
August 8th 1822
This Print Commemorative of Anglo French BRASS & true British Chastity, is inscribed with veneration to that worthy man
Mr Wilberforce who with saintlike regard for the Morals of his Country, has undertaken to make the above fig Decent, from 10 in the Mg till Dusk

Figure 1. "Making Decent," (1822) by George Cruikshank. Courtesy of the British Museum. © The Trustees of the British Museum.

Wellington. It furthermore suggests that women, who presumably uphold the tender virtues of the nation, who, unlike French women, remained true to their womanly nature, betrayed in this incident a Gallic quality unbecoming British womanhood.

The cartoons that ridiculed the monument suggest a further dimension to the scandal of the Hyde Park Achilles. Although the actual statue was cast with a clenched fist in which Westmacott planned to place a sword, the fist remained empty until about 1865.[4] The cartoons of the time, however, all represent the statue holding a sword aggressively held aloft. With a sword, the Achilles is an unmistakably virile and phallic figure who, in the humorous representations of the cartoons, draws women in crowds. One cartoon, representing women congregating under the gigantic fig leaf, offers the caption: "Ladies BUY your LEAF!!" Without the sword, however, the actual statue remained more ambiguous, reminding some of a "prizefighter." For others, the "Achilles looked as if he were running away from a foe" (923). Too martial or too feminized, the statue never succeeded in persuading the immediate post-Waterloo audience of its patriotic power. Like the statue itself, these reactions speak to a larger problem of representation, which is the subject of this book.

Fearful that the nation had become effeminate due to an expanding commercial economy, virile men who promised to empower the nation and the empire fascinated nineteenth-century Britons. However, overt representations of martial and imperialist virility disturbed them, and they preferred to represent successful British leaders as tempered by gentleness, benevolence, and liberality. This fascination with British leaders who both promise and restrain power speaks to a crisis of authority after the French Revolution in a nation that imagined itself to be the most liberal nation in the world but that also feared the radical democratic potential of the French Revolution. With its overthrow of traditional hierarchy, its reliance on paper money over the gold standard, and its emphasis on financial speculation rather than on landed wealth, the Revolutionary government seemed to embody all the fears many Britons associated with modernization. Napoleon's regime added new fears: tyranny, unlicensed imperial expansion, and a military state. To avoid the twin evils of anarchy and tyranny, some Britons sought to reconcile the individual and the public good, controlling individualist excesses in a commercial economy and managing democratic demands while avoiding the other extreme of martial tyranny. Britons sought to appease emerging movements for the rights of women and the lower classes while maintaining traditional hierarchies and expanding the empire. The benevolent leader was a fantasy figure designed to make possible a British nation seemingly sympathetic to individual rights and liberties but wedded to hierarchy at home and to empire abroad.

The nineteenth-century literary representation of leadership creates a figure endowed with charismatic virility, which is characteristically slow to violence, taciturn, unpolished, and reticent, but resolute and immoveable.[5] In these representations, his capacity to replace his followers' multiple desires with his own will allows him to remedy the common fear in the period that commercial and democratic modernity licenses the chaos of competing individual ambitions, the mob effect associated with the French Revolution. After all, predicting that the French Revolution would degenerate into anarchy, Edmund Burke famously wrote, "the age of chivalry is gone.—that of sophisters, oeconomists, and calculators, has succeeded; and the glory of Europe is extinguished forever."[6] Nostalgically bidding farewell to chivalry, Burke actually helped inaugurate an age obsessed with all things chivalric, an age critical of the stultifying and degenerating effects of mere calculators. The age of sophisters and economists, it seemed to many, would create a feminized nation too weak to defeat enemies both domestically and abroad. In literary representations, the leader's virility offers an exciting escape from petty personal concerns and promises a higher commitment to some cause or individual who can establish national unity. The hero's power lies in his ability to promise the follower that modern life comprises not only the mundane concerns of the individual, but also the thrill of a meaningful, chivalric life, which can still be part of modernity if only the proper leaders can be found.

As my brief discussion of the "Ladies' 'Fancy Man'" and the nostalgia for an age of chivalry indicate, gender was a crucial category for Britons in their attempts to control democracy. Recent work in gender studies has pointed out how the "nation and state" became increasingly "entwined" since the French Revolution in ways that were "thoroughly gendered."[7] Masculinity "in particular was deployed in the various political and military projects that aimed at building the modern nation and at opening up the institutions of the state and of political life to this newly imagined collective entity" (6). Historians of gender have emphasized "the essentially gendered nature of politics in nineteenth-century Britain."[8] Although more traditional historians tended to push gender to the sidelines, historians of gender have shown how every aspect of British life was informed by complex and sometimes competing notions of gender. Davidoff and Hall early on offered a crucial study on "the centrality of the sexual division of labour within families for the development of capitalist enterprise."[9] Because they examined the connection "between the formation of the English middle class and gender" and the "male and female experience, they succeeded in bringing gender to the forefront of mainstream social history."[10] Where Davidoff and Hall focused on gender and the middle class, much work has also been done on the roles of men and women in the working classes.[11] Historians have recently begun to emphasize that a British understanding of gender was also crucially connected with imperial power and relations with British colonies.[12]

Work on gender in the period has become increasingly more complex over time often questioning the public–private divide that some saw as defining a clear separation between women and men. Amanda Vickery and Joyce Thomas have been most explicit in their critique of the separate spheres approach.[13] But most historians, including Davidoff and Hall, have long insisted that permeability always existed between public and private.[14] Several critics have pointed to the difficulty of defining the public sphere as well as to the need to be attentive to how the rhetoric of separate spheres changes over time and in different locations.[15] For Joan Scott, gender needs to be studied in areas that have seemed to historians to be divorced from concerns of gender such as war and high politics. Hall, McClelland, and Rendall suggest that Scott's refusal of the separate spheres opposition allows for a better understanding of "the connections between gender and power relations."[16] *Manly Leaders* also relies on a more complex and fluid sense of the public and private and on how representations of seemingly private relationships have crucial effects beyond the home. In fact, my examination of the so-called domestic novel finds that the home becomes a crucial site for enacting the political dramas of the nation and of the empire.

The study of gender has, thus, moved from a focus on recovering women in history to understanding the complex ways in which gender systems operate in different places and times and how gender relates to race, class, ethnicity, and nationality. This opening up of the study of gender beyond a concern with the recovery of forgotten women has also led to the creation of masculinity studies.[17] If some have feared that the interest in masculinity would simply replicate the traditional focus on men, others have argued that a broader study of gender can give us a more nuanced picture of how gender systems work in varied arenas.

Manly Leaders participates in this new interest in masculinities and in the inextricable interconnections between gender, politics, economics, and national identity. One of the reasons gender was so crucial in the nineteenth century was that the emphasis on manliness responded to a fear of democracy and of commercial culture, a culture that many thought might produce an effeminate people. Nineteenth-century Britons feared that modern political and economic systems were devoid of an exciting cause that could attach the people to the nation and to the status quo. Democratic equality and the scramble for economic power could threaten hierarchy as well as suggest that the political landscape had become peopled by ordinary individuals struggling for their share of power, a dull leveling that only imperiled the nation. Modernity required the supplement of gender to eroticize submission and make hierarchy again legitimate.

However, historians have examined various types of masculinity in the period suggesting an ongoing struggle in the nineteenth century to define and canonize maleness. For example, scholarship on gender in the eighteenth and nineteenth centuries has often described a softened masculinity. Historians such as Randolph Trumbach and Alan Bray have pointed to the creation of the molly, a figure connected to both effeminate manners and homosexuality, in the eighteenth century. The fop, too, is an important figure, but his effeminacy is more often associated with heterosexuality and an overeager desire for the company and manners of women.[18] The dandy in the nineteenth century assumes the notorious charge of effeminacy but, like the fop, he is not always or necessarily associated with homosexuality.[19] Although less clearly marked by effeminacy, other versions of masculinity also downplayed violence and roughness in favor of softened manners. John Tosh points out the "decline of bearing arms as a core attribute of masculinity. Along with the exercise of household authority, bearing arms had been the central attribute of manhood since feudal times."[20] Still important during the Napoleonic wars, "it rapidly lost ground after 1815" (222). Others have pointed to a softened masculinity altered by companionate marriage and the cult of sensibility that required men abandon roughness and learn their manners from women.[21] These changes helped make the virile display of martial manhood in the statue for Wellington an embarrassing miscalculation.

Yet, if we see changes in conceptions of masculinity, we also see continuities and resistances to the perceived feminization of men in a commercial and modern culture. Tosh underscores the disturbing continuity and increase of violence against women and children and a greater male authoritarianism in the home despite the new view of companionate marriage: "The theory of middle-class domesticity might be based on marital harmony achieved through complimentary roles, but the reality had to take account of men's continuing insistence on mastery in the home."[22] This new ideal of domesticity, "if anything, increased rather than diminished the incidence of household tyranny" (223). Although the field of masculinity studies is new and many questions remain unanswered, eighteenth- and nineteenth-century masculinity cannot be characterized as simply more gentle, more in harmony with women, and more domesticated than earlier forms. Despite a tendency to minimize martial manhood, a fear of effeminacy in varied arenas and in different forms remains important until at least the 1840s.

By insisting on male violence that persists both in actuality and as a desired but unacknowledged response, this book contests the often-repeated narrative of "beset" masculinity in gender studies. In an admirable effort to demystify an essentialized notion of masculinity, gender studies often claims that men experience the failure of their gender, that they are beset by insecurities and incoherencies. At the heart of all modern masculinity lies the discovery of a disturbing femininity that undermines all claims to real manhood. But, as Bryce Traister, speaking specifically about the American context, puts it, are

> there actually no "real men" out there? What do we say to the African American men still being dragged around behind pick up trucks driven by white men? To the gay college student mercilessly beaten unconscious and left to freeze to death over the course of a cold Wyoming prairie night? To the women and children hiding in underfunded shelters? I just do not know whether the vicious masculinity behind these crimes is enduring a "crisis" in any way comparable to that of their victims, or if instead we are dealing with a manhood smoothly coherent, frighteningly competent, and alarmingly tranquil.[23]

Traister argues that the claims of "the 'crisis theory' of American masculinity" (291) only serve to occlude a historical reality of male violence and power. Traister extends these claims about masculinity studies to the context of British literary studies in which similar claims about manhood in crisis likewise hold pride of place.[24]

A more nuanced view of masculinity studies might emphasize that critics have pointed out how the loss of manly power can produce violent reactions as John Tosh's example of domestic violence suggests. However, I join Traister in pointing to a type of remarkably successful masculinity and, in difference from much recent work in masculinity studies, I claim that representations of loss, incoherence, and benevolence do not necessarily indicate real failure or loss of power. Rather, benevolence can become a seductive means by which followers become even more fully submissive to their leaders.

Manly Leaders examines the work of William Wordsworth, William Godwin, Lord Byron, William Hazlitt, Thomas Carlyle, Jane Austen, and Charlotte Brontë. These writers all imagined charismatic figures who promise to make the nation powerful despite the widespread fear of the individualizing, atomizing, and even feminizing effects of democracy and commercial culture. Although the Romantic and early Victorian periods offered many types of masculinity, Wordsworth's good Governor and his true poet, Godwin's chivalric Falkland, the Byronic hero, Hazlitt's Napoleon, Carlyle's captain of industry, Austen's Darcy, and Brontë's Rochester exemplify the operations of one particularly disturbing type of masculinity, among the competing modes in play during the period. Most of the works I examine had a powerful effect on contemporaries and later generations particularly in their conceptions of masculine behavior. Godwin's novel, widely read in the 1790s and beyond, represents a disturbingly perverse picture of elite manhood as superficially benevolent but fundamentally violent and cruel.

Wordsworth had, as is well known, a lasting effect on our understanding of the value of poetry, but he was also influential as is less often acknowledged in nineteenth-century conceptions of manhood and leadership. Byron created a type of hero famous throughout the world for his seductive power. Carlyle engaged in one of the most successful appropriations of the kind of hero Byron helped create by connecting his type of silent, mysterious hero to the world of capitalist production, thus establishing the influential image of the virile and commanding leader of industry. Austen and Brontë's heroes Darcy and Rochester remain powerfully compelling figures of elite manhood.

Hazlitt, like Carlyle and Brontë, also appropriated some of the features of the charismatic hero Byron had earlier made famous and, yet, had little lasting effect on his contemporaries and virtually none in our own time. Hazlitt's writing on Napoleon has been largely ignored. The one example in this book of a noncanonical appropriation and development of this type of masculinity owes its lack of success at least in part to the fact that Hazlitt explicitly connects the leader's charisma to terror and totalitarian politics and champions the need for spectacles of violence.[25] Like the Hyde Park Achilles, his Napoleon shows too much.

Manly Leaders, then, offers a different approach to gender studies by emphasizing not a manliness in crisis but a successful manliness enlisted to quell those crises of modernization that have so often been represented as threats to masculinity. By seeing masculinity as the victim of a modernizing world, critics have failed to understand the ways in which this narrative feeds a fantasy of enduring masculinity that survives these feminizing conditions to rise again out of the purifying fires of suffering and loss.

This chapter considers the specific historical conditions of the postrevolutionary period that led to this interest in manliness, making a case for a larger historical perspective that sees continuities between the Romantic and early Victorian periods. It furthermore examines the complexity of nineteenth-century political culture that, although often wedded to the values of individualism, retained a serious concern about public unity. It concludes by offering in William Wordsworth's aesthetic and political theory, an example of why the literary was particularly important for creating manly leaders and submissive followers in a developing commercial and democratic culture.

Fear of Democracy: A Crisis of Authority

A widespread belief in the eighteenth century was that Great Britain was the freest nation in the world and for many it was "the only land in which political and civil liberty was possible."[26] Yet, this book argues that Britons nonetheless engaged in an exciting and complex flirtation with submission, demonstrating an implicit desire to maintain unequal political, social, and economic structures, kept in place in extreme instances by violence and imperialist coercion. James Vernon argues that although we tend to point to the period from 1815 to 1867 as the time that "established English political liberty and democracy,"[27] this "founding moment" actually saw "the closure of democratic political forms, the stifling of a radical libertarian tradition" (7). The political culture became increasingly "fashioned from above" and it mostly "told the story the official political establishment wanted to be heard" (102). Jonathan Perry points to the fact that "in 1890 Britain had almost the least democratic franchise in Europe."[28] Historians tend to agree "on the persistent importance until about 1880 of a 'traditional' politics in which local, aristocratic and religious influences remained paramount.... If there is a single theme that predominates, it is the persistence of aristocratic politics."[29] If the strong hold on power by elites was cemented in the course of the century, it was not clear at the beginning of the nineteenth century that elites would maintain control and could stifle democratic desires.

The period from the 1790s to the 1840s is marked by an acute sense of impending political and social collapse, which brought to the fore fears about national virility and coherence. Britons experienced "a constant sensation of fear—fear of revolution, of the masses, of crime, famine, and poverty, of disorder and instability."[30] Historians agree that in the first half of the nineteenth century fear was widespread that democracy would lead to an anarchic leveling of society. To be sure, this fear of democracy was not entirely new. Don Herzog asserts that issues of democracy and the people's rights did not emerge for the first time with the French Revolution and the Enlightenment. England had a history of civil unrest and regicide that made questions of authority part of its political culture. However, for nineteenth-century men and women the French Revolution did inaugurate a new era in which something profoundly different had occurred. Herzog asks, "What's so special about the years 1789 to 1834?... First there were real changes in these years, changes of decisive political importance. Second, the Revolution heightened anxieties, threw things in bold relief, posed worrisome choices that preceding generations managed more easily to evade."[31] Whatever the possibilities of democracy might have been in the past, the present seemed far more dangerously overrun by democratic claims. Alarmed contemporaries referred to the dangers of democracy not as distant possibilities but as a spreading "conflagration" or "as venom coursing through the body politic" (99). Herzog points out that, whereas the Tatler could comfortably ridicule coffeehouse culture and the claims of citizenship and rights openly discussed there, no such ease could be felt after the Revolution (53). Now, "political discussions, it became painfully (or exhilaratingly) clear, might well issue in hated revolutionary politics" (53).[32]

Beyond the years of Revolution and the Napoleonic wars, social unrest in England itself only exacerbated fears of mob rule. Between the "passage of the first Reform Bill in 1832 and the dying-out of Chartist agitation in the Christian Socialism of the early fifties...there was always present in men's minds the possibility that the English working classes would assume political power, perhaps even by some kind of violence."[33] The second half of the century experienced a greater sense of stability: "Against the broadening background of prosperity and social peace traditionally symbolized by the Crystal Palace exhibition of 1851, the militant demands for radical change once so dismayingly expressed in post-Waterloo and prereform Bill periods had through repetition and accommodation...been seemingly brought to a benign and cooperative resolution."[34] By mid-century, Britons, having "escaped the violent revolutions experienced throughout the continent" could imagine that "revolution was a foreign disease."[35] But before then, in the first half of the new century, Romantic-era Britons and early Victorians faced both the threat and the promise of democracy and the commercial economy with a sense of particular urgency.

By moving beyond the confines of the Romantic period, this book joins recent critics in making a claim for the long nineteenth century. The tendency to see a clear demarcation between Romantic and Victorian periods has recently come under some attack.[36] This study of political representations after the French Revolution fruitfully examines continuities between the Romantic and early Victorian periods. For this study, the demarcation might be more interestingly placed at midcentury when the sense that the political order might collapse became less vivid.

Common Ground: Tory, Whig, and Liberal Reactions to Modernity

This section examines some reactions to democratic pressures and to an expanding commercial economy among political antagonists who often shared similar fears about modernity. The following review of recent historical work on nineteenth-century politics, argues that Britons of various political persuasions tended to accept, with varying degrees of enthusiasm, that some accommodation had to be made with demands for civil rights and for commercial development. By the end of the eighteenth century, the "rights of man" were "held to be 'self-evident' and freestanding: no king, no divine authority, no imperial interest, no superiority of race or creed could nullify them."[37] However, this willingness to accept some features of modernity was coupled with a desire to carefully manage and control the new forces that, for many, threatened to lead to anarchy. C. A. Bayly writes, during "the early part of the nineteenth century power-holders and intellectuals sought to find ways—political, economic, and ideological—to constrain the forces of change which had been unleashed" (127).

Much recent work on the desire to control democracy in the period focuses on conservative thought partly because conservatives were often more overt about their concerns with order and partly because they offered innovative analyses of how submission works. Boyd Hilton argues that "neo-conservative ('Throne and Altar') ideology, so far from representing an *ancien regime*, was a *new* development following the American and French revolutions; that it was a reaction against the 'progressive' ideologies associated with those events" (30). As Yoon Sun Lee claims, in "the half century between 1790 and the mid-1840's," Britain valued "the display of loyal feelings" and put a premium "on the civic emotions which were to keep the nation's parts in their places."[38] Lee examines how conservative writers adopted irony as one solution to the problem of deference. Romantic nationalism sought to address the fear of democracy and commercial culture by maintaining "the stern necessity of [social differences] while insisting on the unity and, at some level, the fraternity of the nation. Its mandate was to discover the ideas and emotions that could keep these parts in their subordinate places, in spite of the myths of equality, liberty" (5). Lee sees non-English but British conservative writers as contesting the myth of British nationalism that claimed a "uniform character" for all British subjects" (5). These non-English writers developed an ironic stance that both emphasized the "anomalies of Britain's identity, structure, and relation to its own past" and "license[d] the experience of particular types of feeling beneficial to the state" (5). Irony had a "capacious address" (5) that could acknowledge the failure of national myths while insisting on the need for submission.

At the level of high politics, the Tory party was often understood as the representative of conservative authoritarianism. Critics in the nineteenth-century commonly charged the Tories with support for king and church at the expense of the people. The word "Tory" became widely used by at least 1815 to define those who accepted authority and wished to limit civil and religious freedoms.[39] Orthodox Tories thought that "hierarchy was a natural principle of social organization because it took account of fundamental differences in human capacities and experience."[40] The Tories became particularly authoritarian due to the "great fear inspired among the country gentry by the French Revolution and its aftermath."[41] As a result, commercial "interests were subordinated to an increasingly belligerent foreign policy and ultimately subsumed altogether in the exigencies of war" (26).

Yet even those thinkers and political leaders we tend to define as conservative cannot be understood as mere reactionaries. To see them as only reactionary is to miss how they sometimes grudgingly accepted and sometimes even embraced certain modern ideas and values. The label "conservative" may allow us to forget that before the French Revolution, Pitt's party had been far more congenial to commercial interests than the Whigs. When the revolutionary threat subsided in the 1820s, the liberal Tories, "as they became known, to contemporaries as well as to historians," again came to represent commercial interests and to cement an alliance with those commercially oriented members of the gentry and middle class who had felt alienated by the Tories during the war years (25). Paradoxically, then, the party that tended in moments of crisis to embrace authoritarian politics, was also the party that in more relaxed times embraced economic liberalism: if "government was to promote 'liberty,' it was commercial liberty that the Pittites had in mind, with sweeping tariff reforms a consistent aim of peacetime governments from the 1780's to the 1820s" (25).

The liberal Tories were more enthusiastic than many other conservatives about the political economy, but they were not alone in supposing that some accommodation had to be made with commerce. Important conservative thinkers such as Coleridge warned against "the overbalance of the commercial spirit."[42] Yet, even as Coleridge warned about the danger posed by the absence of "counterweights" to the commercial spirit, he was careful to point out that his "opinions would be greatly misinterpreted if I were supposed to think hostilely of the spirit of commerce to which I attribute the largest proportion of our actual freedom (i.e. as Englishmen, and not merely as landowners)" (662). Critics of modernity were not simply reactionaries who wished to turn back the clock. They were interested in "counterbalances," in ways of controlling modern forces. Coleridge attempted to be "useful in the modern world."[43] He tended to reiterate the concerns of civic republicanism about the dangers of commerce while ascribing to some of the "values derived from a rival tradition of 'commercial humanism'" (126). He connected "the growth of commerce" with "expanding opportunities for the exercise of human freedom" (129).

If conservatives had to come to terms with economic liberalism, they were also not simply able to ignore demands for greater civil rights. Although the kind of liberalism associated with civil rights "sparked off a violent conservative backlash," it could not, however, be completely denigrated.[44] Don Herzog finds in much conservative commentary an effort to come to terms with the liberal idea of universal equality. Herzog examines the scandal of Burke's phrase, "a swinish multitude," which became particularly evocative and infamous.[45] If the image of the people as swine was initially thoroughly dismissive, it took on a new life when radicals appropriated it to ridicule the ruling elite and to demonstrate "the contempt that the reigning establishment had for the people of England" (512). Herzog makes the point that this sort of phrase, unacceptable today, was already becoming so in the late eighteenth and the early nineteenth centuries (544). Exposing this degree of contempt for the people was neither safe nor sound policy.

Despite crackdowns on radicals and serious threats to rights and liberties during the years of the Revolution, Great Britain was not simply an authoritarian state in which hierarchy could be unproblematically defended. Certain values, that by midcentury would become clearly associated with liberals such as the right to property, certain civic freedoms such as freedom of religion, and the belief in universal human equality, were earlier widely disseminated across the political spectrum.[46] Dismissing the rights and liberties of the individual in a commercial economy and in a modern political universe in which middle and lower classes demanded more share in national government was unhealthy. The problem for many was how to persuade the post-Enlightenment individual that her true interests lay with hierarchy, order, and empire.

A sense that denigrating equality, liberty, and the swinish multitude was no longer healthy made the defense of hierarchy particularly urgent and particularly difficult. As Herzog makes clear, the problem the general assumption of human equality raised is that if "people are naturally equal and if we're not trying to conceal that behind the veil of secrecy, how successfully can [social inferiors] carry off the routines of deference and hierarchy? Why won't their role playing always be ironic, detached, not fully sincere or committed? And if their role playing isn't sincere, won't the social drama of inequality collapse?" (220) Herzog offers innumerable examples of masters worrying about the loyalty and deference of their servants. For instance, one contemporary observed, "a serious Rumpus among the servants. That tribe of beings are much altered of late years, no subordination among them. The Glorious Effects of the French Revolution" (226).

If some powerful Tories embraced economic liberalism and if conservatives had to find careful ways of managing the modern belief in equality and liberty, Whigs, who have often been understood by historians as the proto-Liberal party before the Liberal party came into being, were at times guided by a High Whig faction that was resistant to liberal economics and very committed to strong aristocratic government. Although the Tories reacted to the threat of democracy by becoming more authoritarian, this concern with strong central leadership cannot be defined as only an Ultra Tory reaction. A study of nineteenth-century political culture reveals a more complex situation.

Historian Peter Mandler argues that in the age of reform, the High Whigs were able to rally support for their idea of strong government led by virtuous aristocrats. Yet, their interest in elite power could not completely ignore modern forces. Whigs sought to marry central authority with certain kinds of civic freedom and commercial interest. For Mandler, our frequent tendency to see a liberal ascendancy in the early nineteenth century that supported the free market and downplayed government power is complicated by the realities of Whig power from the 1830s to the 1850s. The Whigs in the early nineteenth century developed a conflicted relationship between Foxite whiggism and a "liberal style" associated with "Scottish intellectuals and commercial men far from the centers of landed power," which "came to challenge Foxite supremacy even in the aristocratic strongholds of the Whig party itself" (23). For Mandler, the Whigs who challenged Fox's aristocratic power depended on the ideas of the philosophers of the 1760s and 1770s who:

> cast doubt on the traditional identification of liberty with political participation and constitutional forms. People did not possess rights in common, it was argued, they possessed only real things, as private individuals. In a modern, commercial society, therefore, liberty lay not in "the share which the people possess, directly or indirectly, in the enactment of laws," but rather in the individual's passive enjoyment of his property and his private cultivation of his moral and intellectual faculties. (23)

From this perspective, the "scope of politics" needed "to be dramatically limited" (23). These views had great purchase in the first decades of the nineteenth century when liberal Whigs and Tories tended to embrace modern commercial forces: "To onlookers of all persuasions, it was evident that Peel was swallowing up not only the philosophy but also the mass base of liberalism" (118). In "the 1820's, then, the values and principles of liberalism registered all across the political spectrum, among liberal Tories, independent Whigs...and circles detaching themselves from Foxism like the Young Whigs" (31).

Yet, Foxite Whigs embraced a seemingly older notion of strong leadership. If the liberal Whig had the ascendancy in the party before the 1830s, afterward Foxite whiggism became more influential. For Mandler, Fox's political heirs were better able to represent the demands of the "'Angry Thirties' and the 'Hungry Forties'" by making an explicit connection "between aristocracy and the people," who should not exercise power directly but whose interests were "vested in a kind of trust. The trustees were that band of virtuous and disinterested men who had wrested acknowledgement of the people's rights from the hands of absolutist kings: that is, the whig aristocracy" (19). These Whigs insisted on the continued importance of politics because politics, "not commerce or religion, was the proper enthusiasm—even fanaticism—of the aristocrat" (20). The fortunes of the Whig party revived with the rise of popular politics and demands for Reform. The Whigs "made respectable again that old language of natural rights and popular sovereignty which government had laboured so patiently to bury from the

1790's" (33). For the Whigs, the people needed strong "political leadership" (35) and did not see "the process of improvement as largely a business of individual striving" (37). They struggled to establish a "popular but not democratic government" (39). They alone seemed able to speak to and yet control popular movements and to prevent radical democratic change. Although Foxite Whiggism was short lived and by the 1850s was overcome by a Liberal party that "not only embraced both whigs and liberals, but [also] virtually swamped and drowned the whigs" (42), their brief success suggests a desire for strong leadership in times of political turmoil.

Mandler's work shows how for a brief period those politicians who emphasized leadership galvanized the public even as they gingerly accepted the necessity of a commercial economy. The Whigs were not simply a throwback to landed aristocratic interests. They combined their concern with citizenship and strong government with commercial interests even, if only grudgingly, among the Foxites. They attempted to "link free trade to an unambiguous espousal of interventionist social reform" (218). William Anthony Hays reminds us that the Whig MP Henry Brougham was a crucial architect in the revival of the Whigs due to his interest in political economy, an interest unusual among Foxites.[47] His influence "over liberal opinion" (7) was almost unmatched among the Whigs; he brought the "Whigs out of the margins and lay the basis of Victorian liberalism" (184) by "constructing a sustainable working coalition of varied interests that reached beyond the metropolitan preoccupation of high politics" (177). "Coalition building," according to Hays, shaped the party's "transition from Whig to Liberal" (177). The Whigs did not simply turn their backs on a commercial economy, then, but they often gave priority to strong government and leadership while supporting commercial interests during their ascendancy. Later, they joined others in the widespread support for the free market by the midcentury.

Although Mandler tends to emphasize a liberalism that was unproblematically allied to laissez-faire individualism, other historians have shown that not only Foxite Whigs feared the excesses of modernity, but also liberals and even political economists were sometimes troubled champions of a commercial economy and of democracy. Other historians' close readings of theorists such as Adam Smith suggest that liberals were in different ways also concerned about leadership and the dangers of individual interests.

The term "liberal," as Hays reminds us, was "an adjective that originally described openness or generosity, [that] took on a political meaning in the late 1810's and 1820's as counterpoint to orthodoxy or authoritarianism that brought it into general usage as a noun. Liberalism then became reified into a concept that described the shared agenda of Whigs and reformers into the 1840's and beyond."[48] Although the term did not point to any clearly defined political program until midcentury, if even then, the tendency is to imagine a clear liberal tradition that was strongly supportive of liberal individualism and laissez-faire economics.[49] More recent work suggests that certain ideas we have come to associate with liberalism could be seen among many people of various political persuasions, even Tories, who were at times sympathetic to a free market, or to religious freedoms, or even to a broader franchise. Furthermore, historians have shown that nineteenth-century liberals were especially "protean,"[50] and those groups and thinkers most commonly associated with liberalism were often not simply the supporters of free market economics and liberal individualism we often suppose them to be.[51] Liberalism is a notoriously complicated and multifaceted term. As Lauren Goodlad writes, in "Victorian Britain, liberalism most persistently asserted itself as antipathy toward statist interference—a discourse that anticipates neoliberalism...of our own day."[52] But "there is another and broader liberal tradition....If the first discourse seems naively to exalt the 'free' economic and voluntary activities of discrete individuals, the broader tradition...is more demanding in its conception of citizenship and, at the same time, more likely to view the state as a potential aid to individual and social welfare" (viii). Richard Bellamy claims that if formerly historians and theorists of political thought understood "the liberal agent [as] a self-interested, atomistic individual, driven by a series of self-referential desires to acquire and produce material goods," and if they understood liberalism as a politics that allowed the "fullest range possible to these passions," recent historians would claim that a "more accurate version of the liberal ideal would consist of a meritocratic society of self-reliant and responsible citizens, co-operating together in pursuit of individual, social, material, and moral improvement."[53]

That liberal thinkers were themselves critical of certain liberal tenets is not only a Victorian phenomenon. Even in the eighteenth century support for individual freedom and a market economy were not unproblematically embraced by liberal thinkers. H. S. Jones argues:

> Classical liberals typically perceived that the advent of a modern commercial and industrial economy overturned old forms of social cohesion built upon ascribed social roles, prescriptive authority, and shared beliefs derived from the teachings of the churches. A new kind of social bond must therefore be forged, one based upon the spontaneous harmony of individual interests in what Adam Smith termed a system of natural liberty. Smith had perceived that the distinctive feature of a market-based society was that social relations would no longer depend upon communal solidarity but would instead be conducted on the basis of interest alone.[54]

But, for Jones, the question of whether "the interest of individuals" was "sufficient to hold society together" haunted "European social theory in the age of revolutions that stretched from Rousseau and Smith to Tocqueville and Marx" (2). If Victorian thinkers complicated our tendency to see liberalism as merely the champion of laissez-faire economy,

> it is important to recognize that the complexity was present in classical liberalism from the outset. Just as Benthamism was marked by a tension between self-interest and the general good, so a tension between "wealth" and "virtue" pervaded Adam Smith's thinking, rather than serving to characterize the distinction between his outlook and that of his critics. No more in Smith than in Bentham was the harmony of interests unproblematical. (8)

Smith recognized that the "social and political institutions had to be developed which would foster an ethos of devotion to the common good" (8). Yet, the market "threatened to erode that very devotion to the public good," making individual interest and the public good difficult to harmonize. For Smith, the commercial classes represented a serious challenge to the public good because they "have an interest which can conflict with that of society at large."[55] By complicating the relationship between private interest and the public good, Smith "posed one of the central dilemmas of modern political theory."[56]

What this historical survey of some early-nineteenth-century political views suggests is that a fear of political and social disorder was pervasive, that various parties and thinkers sought to find ways to manage democratic aspirations, which they often saw as connected to economic liberalism or the free market. As this book argues, an attention to the literary representation of the crisis of authority in the period indicates that one response to this fear was an interest in elite male power and in the unifying powers of a seductive virility.

This concern with leadership is not merely an anachronistic attempt to turn back the clock to an earlier aristocratic and agrarian age, but rather to harmonize order and hierarchy with some very muted degree of civic freedom and a cautious management of the market. In this situation identifying wholly different conservative or liberal strains working in opposition is difficult. This is why, as this book argues, we can find shockingly authoritarian views associated with liberals and radicals and liberal individualist values associated with conservatives.[57]

The "manly" leaders examined combine an attachment to hierarchy and order with certain liberal values, finding a way to control democracy, paradoxically, by adopting liberal manners. In response to the complexity of liberalism in the nineteenth century, I use the term "liberal" in this book not to refer to a clearly defined political position, but rather to the support for merit over rank, the right of individual self-development (a right, however, often qualified), and an emphasis on benevolent manners that eschew overt coer-

cion. As the previous discussion of eighteenth- and nineteenth-century political theory has made clear, many of these values can be connected to other
political traditions, among them civic humanism, Scottish Enlightenment
thought, and various strains of whiggism. However, by the mid-nineteenth
century and beyond, these values have often been labeled as liberal. I use the
term "liberal" somewhat anachronistically for the practical purpose of giving
a name to those values and manners espoused by most of the "manly" leaders
discussed. The use of the term "liberal" in the following chapters should not,
however, obscure one of the book's major claims that these values cannot be
aligned only with those thinkers we have usually defined as liberal.

Republican Manhood

Manly Leaders argues that one reaction to the fear of modernity in the nineteenth century was the formulation of a fantasy of heroic male leadership
that would infuse much-needed virtue in the body politic and in society at
large. This fantasy in many ways speaks to a political tradition inherited from
the eighteenth century.

The interest in manly leadership recalls civic republican concerns with
national effeminacy and the need for virile citizens.[58] Historians have long
debated the place of republicanism in modern times. For a long time historians tended to tell a story of strong opposition between a modernizing liberalism, which supported individual rights and a laissez-faire commercial society,
and a more conservative republicanism, which emphasized the public good
and the virile citizen's duty to the polity. Like team cheerleaders, historians
went back and forth, emphasizing the victories of one side over the other.
According to a once widely accepted historical account, liberalism, after a
long struggle with authoritarian and royalist forces, gained a significant
ascendancy over the social, political, and economic culture of Great Britain
by at least the eighteenth century.[59] Particularly after the publication of Louis
Hartz's *The Liberal Tradition in America* (1955), historians tended to see liberalism as the hands-down winner in the formation of eighteenth-century
political thought and John Locke as the crucial figure in this victory.

But later, historians, led by J. G. A. Pocock, showed that this ascendancy
was not uncontested. If modern-minded thinkers came to value individual
development over the static entitlements of rank, if they believed in the
importance of the market and of the right of each individual to compete for
economic improvement, an opposition grew in the eighteenth century that
looked not to the market and to the future but to the past and to the land for
sources of value. With the publication of Pocock's *The Machiavellian Moment*
(1975) historians began to argue that civic humanism or republicanism played

as crucial and, for Pocock, a far more crucial role in eighteenth-century political discourse and that Locke was a less important figure than those backward-looking thinkers Machiavelli influenced.

More recently, historians have questioned the narrative that sees republicanism and liberalism as strongly oppositional political discourses. Some historians now tend to see how liberal and republican ideas could often work together rather than as competing discourses.[60] Vicky Sullivan argues that, imagining two political discourses, a republican one "associated, for the most part, with antiquity" and a liberal one associated with modernity, is a mistake.[61] For Sullivan, scholars have offered "an excessively polarized view" in which "republicanism is necessarily ancient and is thoroughly hostile to liberalism and its purposes" (5). Instead, "the relation between republicanism and liberalism need not result in a hostile antinomy" (7).[62] Sullivan sees a certain synthesis occurring as early as the seventeenth century.

This book argues that in the nineteenth century an interest in commercial economy and in civil rights did not necessarily preclude also a fascination with virile leadership. As recent work has shown, liberals, much like republicans, were preoccupied with questions of the public good. Furthermore, as previously argued, the fears associated with republican thinkers were also shared by some of those who supported and participated in the new commercial economy and who, in many of their views, were sympathetic to liberalism. They were troubled by certain aspects of liberalism that, they believed, threatened the integrity of the nation. Recent historical work on liberalism and republicanism does not suggest a strict antagonism between agrarian and commercial interests, but rather a more complex situation in which different backgrounds could still lead to common desires, fantasies, and ideologies.[63]

Manly Leaders argues that the nineteenth-century leader responds to a republican ideal of virility but is adapted to certain liberal concerns and values. To understand the interest in powerful leaders in the nineteenth century, examining a civic republican discourse that had earlier declaimed against the degenerate effects of commercialism is necessary. In the eighteenth century, the republican ideal revived an ancient view of citizenship as firmly rooted in both the ownership of land and in the practice of war. J. G. A. Pocock writes:

> Military *virtu* necessitates political virtue because both can be presented in terms of the same end. The republic is the common good; the citizen, directing all his actions toward the good, may be said to dedicate his life to the republic; the patriot warrior dedicates his death, and the two are alike in perfecting human nature by sacrificing particular goods to a universal end.[64]

Death is the ultimate sacrifice that proves the absolute willingness of the citizen to put aside private interest in favor of the public good. The fear of the eighteenth-century republican is that with modern specialization every citizen need not take up arms but can rely on "professional soldiers" (430). Pocock argues that the opponents of modernity feared luxury, which distracted the citizen from his true concerns: liberty and virtue. Luxury was another word for culture, "which, more than commerce itself, opened up the problem of the diversity of human satisfactions. The freeman must desire nothing more than freedom, nothing more than the public good to which he dedicated himself" (431). However, in a modern commercial culture in which satisfactions are varied and accessible, the citizen becomes distracted: "once he could exchange his freedom for some other commodity, the act became no less corrupting if that other commodity were knowledge itself" (431). Some eighteenth-century citizens were appalled by financial speculations, standing armies, and leisure culture, the signs of a new commercial culture that threatened to overwhelm a largely agrarian order. A specialized society in which one gained leisure and culture by giving up one's ability to defend the nation was a clear sign of degeneracy. In the nineteenth century, I argue, this figure recurs by continuing to allay the dangers of individualism and the anarchic potential of democracy while maintaining a commitment to liberal values, such as the importance of merit and, in a cautious, limited way, supporting a commercial society, despite fears of degeneracy.

Often, like his eighteenth-century precursor, this leader is associated with a willingness to take up arms for the community, but this penchant for war is both a source of fascination and of embarrassment for nineteenth-century writers. Vickie Sullivan has argued that for a synthesis between republican and liberal ideas to occur by the early eighteenth century, the republican emphasis on war and on warrior males needed to be downplayed.[65] Nineteenth-century liberal theorists such as Benjamin Constant contended that a modern commercial culture must do away with war to promote successful commerce.[66] At times, however, the warrior could function as a desirable figure, particularly during the war with France, when he could appear as a defender of the modern British state preserving its liberties from the militaristic tyranny of Napoleon. But such a figure, as Sullivan and the reaction to Wellington's statue suggest, was not easily accommodated to a nation that sought to define itself as essentially peaceful and benevolent.[67] Sometimes the steadfastness and virility associated with the warrior needed to be distanced from actual battle and adapted for British males, such as Austen's Darcy, who fight their enemies by other means and in other spheres while nonetheless protecting their communities from disruption. Godwin's Falkland, although dependent on violence for his power, must hide his commitment to brutality from public exposure. Some writers, on the other hand, persisted in embracing the ideal of the warrior and even his use of violence. This was a controversial move that relegated William Hazlitt to the sidelines of historical memory.

The nineteenth-century leader in the works I consider, such as the eighteenth-century republican Pocock describes, appears often juxtaposed to an effeminate figure addicted to consumption. Examples include Edmund Burke's virile Englishman and the effeminate French revolutionary; Wordsworth's leader/poet who counteracts the effeminate public's fascination with literary commodities and theatrical spectacles; Byron's virile Salemenes, the king's brother in law, and the king Sardanapalus, addicted to luxury and the incessant consumption of goods, who abandons war for pleasure; William Hazlitt's Napoleon and the modern citizen, dedicated to theatrical spectacles and the consumption of novels, who forgets his political commitments in favor of private fantasies; Carlyle's warriorlike captains of industry who give up self-interest to dedicate themselves to the public good by leading their workers out of a state of effeminacy; Austen's manly Darcy and the upstart Wickham who consumes women and goods indiscriminately; Brontë's virile Rochester who sets himself apart from the pampered darlings of his class. If something like the effeminate consumers and the virtuous males of Republican thought appear in the nineteenth century, however, they are often modern characters who borrow from an older vision of a landed society not to halt modernizing tendencies but to supplement them. Efforts to create a modern chivalric glamour are not necessarily antiliberal or reactionary. As Sullivan argues, imagining clearly divided modernizing and conservative forces pitted against one another is not always useful.[68] A more accurate picture would account for how republican and liberal views could often bolster the appeal of a modern political and commercial society. A seemingly old-fashioned prescription for authority becomes part of a modern effort to control the new political and economic conditions of the postrevolutionary period with an exciting dose of chivalric masculinity.

Literature and Politics: Wordsworth and the Fantasy of Leadership

Although the first half of the nineteenth century may be a particularly rich period for the study of leadership in a time of crisis, why a study of political and social authority should focus on literature is not immediately clear. With M. H. Abrams and the ascendancy of new historicism in Romantic studies, critics tended to claim that Romantic literature was rarely concerned with directly political issues of statehood, political representation, and leadership. Romantic poetry was influentially described as a poetry of evasion that escaped the hard realities of history and politics.[69] The Romantic hero, in particular, seemed to be overwhelmed by his own failure, cut off from society and unable to claim his traditional male privileges. Understanding this figure as a profoundly solipsistic individual, committed to the expression of his creative genius and unable to integrate his vision into society, was a commonplace of literary criticism. We also see a tendency, borrowing from historical work on gender that emphasized a culture of separate spheres, to read the domestic novel as concerned with representing a private domain removed from the masculine public sphere of governance and economics.[70] Critics saw these novels as attempts to define a woman's sphere that preserved the values of the heart against the encroaching and destructive values of the male sphere of politics and business.

Yet, more recent work on the nineteenth century has turned away from the new historicist tendency to emphasize political evasion. Critics often see inextricable continuities between political and economic concerns and those literary representations that seem to be about the individual self or the private sphere of the home.[71] Participating in this more recent turn toward the political, *Manly Leaders* argues that the heroes of the early nineteenth century, such as the Byronic hero who seems disgusted with humanity and Austen's Darcy who seems concerned only with establishing a personal romantic relationship, are leaders who organize modern political and economic communities, sometimes by example, and sometimes by direct engagement. Romantic heroes and the heroes of domestic novels are profoundly social figures who help make hierarchical society possible.

If we are more likely now to see literature as responsive to economic and political concerns, however, the literary is not just another kind of political theory embellished with narrative. Literary representations are particularly useful in understanding the fantasies of power that operate in a culture because literature often engages with fantasy in more powerful ways than nonnarrative writing such as theory and philosophy.[72] Fantasies of power turn out to be often most interestingly represented in those works that appear to be largely removed from questions of governance. In the domestic or Gothic novel, for example, nineteenth-century writers laid out the most powerful coordinates for how liberal ideas and the respect for authority and submission could coexist. Nineteenth-century literature reveals the particularly complex and disturbing ways in which male power becomes particularly appealing in modern times. The writers this book examines negotiated questions of political authority and created, reflected, and critiqued the erotic fantasies that legitimized submission.

In this book, the use of the word "fantasy" speaks to the psychoanalytic account of the reality-making effects of narrative. In psychoanalysis, fantasy is not a daydream but a construct that creates our sense of reality by organizing desire within a temporal narrative. According to Slavoj Žižek, "*narrative as such* emerges in order to resolve some fundamental antagonism by rearranging its terms into a temporal succession."[73] As Todd McGowan suggests, fantasy is a quest narrative because "desire always involves not knowing, being confronted with a question that does not have an answer. The desiring subject confronts a mysterious, enigmatic object that is never isolatable as *the* object."[74] The illusion put forth by fantasy is that some object exists that can fulfill the subject's desire: "The attractiveness of fantasy stems from this ability to deliver the goods, to provide the subject with a narrative in which it is possible to access the inaccessible *object petit a*," the object cause of desire (76). Žižek writes, "fantasy constitutes our desire, provides its coordinates; that is, it literally 'teaches us how to desire.'"[75] Fundamentally, it seeks to answer the subject's question: *Che vuoi?* What does the other want from me or "What does society want from me?" (9). The subject fantasizes that something in her fascinates the other, a *"secret treasure"* (10).

Fantasy, thus, organizes our experience of reality by hiding the impossibility of answering the subject's question. Experienced as a story about the individual self, fantasy offers the subject the means to see himself or herself as the hero or heroine of a romantic quest to find one's place. The question of what one is for society becomes particularly important in moments in which traditional order and authority appear fundamentally in crisis. Psychoanalysis is a science of bourgeois subjectivity, of a subjectivity that has lost its traditional place in the world.[76] Narratives of self-development, of finding one's proper place, become important in nineteenth-century literature in the historical moment when the liberal individual becomes a crucial if problematic figure.[77]

In the fantasy with which I am most concerned, a protagonist searches for the proper master, for the properly liberal/subservient place, or, in the case of the master himself, for the proper means of mastery in an enlightened age. The works herein reveal how liberal values could coexist with submissive desires when Britons learned to eroticize power on a very intimate level. One must experience the erotic, domestic, and personal fantasies of nineteenth-century Britons to comprehend one reason why elites remained so powerful despite potentially serious threats. Literature often makes those fantasies available in powerful and disturbing ways because literature deals with seduction, its mechanisms and strategies, far better than political philosophy. To become normative and self-evident, the type of political culture that endorses both freedom and hierarchy needed to be brought into the home and into the bedroom. The nineteenth-century writers this study examines are often concerned with a story of seduction in which women, servants, and sober middle-class subjects who have freed themselves from the aristocracy become seduced by a new kind of attachment to power. Having forsaken his or her allegiance to the aristocrat, the middle-class subject finds a new source of idolatry in the man of merit, a leader who appears naturally endowed with the right to power. Although Godwin's Caleb Williams, Hazlitt's true democrat, Carlyle's working man, Austen's Elizabeth Bennet, and Brontë's Jane Eyre all scornfully eschew any allegiance to the aristocracy in the name of liberal notions of freedom, they finally accept a master. Freedom, for them, becomes finding one's proper master, to paraphrase Thomas Carlyle. This narrative of submission is told in such a way that the subordinate appears to flaunt social conventions and oppressive institutions to liberate himself or herself into submission. The process of submission is cast as a story about personal liberation and fulfillment. In the historical moment in which the term "literature" comes to have its modern meaning of special, inspired, and creative writing, Romantic and early Victorian writers offer claims about how a certain kind of literary production can do the work of making one fall in love with one's leader.

William Wordsworth has, of course, had a lasting effect on our conception of the literary.[78] In the historical context that I have sketched out here, we can better understand why his essays on poetry describe a poet who functions very much like the leader who saves an effeminate and atomized people from the debilitating conditions of modernity.[79] But in his lesser known political writing, *The Convention of Cintra*, Wordsworth goes beyond the role of poetry to consider the role of war as a means of creating community. As this section of the chapter shows, his claims about poetry's function and that of war are strangely similar and suggests, as the subsequent chapters argue, that literature in the period could be understood as part of a project of unification that could work hand in hand with violence to bring excitement and meaning to modern life. In "Essay Supplementary to the Preface of 1815" Wordsworth explicitly compares the relationship between writer and reader to that of leader and follower. The "original writer," he claims, must "communicate *power*."[80] He writes, "What is all this but an advance, or a conquest, made by the soul of the poet? Is it to be supposed that the reader can make progress of this kind, like an Indian prince or general—stretched on his palanquin, and borne by his slaves? No; he is invigorated and inspirited by his leader, in order that he may exert himself; for he cannot proceed in quiescence, he cannot be carried like a dead weight" (82). The reader is orientalized as a passive and indolent eastern prince or general who cannot act without the inspiration of a master. The master is not directly the man of war but he offers the necessary leadership to invigorate the general.[81] The writer is the leader who rouses the reader to action.

In Wordsworth's portrayal, the original writer who conveys real power intervenes in a culture of publicity that only distracts and sickens the public imagination. In the famous "Preface" to *Lyrical Ballads* (1800), Wordsworth argues that the writer's greatest purpose is to excite the mind "without the application of gross and violent stimulants."[82] Wordsworth bemoans a cultural, moral, and political crisis in which modern mass commercial culture has destroyed the capacity of the public to remain true "to the beautiful and permanent forms of Nature" (124).[83] The modern public has become fickle and is drawn to every new and ever-changing spectacle. If one of the writer's "best services" is to draw the reader's attention to the permanent forms, then that service is needed more at the present time than ever before: "For a multitude of causes, unknown to former times, are now acting with a combined force to blunt the discriminating powers of the mind, and, unfitting it for all voluntary exertion, to reduce it to a state of almost savage torpor" (128). Orientalized, the public has become paralyzed by a lassitude that destroys all possibility of action. The causes of this passivity are the "great national events which are daily taking place, and the increasing accumulation of men in cities, where the uniformity of their occupations produces a craving for extraordinary incident, which the rapid communication of intelligence hourly gratifies. To this tendency of life and manners the literature and theatrical exhibitions of the country have conformed themselves" (128). The war with France, urbanization, and a commercial culture that disseminates ever new spectacles and reading material create a feverish desire to consume new objects of entertainment that distract the public from "permanent forms." For Wordsworth:

> The invaluable works of our elder writers, I had almost said the works of Shakespeare and Milton, are driven into neglect by frantic novels, sickly and stupid German Tragedies, and deluges of idle and extravagant stories in verse.—When I think upon this degrading thirst after outrageous stimulation, I am almost ashamed to have spoken of the feeble endeavor made in these volumes to counteract it; and, reflecting upon the magnitude of the general evil, I should be oppressed with no dishonourable melancholy, had I not a deep impression of certain inherent and indestructible qualities of the human mind, and likewise of certain powers in the great and permanent objects that act upon it, which are equally inherent and indestructible: and were there not added to this impression a belief, that the time is approaching when the evil will be systematically opposed by men of greater powers, and with far more distinguished success. (128, 130)[84]

Wordsworth's analysis is similar to the warnings of earlier eighteenth-century writers who feared that specialization would produce citizens incapable of action or self-defense. Commodity culture has disseminated textual and visual stimulants to "hourly" gratify the senses of torpid people whose minds have been put to sleep by their repetitive labors. People involved in industrial labor, office work, the business of the petit bourgeois, removed from land, independence, and rural places where old traditions flourish, become lost in every new form of entertainment. Only those who live off the land have a connection to what Wordsworth calls the permanent forms. In rural places "the essential passions of the heart find a better soil in which they can attain their maturity, are less under restraint, and speak a plainer and more emphatic language; because in that condition of life our elementary feelings co-exist in a state of greater simplicity, and, consequently, may be more accurately contemplated, and more forcibly communicated" (124). People in cities are prey to changing fashions ("under the influence of social vanity" [124]) and cannot fix on anything really lasting or valuable. Under the hourly influence of "outrageous stimulation" from trivial but ever varied and exciting commodities, the public becomes incapable of being fixed. Their minds seem alive to the mass culture around them, but this excitement is really only a sign of mental death, a torpor that renders them incapable of really reacting at all. Essentially, Wordsworth imagines a public united only to consume. However, it cannot create any unity of purpose or action because consumers are addicted to change and the experience of ever new stimuli. They become disconnected from tradition; their literary culture is lost to them as they become enchanted with the latest commodity. They can have no permanent belief or view that would guide their political choices or that would convey a sense of who they are. For Elizabeth Fay, Wordsworth's "return to origins" is the "object of manly poethood."[85] The attempt to "re-connect the urban reader to a purer linguistic experience" is to "knight the reader and charge him with a quest of his own." The function of Wordsworth's poetry, then, is to revive the manhood of the nation.

This chivalric manhood requires that the people understand themselves as an entity with a character and a sense of itself as connected to something permanent. The "men of greater powers" will reconnect the people to Milton and Shakespeare, to a tradition that comes from the land where the permanent forms can be experienced. The function of great writers, ultimately, is to sustain and be sustained by "the People," as Wordsworth claims in "Essay Supplementary." Good poetry survives "through the People," preserved by "their intellect and wisdom" (84). The author, on the other hand, "as far as he is great and at the same time *original*, has had the task of *creating* the taste by which he is to be enjoyed...he will be in the condition of Hannibal among the Alps" (80).[86] The poet, then, creates the values that make the people at the same time that he is preserved by that entity that he has helped bring into being. Whereas the Public is created by outrageous entertainment, the People come into being through the great men who, like Hannibal, conquer new territory while reconnecting to earlier glory. Gaudy and popular writing seduce the public; only original art appeals to the people.

Wordsworth claims a total separation between the two: "It is in the fine arts as in the affairs of life, no man can *serve* (i.e. obey with zeal and fidelity) two Masters" (64). Wordsworth adopts the metaphors of mastery and submission to differentiate the taste of the people and public. For the "People, philosophically characterized," (84) are that fictional entity imaginatively set apart from a commodity-addicted public. The people have submitted to the right master and are, therefore, connected to something, however vaguely defined, that is greater and better than the vanities of the latest vogue. By choosing a true "Master" the people avoid the passive, "languid" (65) state of an overexcited public. In the language of republican discourse, Wordsworth's public is effeminate and incapable of properly addressing the current political and social crisis. A true master is needed.

In his later political writing, Wordsworth makes similar claims about the community producing effects of war. He acclaims the public outcry against the convention of Cintra in which the British signed a treaty with France. He writes:

> I have to defend my countrymen: and, if their feelings deserve reverence, if there be any stirrings of wisdom in the motions of their souls, my task is accomplished. For here were no factions to blind; no dissolution of established authorities to confound; no ferments to distemper; no narrow selfish interests to delude. The object was at a distance; and it rebounded upon us, as with force collected from a mighty distance; we were calm till the very moment of transition; and all the people were moved—and felt as with one heart, and spake as with one voice.[87]

For Wordsworth this unifying feeling made every "individual" who "if his father, his son, or his brother, or if the flower of his house had been in that army, would not rather that they had perished, and the whole body of their countrymen, their companions in arms, had perished to a man, than that a treaty should have been submitted to upon such conditions" (289). The cause of the oppressed people of Spain and Portugal unites the British people in sympathy so that they no longer act for selfish reasons but for a higher motive, which makes them ready for self-sacrifice.

The British statesmen who approved the treaty failed in leadership because they did not have "knowledge indispensable for this service" (302) and because they had "a lack of power" (302). Wordsworth understands it as his duty to enlarge the understanding of statesmen, to "offer instruction to men" who fail to understand the "principles and passions which are the natural birth-right of man" (303). Wordsworth avers that the knowledge he wishes to teach is "not locked up in cabinets, but is accessible to all; as it exists in the bosoms of men—in the appearances and intercourses of daily life—in the details of passing events—and in general history" (303–304). Like the poet in the "Preface" who understands the nature of the people, rather than the passing fad, here, Wordsworth is "more alive to those genuine sensations which are the materials of sound judgment" rather than to "the changes of things" (304). Wordsworth claims to address his words to those:

> who have feeling, but whose judgment is overpowered by their feelings:— such as have not, and who are mere slaves of curiosity, calling perpetually for something new, and being able to create nothing new for themselves out of old materials, may be left to wander about under the yoke of their own unprofitable appetite.— Yet not so! Even those I would include in my request: and conjure them, as they are men, not to be impatient. (230)

His less immediate audience, those people addicted to the new, slaves of their appetites, recall those urban dwellers in the "Preface" who cannot focus on the essential things that Wordsworth would impress on them. But these people are not alone. British leaders have a similar lack of understanding. Like the public in the "Preface," statesmen are not in a position to focus on "a knowledge of human nature" (304) because "they are in a situation exclusive and artificial" (304). These statesmen live in a world of rank and pride (304–305) and so learn nothing about the "instincts of natural and social man" and "the spacious range of the disinterested imagination" (305). These men, who live in a world of individual ambition, cannot understand the desire to serve the nation "not from personal motives, but for a reward which is undefined and cannot be missed; the solemn fraternity which a great nation composes—gathered together, in a stormy season, under the shade of ancestral feeling" (305). Faced with an enemy, the people unite in a "solemn fraternity" that allows them to transcend selfish motive. If the statesman cannot understand this capacity, the poet and tract writer can teach a true sense of the people to the mere politician. If the tract creates a role for Wordsworth like the role he imagined for himself as the man who could make the nation chivalrous again in the "Preface," it also goes beyond his earlier arguments to clarify how violence is necessary to this process of national unification and virility.

For Brian Folker, Wordsworth responds to a crisis in British leadership by touting the value of violence as a means of unifying the people. Wordsworth sees an opportunity in the war against Napoleon to unite Britons against a common enemy. Paradoxically, war in Wordsworth's *Convention of Cintra* "is seen as a moral opportunity that allows the conscience-governed individual a scope of action unavailable in the more familiar realm of domestic social life."[88] But this scope of action for the individual at war is really an occasion for "the nation as a whole" so that the nation functions, in its self-defense and its moral purpose, like the individual soldier. If Wordsworth celebrates the individual's moral "self-sufficiency" at war he is not so sanguine about it under normal, domestic conditions when the individual threatens to become anarchic (174–81). If war offers an exception in which individuals must rely on their own judgment and not on preordained institutions and legislation, war, nonetheless creates a "community of war"[89] in which each individual functions like a stand-in for the nation so that the warriors in the Iberian Peninsula reconcile "the free will of the democratic citizen" with "the coercive force of institutions. They appear to have bridged the gap between will and order" (193). This liberty of the individual can be allowed because the threat of external violence produces unity among individuals who must fight to defend the nation. External threat alleviates Wordsworth's concern with "the potential internal danger of coercive and alienated domestic institutions" (193). By placing coercion outside the nation, Wordsworth imagines a situation in which outside threat inspires the most aggressive manly individualism but only in the service of a common national cause. Wordsworth looks enviously on the Spanish because "Oppression, its own blind and predestined enemy, has poured this of blessedness upon Spain,— that the enormity of the outrages, of which she has been the victim, has created an object of love and of hatred—of apprehensions and of wishes—adequate (if that be possible) to the utmost demands of the human spirit."[90] For Wordsworth the Spanish are fortunate because the "true sorrow of humanity consists in this;— not that the mind of man fails; but that the course and demands of action and of life so rarely correspond with the dignity and intensity of human desires" (339). Those who can live up to this dignity of human desires form "a spiritual community binding together the living and the dead; the good, the brave, and the wise, of all ages" (339). For Folker, in his pamphlet, Wordsworth "came to regard external threat—the cause of so much anxiety in his early political sonnets— as itself a valuable cohesive force" (194). Unity depends then on "the presence of the common French enemy" (194) who create a spiritual community among men who have given up personal interest for a larger cause.

Wordsworth's understanding of the enemy resembles his claims about his own function as a poet who will reconnect the public to permanent forms that reveal the real nature of the people and unify them. This similar function of war and poetry might help to explain why so often in Wordsworth's poetry nature has a terrorist function. In "Tintern Abbey" the boy Wordsworth experiences nature as something to fear and responds to it

> more like a man
> Flying from something that he dreads, than one
> Who sought the thing he loved (71-73).[91]

In *The Prelude*, nature is a "great school" (III.586) that impresses

upon all forms the characters
Of danger and desire, and thus did make
The surface of the earth
With triumph, and delight, and hope, and fear
Work like a sea (I. 497-501).[92]

Throughout the autobiographical poem, nature teaches the poet through fear and joy, exposing him to death, loss, and punishment. If the poet learns from nature and nature has a coercive power, the poet's own function is to remind the reader of a dread that produces proper readers, proper citizens, and proper men in difference from the motley crowd of the city. Fear is crucial for the poet, the reader, and the people.

⟨⟨◎

Adopting this Romantic conception of literature as the kind of writing that both represents the true identity of the people and creates that identity and often sharing Wordsworth's interest in violence, writers as different as Godwin, Byron, Hazlitt, Carlyle, Austen, and Brontë develop the role of literature as that special discourse that can seduce the people into loyalty to a leader. Some of these writers celebrate the seductive powers of literature whereas others warn us against them. William Hazlitt imagines a type of writing that will provide an alternative to the false visual stimulants of a commodity culture and that will create a lasting attachment to Napoleon as the true liberator of Europe. Thomas Carlyle creates a complex style that is a combination of history writing, poetry, philosophy, and narrative to produce a famously compelling and seductive prose that invites the reader to enjoy a new submission. In the "Preface" to *Jane Eyre*, Brontë theorizes her writing practice by claiming that it depends on her submission to a man of merit, William Thackeray, who has taught lesser writers to join him in a mission of social change. Even as some of these texts represent the seductiveness of masters, however, they also show the limits of the master's power. Godwin represents the seductive powers of romance and chivalric literature while counteracting them with a narrative of "things as they are" that exposes the perverse eroticism of the master/servant relationship. Byron addresses how literature and theater produce dangerously submissive subjects and becomes a strong critic of the seductive Byronic hero. Hazlitt exposes the destruction of the hero's aura by a consumer-addicted public. Carlyle can only save that aura by inspiring a necrophiliac desire. Austen imagines a subject who is beyond seduction, a consumer of goods and people who can never be satisfied or therefore controlled. Brontë emphasizes the claustrophobic quality of the master/servant relationship and the Gothic perversity of ordinary domestic life. Although these writers portrayed literature as seductive and compelling, they also showed it to be importantly self-reflexive on questions of power and submission.

This book considers the development of the leader in different realms: the state, the battlefield/army, the factory, and the home. They examine the effect of the leader in both homosocial and heterosocial spheres. If Godwin, Hazlitt, and Carlyle focus particularly on homosocial spheres, nineteenth-century writers also see women as crucially important for the legitimation of the modern leader. The heterosexual love affair in the work of Austen and Brontë offers a narrative that justifies eroticized hierarchical bonds. Women often represent the democratic subject, striving toward freedom and equality. Jane Eyre and Elizabeth Bennet are important examples. This subject, however, finds her ultimate freedom and equality when, paradoxically, she finds her master. I argue that women, lower-class men, and the masses are particularly important as subjects who can testify with a certain authority about the desire for submission. After the Revolution these types are marked by a particularly strong desire for democratic freedom and equality and their capitulation to their masters stands for a highly cathected assertion of the value of hierarchy.

The chapters also examine how the manly leader, when successfully seductive, blends a softness or benevolence with steadfastness and even violence. Most of these authors represent a manly leader who gains strength in part by appearing gentle, distanced from violence, while covertly promising necessary action in dangerous times. If masculinity exposes its weakness in the texts I study it does so to gain power. "Beset masculinity" is only a successful pose for effective leaders.

The book is divided into three parts. The first part examines Godwin's and Byron's critiques of the seductive master. Both see this figure as particularly compelling but, unlike the other authors in this study, Godwin and Byron attempt explicitly to expose the dangers of submission and to reveal the illusions necessary for seduction to take place.

Chapter 2, "'A Left-Handed Way': Modern Masters in William Godwin's *Caleb Williams*" considers the perverse homosocial relationship between a master and servant whose conflict offers a particularly lucid example of the nature of modern mastery. A powerfully influential novel during the period of the French Revolution, *Caleb Williams* represents the shift from an ancien regime past to a modern form of power in which leaders present themselves as benevolent and egalitarian. The novel reveals how the modern leader's real power depends on a secret and disavowed violence that underpins the public law. Godwin's representation of the relationship between the master, Falkland, and his servant, Caleb Williams, examines how modern subjects are fascinated by a violent power that persists despite a liberal egalitarian public façade. But the novel offers a strange twist or a "Left-Handed" representation of power suggesting that modern leaders must shift between embodying obscene power and weak mortality. Caleb Williams becomes fascinated by his master's brutality but is only thoroughly enslaved by him when he recognizes his weakness. The novel claims that weak men in modern times are far more dangerous than cruel tyrants. Falkland's devolution into the wounded and ailing father produces a repentant and servile Caleb far more thoroughly subjugated than the victim of tyranny. Godwin's representation of the dual nature of modern power (the cruel tyrant and the weak father) speaks to contemporary representations of monarchy, which sought both to engage the hatred of monarchical power and to expiate it with images of the king's ordinary mortality.

Chapter 3, "Political Seductions: The Show of War in Byron's *Sardanapalus*" considers Byron as a crucially important figure because he was famous for creating the kind of exciting hero whose powers of fascination seemed to inspire subordination in others. Byron's self-description as the "Napoleon of the realm of rhyme" captures nicely the public's sense of Byron as a kind of literary despot who seduced his readership. Byron lends himself to this study not only as the writer who most visibly embodied the seductive master both in his person and in his writing, but also as a writer who explicitly turned against his early work and offered a critique of political seduction in many of his later works. I address Byron's critique, in his late play *Sardanapalus*, of Great Britain's claim to benevolent and enlightened values and its unacknowledged commitment to a politics of brutality sustained by exciting spectacles of violence on the battlefield. The chapter describes a conflict between liberal values that insist on benevolence and the pleasures of commercial consumption, on the one hand, and the martial values of civic republicanism, on the other. The play represents how liberal and republican values become reconciled in Great Britain by energizing the consumption of luxuries with the glory of war. The chapter connects Byron's interest in theater with his interest in the theater of war.

The second section compares the work of William Hazlitt and Thomas Carlyle, two authors whose political views have always been understood as poles apart. Yet, these chapters show how the radical Hazlitt and the conservative Carlyle share much common ground at a time when the desire for authority was a pervasive concern.

Chapter 4, "Sublime Democracy and the Theater of Violence: Authoritarianism in William Hazlitt's *The Life of Napoleon Buonaparte*," studies Hazlitt's largely ignored celebration of Napoleon. Hazlitt's defense of the emperor offers an extended defense of political terror as the necessary means to inspire unity in a modern world. This defense of Napoleon has been excused as an unfortunate failing in an otherwise admirable career. Precisely the embarrassment over Hazlitt's support for Napoleon, however, makes Hazlitt interesting for my purposes. His work represents a particularly embarrassing example of the authoritarian temptations facing democrats. I see a troubling continuity between Hazlitt and the fascist theorist of the Weimar Republic, Carl Schmitt. Hazlitt claims the only alternative to a culture of competition and individualism is to offer a sublime theater of violence that replaces the distracting spectacles and commodities offered to the public. By fixating the public's attention with a spectacle of virile prowess, Napoleon ensures a type of unity that keeps the people loyal. For Hazlitt, a modern culture creates the need for war, for a thrilling struggle against the enemy, to overcome the divisive effects of economic and political modernity. Hazlitt's Napoleon uncomfortably exposes the fantasy of martial virility that contemporaries sought to veil behind the representation of a softened and chastened leader.

Chapter 5, "Communities in Mourning: Making Capital Out of Loss in Thomas Carlyle's *Past and Present* and *Heroes*," moves from the state and the Napoleonic battlefield to the factory. Carlyle, like Byron, is a crucial figure for the study of leadership because of his enormous effect on his contemporaries. His model of leadership had a very direct effect on how captains of industry understood their position and their duties. More than any other writer on capitalism and leadership, he offers an example in his writing of the kind of sway that Byron's heroes claim. For Carlyle, the leader is the means by which modernity, enervated by individualism and by rampant competition, becomes energized and strengthened. The problem for Carlyle's heroes is that publicity, the market, and exposure to the public's rude gaze feminizes and diminishes the hero's aura. Critics such as James Eli Adams argue that the Carlylean hero is a social failure who cannot engage the public. I argue instead that the apparent failure of Carlyle's leaders (their inability to speak to the public, their fear of the public gaze, their impotent despair) actually constitutes their success. Carlyle represents heroes whose very avoidance of the public marks them as mysterious and fascinating. Their reticence, paradoxically, engenders a desire for submission in the public. Carlyle proposes the worship of dead heroes who cannot be smeared in the daily papers and who provide the erotic energy that energizes capitalist production.

The third section turns to the domestic sphere and examines the role of women in relation to the master. Both Jane Austen and Charlotte Brontë see women as representatives of liberal democratic desire but for both this figure is also crucially important for legitimizing the seductive hold of the master.

Chapter 6, "'To Please a Woman Worthy of Being Pleased': Darcymania in Jane Austen's *Pride and Prejudice*," like chapter 7 on Brontë, represents how the domestic sphere functioned as a space wherein political relations were naturalized and transformed into intimate love affairs between leaders and followers. *Manly Leaders* claims that the fantasy of mastery needed to be communicated through the home to become powerfully seductive. Austen and Brontë show how a distinctive type of politics, committed to both subordination and equality, took hold of the most intimate spheres of human experience. This chapter describes Austen's efforts to define a specifically British type of leader. Austen's *Pride and Prejudice*, written during the Napoleonic wars, manifests a fear of the warrior figure whose glamour can be used to justify the appeal of Napoleon. Darcy functions as a British and aristocratic answer to the allure of Napoleon. To assume an effective modern form of leadership, Darcy must distance himself from both war and from the arrogance of the aristocratic past. He must assume liberal manners, paradoxically, so that he can maintain traditional hierarchies while embracing an enterprising commercial and professional culture. I consider how egalitarian and humble manners, which respect liberal claims about the value of the individual rather than the value of rank, actually legitimize the master's power and make him able to control upstarts. Darcy learns to assume the humility that Wordsworth in his sonnet "I griev'd for Buonaparte" ascribes to the good British Governor as opposed to the merely bellicose Napoleon. The great landowner, under the liberal influence of Elizabeth Bennet, learns to respect merit and the commercial classes while maintaining an "obstinacy" that allows him to protect his community from disruption and change.

Chapter 7, "Dependent Masters and Independent Servants: The Gothic Pleasures of British Homes in Charlotte Brontë's *Jane Eyre*," examines a later period after the years of protracted war with France. Writing when Napoleon was no longer a threat but maintaining a lifelong fascination with Wellington, Brontë integrates the warrior into the domestic sphere to eroticize the relations between masters and servants. Violence is a far more exciting possibility in Brontë's homes than in Austen's. *Jane Eyre* represents an erotic power struggle between the liberal desire for self-development and independence and the countervailing desire for submission to a worthy master. This struggle leads to a condition of apparent social and economic equality, which is nonetheless underwritten by the unacknowledged presence of the master. Rochester gains Jane's servitude, paradoxically, because of his weakness and Jane gains the right to submit in good conscience by freely choosing servitude to a master who can no longer compel her. But, behind Rochester's apparent weakness lies another figure of the master, a sublime master whose power survives all purifying fires, even the destruction of his social and economic superiority to his subordinate. Figured as Samson, this master holds in reserve a power that cannot be actualized under ordinary conditions but which promises, in times of need, to reveal its explosive force.

Chapter 2

"A Left-Handed Way"

Modern Masters in William Godwin's *Caleb Williams*

*W*illiam Godwin's representation of mastery in the early years of the French Revolution responds to a widespread British sentimental discourse about monarchy which threatened to reconcile subjects to their kings and to the status quo. *Caleb Williams* (1794), Godwin's most famous novel, offers a powerful representation of how modern power depends on a fascination with illegal violence, a fascination that, however, must be covered by the leader's vulnerability. The modern leader vacillates between omnipotence and victimhood, inspiring the fascinated gaze of lesser men who, by placing "a watch upon [their] patron[s]," learn how to become fully subjugated to their masters.[1]

The novel represents the shift from an overtly patriarchal to a more modern form of leadership in which masters find subtler means of maintaining the status quo. In the world of Godwin's novel, modern power must assume a benevolent public form while maintaining a disavowed connection to illegal violence. As liberal and enlightened ideologies domesticate the leader into a benign figure, the leader's violence becomes the invisible underside of his power.

Speaking to eighteenth-century representations of monarchy such as that of Edmund Burke, who reacted to the threat of the French Revolution by privileging weak and benevolent images of male leaders, Godwin claims that tyrants can be redeemed in the eyes of their victims. By enacting a vulnerable and beset manhood that allows them to assume the place of their victims, modern leaders preserve the power of the law and inspire renewed love of submission in modern times.

This chapter begins by examining the power struggle between the outdated tyranny of Barnabas Tyrrel and the modern mastery of Ferdinando

Falkland.The novel's representation of power in some ways anticipates psychoanalytic accounts of modernity. Whereas most critics read the novel in Foucauldian terms, this reading misses some crucial aspects of Godwin's representation of modern power. Psychoanalytic theory allows us to see how Godwin represents a debilitated public law rather than the Foucauldian model of pervasive power. But Godwin's representation of power is, furthermore, responsive to the sentimental discourse about monarchy that stimulated the public's pity for the French king in the 1790s. The effects of this discourse allow Godwin to address how modern power is sustained by a debilitating sentimentality that, unlike the psychoanalytic account, emphasizes the power of pity.

The Patriarchal Past and Enlightened Power

The first volume of the novel examines the violent conflict between two local squires, Tyrrel and Falkland, representatives of ancien regime and modern power. Tyrrel follows the law of the ancien regime, which demands that men of power fulfill their own will even by brutal and unjust means. Tyrrel appears as a "hero of antiquity, whose prowess consisted in felling an ox with his fist.... Conscious of his advantages in this respect, he was insupportably arrogant, tyrannical to his inferiors, and insolent to his equals" (17). His is a code of overt patriarchal power unmitigated by a more universal or impersonal sense of justice that takes humanity into account.

However, Falkland ascribes to the law of chivalry that demands fidelity to universal justice and to carefully codified and public forms of violence often in the service of benevolent ends. At the center of his life is a concern with honor, which depends fundamentally on the approving eye of the public. Public opinion, a good name, and good character are crucial to him. In this way he suggests the modern aristocrat's concern with the public, with the need for a modern elite to lead benevolently and to maintain the good opinion of the people. The people were making themselves heard in France and for many the overt tyranny of the French aristocracy brought on a violent reaction. Modern aristocrats in Great Britain needed to appear as men worthy of their station, not as mere bullies.[2]

Tyrrel, however, does not understand the need to court public opinion, believing that his status and his power are enough to subdue the people. When, after a series of brutal public acts inspired by his rivalry with Falkland, Tyrrel discovers that he has alienated public opinion, he appears to crumble before the weight of historical change. Unable to adapt to a historical moment that requires more subtle forms of leadership, Tyrrel sneaks away from a public assembly where he has been humiliated by Falkland who accuses Tyrrel of having incurred the "universal indignation of mankind" (95). At first, "Mr. Tyrrel began to obey his imperious censurer. His looks were full of wildness and horror; his limbs trembled" (95). But, if Falkland's code of benevolent chivalry seems to have superseded Tyrrel's brute power and Tyrrel appears about to exit the historical stage, Falkland's law of chivalry turns out to be insufficient to protect him from brutal assault. Encouraged by drink and a desire for revenge, Tyrrel returns to the assembly and attacks the physically smaller Falkland without warning. Unable to compete on Falkland's terms, Tyrrel resorts to a violence that denies the carefully codified and gentlemanly violence of chivalry: "Mr. Tyrrel kicked his prostrate enemy, and stooped, apparently with the intention of dragging him along the floor" (96).

In an instant, Tyrrel destroys all of Falkland's chivalric pretensions, bypassing the laws of gallantry and felling his opponent with brute force. Tyrrel exposes the stakes of power: behind the most adept follower of chivalry must be a commitment to violence and brutality that maintains the leader's power. As we learn later from Falkland's own confession to Caleb, Falkland murders Tyrrel by stabbing him from the back out of sight of any witnesses. If Tyrrel exposes the stakes of power, however, he fails to understand that brute force can no longer appear in public. Falkland survives their struggle because he murders Tyrrel in secret. Violence persists after Tyrrel's death but it is hidden and disavowed. The murder of Tyrrel represents a shift from an overtly patriarchal culture to a more modern and superficially benign power. Modern patriarchal figures abjure public violence and present themselves as the impartial and just administrators of a neutral law while founding their power on a violence that remains hidden, yet suspected.

Godwin's description resembles the psychoanalytic explanation of modern power. Psychoanalysis has described the power that replaces the directly patriarchal one as split between a public law and a disavowed supplement. For Slavoj Žižek "where the Law—the public Law, the Law articulated in public discourse—fails" another kind of power steps in to support it: "at this point of failure, the public Law is compelled to search for support in an *illegal* enjoyment," which is an "obscene 'nightly' law that necessarily redoubles and accompanies, as its shadow, the public Law."[3] This split between the public Law and its shadow takes on a new form with the rise of liberal and enlightenment values. Žižek writes:

When, as a consequence of the bourgeois egalitarian ideology's rise to power, the public space loses its direct patriarchal character, the relationship between the public Law and its obscene superego underside also undergoes a radical change. In traditional patriarchal society, the inherent transgression of the Law assumes the form of a carnivalesque reversal of authority...

However, once the public Law casts off its direct patriarchal dress and presents itself as neutral-egalitarian, the character of its obscene double also undergoes a radical shift: what now erupts in the carnivalesque suspension of the "egalitarian" public Law is precisely the authoritarian patriarchal logic that continues to determine our attitudes, although its direct public expression is no longer permitted. (55–56)

Similarly, Falkland's secret violence produces a split in the bearer of the public Law. Falkland becomes both the benign administrator of justice, patently weak and unstable, and the obscene manipulator of lesser men's fate.

For psychoanalysis, this new political sensibility allows for a strong sense of the public leader's powerlessness, of his being merely a functionary in a system of rules only as long as post-Enlightenment subjects also believe at the same time "that there is an 'Other of the Other,' that a secret, invisible and all powerful agent actually 'pulls the strings' and runs the show: behind the visible, public Power there is another obscene, invisible power structure."[4] The desire for this other master lies in the fact that only he appears to hold real power and functions as "the meta-guarantee of the consistency of the big Other (the symbolic order that regulates social life)" (362). The weak, helpless Falkland dragged along the floor by his muscular opponent proves that the humiliated public law that seems incapable of compelling submission has another side. This secret "Other of the Other," must be kept hidden but it ensures that a real power underlies the public law. In destroying Tyrrel for his overly public manifestations of violence at a time when such publicity is no longer possible, Falkland assumes Tyrrel's tyranny in a much more effective way, in a manner more fitting modern times.

Much of the critical work on Godwin's novel, however, engages a Foucauldian vision of a modern disciplinary society organized around the panopticon, rather than a psychoanalytic model to explain Falkland's power.[5] Yet, Falkland's power does not quite replicate disciplinary mechanisms because it emerges not as an extension of the law but as a result of its failure. In one of the best and most subtle Foucauldian readings, James Thompson claims that the novel "evidences Godwin's sense of the larger political crisis of the new bourgeois state, and the continuing power of the novel owes much to Godwin's uncanny recognition of the new form of the state and state punishment."[6] In the novel, "Great Britain becomes one huge Panopticon" (182). But, Thompson points to the problem that, in *Caleb Williams*, punishment does not "proceed from the anonymous body of the state," but from "a particular figure" who stands in for the sovereign

(185). Although the novel is obsessed with individuals and the causes of their actions, Thompson claims that this emphasis only replicates the disciplinary procedures Foucault describes and demonstrates "the penetration of state apparatus into the everyday lives of individuals" (192). Falkland becomes a stand-in for the modern disciplinary state. According to this reading, the disciplinary mechanisms pervade every facet of social, political, and economic life compelling individuals who imagine they enact their own personal dramas, in fact, to play out the logic of this modern punitive mechanism. This Foucauldian reading imagines a law that is pervasive, infallible, and undaunted.

Caleb Williams, however, represents a failed law, and psychoanalysis most clearly describes the consequences of this failure. Psychoanalysis helps us see that Falkland is not the victim of an overwhelming power, the dictates of chivalry that compel his actions, as Caleb comes to believe by the end of the novel ("But thou imbibedst the poison of chivalry with thy earliest youth," which hurried "thee into madness" [326]). Instead, his violence and duplicity emerge to supplement the law's weakness. Looking ahead to the conclusion of this chapter, the one aspect of modern power that Caleb never perceives is that the chivalric law to which Falkland ascribes might actually be impotent. At first, Caleb imagines that the law is embodied in a terrifyingly powerful Falkland only to believe by the end that it is a disembodied force that compels the master like a puppet. In neither case does he suspect that chivalric values have actually failed. By ignoring this failure, Caleb only safeguards the very power that Falkland has all along sought to protect and thus becomes a guardian of the very ideology he would dismantle.

Both Falkland and Caleb function in such a way to mask the law's impotence. We might imagine the possibility of a Falkland who accepts the failure of his chivalric code. The law's failure opens a moment of choice for Falkland to assume a destiny as something other than the law's obscene support. That this possibility does not happen does not mean that Falkland is compelled to act as he does. Falkland makes a choice when he murders Tyrrel that is not the inevitable fulfillment of the law's mandate. The consequence of not understanding the failure of the law is that one continues to perpetuate a belief in its omnipotence. The Foucauldian reading, then, is too similar to Caleb's own and tends to replicate the failure of his vision.

Burke's Ailing King and Chivalric Love

If Godwin predates many of psychoanalysis's claims about modern power, he represents the split between law and obscene master as complicated by the discourse of sentimentality that became so important in the period of the

French Revolution. He offers a twist on the story of modern power in which really successful power requires that the leader become not only split between his public and his disavowed function, but also that he suffer for it, that he appear to be the victim of the system that sustains his power. Under threat of public exposure, the master separates himself from the power that otherwise seems to belong to him and transforms into the victim of that power, "the other of the other," the power that really pulls the puppet strings. The narrative leads to a role reversal in which the servant finds he has become the agent of this other power and the master has become its victim. The reversal of roles in which, as in the trial of Louis XVI, the victimizer exchanges place with his victims, is a necessary stage in modern times to cement the loyalty of subordinates and to safeguard the power of the patriarchal law.

Godwin's account of the hold of modern power on the minds of subordinates resembles contemporary accounts of monarchy. Monika Fludernik has argued, "Falkland stands in the symbolic place of a king or a God" and Caleb commits "symbolic regicide."[7] In particular, Godwin's representation of Falkland's power recalls Burke's famous account of the British king. Critics have long noted Godwin's fascination and ambivalent admiration for Burke, but whereas some have pointed out how Falkland recalls Burke himself, I wish to point to how Falkland, in his capacity as ruler, resembles Burke's representation of modern monarchy.[8] In 1792 in his *Reflections on the Revolution in France*, Burke claims that modern British kings do not subdue their subjects but woo them. Describing a system of chivalry, Burke writes:

> It was this, which, without confounding ranks, had produced a noble equality, and handed it down through all the gradations of social life. It was this opinion which mitigated kings into companions, and raised private men to be fellows with kings. Without force, or opposition, it subdued the fierceness of pride and power; it obliged monarchs to submit to the soft collar of social esteem, compelled stern authority to submit to elegance, and gave a domination vanquisher of laws, to be subdued by manners.[9]

Burke offers a historical narrative in which a once barbaric lord transforms, under the pressure of chivalric values, into a mild-mannered ruler who "mitigated" hierarchies by making power gentle. If this is what the French have forfeited, it is still a reality in England where Britons maintain their traditions. But what Burke describes as a tradition in England was in some ways only just becoming fashionable. According to Mark Girouard's important study of chivalry, shortly after the Elizabethan period and up to the eighteenth century, chivalry had "gone almost entirely underground."[10] By the eighteenth century, however, "chivalry was on the way back" (19). For Girouard, the Age of Reason and the French Revolution created a nostalgic desire for a chivalric state in which loyalty to the king was unquestioned (23).

If chivalry was again fashionable and if it responded to modern crises, then Burke's chivalry is not so much a feature of the past but a modern way of conceiving monarchical power. Despite his emphasis on a venerable tradition, Burke tells a narrative of historical change. In England a hierarchical society, in which ranks were not confounded, produced nonetheless a "noble equality" because modern monarchs learned to moderate "the fierceness of pride and power" to the demands of "social esteem." Social esteem, unlike the revolutionary demands of the French, was but a "soft collar" that persuaded, rather than compelled. The monarch, made apparently gentle by modern manners, appears to allow citizens of a chivalrous society to choose their submission so that differences in status seem less marked. The leader who confers a "noble equality" that requires no actual political equality, sways his people by elevating them because he recognizes their value. The chivalric system in which rulers flatter their inferiors creates passionate attachments, which make the nation "lovely" (241).[11] Burke's chivalric nation is thoroughly modern: a modern conservative attempt to integrate ideals of equality and liberality with hierarchy. Like Falkland, modern kings have learned to set aside the overt brutality of power in favor of a more enlightened style of rule in which superiors elevate their subordinates with a flattery that maintains actual inequalities in place.

The paragraph that immediately follows in *Reflections*, however, leads to a somewhat different emphasis on the relationship between king and his subjects. Writing about the French revolutionaries' attack on the king, Burke claims:

> But now all is to be changed. All the pleasing illusions that made power gentle, and obedience liberal, which harmonized the different shades of life, and which, by a bland assimilation, incorporated into politics the sentiments which beautify and soften private society, are to be dissolved by this new conquering empire of light and reason. All the decent drapery of life is to be rudely torn off. All the super-added ideas, furnished from the wardrobe of a moral imagination, which the heart owns, and the understanding ratifies, as necessary to cover the defects of our naked shivering nature, and to raise it to dignity in our own estimation, are to be rudely exploded as a ridiculous, absurd, and antiquated fashion.
>
> On this scheme of things, a king is but a man; a queen is but a woman; a woman is but an animal; and an animal not of the highest order. (239–40)

At first, the pleasing illusion consists of incorporating "into politics the sentiments which beautify and soften private society." Presumably, family life was less marked by hierarchical difference so that when applied as a model to the realm of politics, it "made power gentle." This claim is in line with the earlier paragraph about the effect of modern manners on the "domination vanquisher of laws." Here, private life adds to the civilizing effect. This representation suggests that the violence of even the civilized ruler remains a viable threat and that the king's subjects are at the mercy of his willingness to accept the "soft collar." But then Burke adds an odd twist to his argument. Burke claims that beneath the "super-added ideas" lies, not a despot, but "our naked shivering nature," which reveals that a "king is but a man; a queen is but a woman; a woman is but an animal." In other words, the super-added ideas do not soften monarchical power; rather, they cover up the lack of that power and hide the fact that the king has all the "defects of our naked shivering nature." Chivalry, according to this account, is a desire to hide the monarch's inherent weakness and to protect him from exposure. Burke's sentimental view of power, then, requires a double and contradictory representation: on the one hand, violent and powerful kings are reformed by the civilizing tendency of chivalric values; on the other hand, kings are weak and require the chivalrous protection of their people to stay in power. The second representation denies the first by claiming that kings have no power and, like the expiring Louis XVI, exist only at the will of the people.

These contradictions emerge when Burke attempts to reconcile traditional hierarchy with democracy. Revolution is unnecessary because British kings are already quasi-democratic in that they comport themselves in a civilized manner. But a self-restrained tyrant is still a tyrant, vulnerable to the critiques of reformers and revolutionaries. Burke's second image of the king as a feeble and ineffectual man, however, represents the king as entirely vulnerable and entirely dependant on the good will of his people. Like a damsel in distress, the monarch depends on the chivalrous attention of his subjects who hold the actual power of the realm.

Burke keeps two images of power in play at the same time. In the first, the place of power is filled by a-would-be tyrant who has learned to control his violent impulses for the sake of modern manners. In the second, the place of power is essentially empty, filled only by the people's willingness to believe in an illusion. Burke's king, decked in the regalia of office, is only a super-added idea with no real substance. Far from being simply contradictory, these two accounts of monarchical power crucially elaborate the coordinates for how to create loyal attachments to one's superiors in modern, post-Enlightenment times.

This desire to represent the king as a benevolent father responds specifically to the conflict with France but also fits into a larger modernizing cultural trend evident in Enlightenment and liberal theories of power and progress. Attention to the representations of monarchy before and during the

French Revolution can shed light on this modern cultural logic. As Linda Colley has argued, the British monarchy under George III recreated itself in the image of the private family to gain sympathy and loyalty.[12]

John Barrel argues, however, that the picture of the sympathetic king is complicated by the perverse effect of sentimental discourse: "the sensibility which is outraged by the representations of suffering also finds pleasure and gratification in them."[13] Alluding to Burke who claims that the people tend to fear their king, Barrell argues, "though we may sympathize with, we may also exult in the distress of unhappy kings, for though kings are human like us, and never more so than when brought to grief, they are also alien objects of terror whose destruction we can hardly help desiring" (95). For Barrell, the "language of sentiment masks power with weakness, fear with tenderness, hate with love, but the mask is always transparent" (96). Briefly mentioning *Caleb Williams*, Barrell offers it as an example of how the language of sentiment produces both love and "the guilt and hatred of family life" (98). The hate of kings was aroused, for Barrel, by the very discourse of sentiment that loyalists helped put into circulation. If the new monarchical image suggested that the royal family and the royal father functioned as a typical, ordinary bourgeois family, the fascination with this family depended on the never-forgotten acknowledgement of the king's actual power beneath the manifestation of homely simplicity. The homely king who nonetheless held great power could stimulate both amicable and hostile reactions.

If sentimental discourse did elicit both hate and love, Marilyn Morris points to a crucial difference between British and French representations of monarchy. In Great Britain, even the critics of monarchy tended to offer less vicious critiques than their counterparts in France: "Satires that made use of George III's bodily functions were generally not as censorious as the graphic depictions of Louis XV and Louis XVI had been."[14]

The king's protracted illness offered the opportunity both to ridicule and to sentimentalize him: "during his illness of 1788, his mental and physical functions became the subject of great public interest. The ability of artists to muck about in the bathroom habits of the king and the heir apparent signified a new degree of intimacy with royalty after George's illness."[15] The curious fact about this publication of intimate details is that "acknowledging that the king goes to the privy like everyone else, and being able to imagine him doing so, gave the monarchy a sympathetic, human quality that was not possible in an absolutist, divine-right regime" (178).

What was so powerful about the intimate, if often hostile, representation of the king's body was that it could elicit fear and hate of the monarchy while minimizing that hostility by humanizing the actual man, the ailing George. By masking great power in ordinary frailty, the scatological imagery gave occasion for ridicule and debasement that, however, did not reach the dangerous level of hostility expressed in France. If radical Britons hated the tyrant, they could, nonetheless, love the ordinary, flatulent father or at least satisfy a degree of hostility with scatological humor.

The Pleasures and Political Limits of Transgression

Caleb Williams offers similar pleasures of hostility that emerge from an investigation into the great man's privacy. Although Falkland's private world does not consist of George's various bodily eruptions, but, rather, of mental quirks, and emotional explosions, Caleb investigates Falkland's mind in a sadistic effort to expose him. Caleb's investigation produces a supernaturally powerful agent of persecution who ultimately transforms into a wounded victim, leading to a seductive intimacy that ensnares Caleb.[16]

From the beginning, Caleb's interest in Falkland's past exceeds the desire to reveal an injustice and evidences a more perverse desire.[17] The pleasure of transgression initiates the investigation because "to do what is forbidden always has its charms, because we have an indistinct apprehension of something arbitrary and tyrannical in the prohibition. To be a spy upon Mr. Falkland!" (107). But, in this novel, transgression against the master may not, much like the satires of George III, lead to powerful social critique. What makes Caleb obscene and his investigation erotic is that his efforts to unmask Falkland's cruelty function not to render justice but to become more intimate, more truly connected, and subservient to the master. As Eve Kosofsky Sedgwick argues about Gothic novels such as *Caleb Williams*, "the hero intrusively and in effect violently carves a *small, male, intimate* family for himself."[18] Intimacy, for Caleb, is achieved through hostile investigation.

The novel suggests a possible explanation for Caleb's actions in the genre of his favorite reading. Caleb claims that the key to his own character is curiosity and that the literary form that suits his curiosity is "books of narrative and romance" (4). Caleb's "spring of action" is a desire to trace "the variety of effects which might be produced from given causes" and this interest produces in him "an invincible attachment" to romance (4). When he reads, Caleb "panted for the unravelling of an adventure, with an anxiety, perhaps almost equal to that of the man whose future happiness or misery depended on the issue. I read, I devoured compositions of this sort. They took possession of my soul" (4). Caleb defines romance as a form of investigation, which examines the effects of causes to produce great "adventure." As the self-patterned hero of chivalric romances, Falkland functions as the ideal protagonist of Caleb's romance. Romances for Caleb are mysteries in which the reader is invited to read the master and investigate the makeup of his power. But in so doing, the reader identifies with the protagonist whose pain he feels almost as if it were his own. As Gary Handwerk points out, Caleb experiences an "obsessive identification" with Falkland.[19] Connection to and exposure of the master allows the servant to participate in an exciting adventure that thrills him ("My mind was worked up to a state little short of frenzy. My body was in a burning fever with the agitation of my thoughts...I panted with incessant desire that the dreadful crisis I had so eagerly invoked were come, and were over" [318]). Caleb's efforts do not, despite his stated intentions, tend toward exposing the wrongs of society to change them.[20] Instead, his efforts tend toward establishing a romance between himself and the master, a romance in the sense both of a perilous and extraordinary adventure and in the sense of a love story.

In a memorable scene, the master and servant reveal how romance works by creating an intimacy born of transgression. Caleb critiques Falkland's admiration of Alexander the Great by pointing out that "he overr[a]n nations....How many hundred thousands of lives did he sacrifice in his career?" (111). To Falkland's claim that Alexander's wars spread "knowledge and virtue" (111), Caleb replies, "it seems to me as if murder and massacre were but a very left-handed way of producing civilization and love" (111). Caleb points to the perverse connection between violence and civilization, a connection whose exposure seems capable of undermining all the pretensions of power. But this exchange takes a strange turn.

Caleb accuses Alexander of reacting to "a momentary provocation" to commit murder. This reference is intended as a direct provocation of Falkland who, likewise, has committed murder in a moment of anger. Caleb realizes the effect on Falkland the "instant I had uttered these words." But this provocation produces not hatred and alienation but "a magnetical sympathy between me and my patron" (112). Caleb's provocation creates an exciting connection with his master in which the two become thrillingly aware of each other.

Pages later, Falkland declares his sense of the unbreakable connection between himself and his servant: "You want to leave me do you? Who told you that I wished to part with you? But you cannot bear to live with such a miserable wretch as I am!" (120). Falkland avows a dependence on the servant which raises Caleb in his own estimation. Caleb:

> thought with astonishment, even with rapture, of the attention and kindness towards me I discovered in Mr. Falkland through all the roughness of his manner. I could never enough wonder at finding myself, humble as I was by my birth, obscure as I had hitherto been, thus suddenly become of so much importance to the happiness of one of the most enlightened and accomplished men in

England. But this consciousness attached me to my patron more
eagerly than ever. (121)

Like Burke's king who creates a "noble equality," Falkland flatters his servant
into loyalty. When Caleb feels his own "importance to the happiness of one
of the most enlightened and accomplished men in England," he becomes
most attached. The master elevates the servant by revealing the master's
dependence. But this revelation leads to no rebellion. It is a means of keeping the servant in check. Falkland stimulates the hatred for kings that
inspires a hostile investigation into his life, but this investigation, which initially produces the violent master, leads to a manifestation of the weak and
wounded father, a manifestation that leads from hate to love.

The third part of the novel in which Caleb leaves Falkland's home to
escape his persecution plays out in more extreme form this struggle in which
the master inspires hatred and the desire to expose him. Falkland appears
supernaturally powerful to Caleb, able to penetrate any hiding place and disguise. If this power produces Caleb's hatred and desire for retaliation, it also
produces a fascination with and desire for Falkland to exert his power. Slavoj
Žižek argues that the "betrayal of the father is a desperate attempt to test his
(im)potence, sustained by a contradictory desire: a desire to catch him in his
impotence, to denounce his imposture, yet simultaneously a desire to see him
undergo successfully the ordeal and thus belie our doubt."[21] The novel suggests this dual motive in the character in those moments in which Caleb
manifests disappointment because Falkland seems to have lost interest in the
chase or when Caleb deliberately puts himself in the path of persecution.
Despite his often-repeated statements of self-pity, Caleb often suggests his
own pleasure in being the object of the master's persecution.[22] This game of
provocation and persecution is finally played out in the novel not when Caleb
exposes the master's crime but when the master metamorphoses from terrifying persecutor into wounded and dying father who inspires a crippling pity.

The Power of Pity: Beware a Weak Man

The final trial in which the truth about Falkland is revealed, ironically, produces not liberated subjects who have transgressed against the power of the
father but subjects who, because of their transgression, are now thoroughly
enslaved. The novel proposes the scandalous notion that a way exists to expose
the master's crime publicly without destroying his hold on his inferiors.
Responding to a late-eighteenth-century literary culture overrun by sentimental discourse, Godwin perceives how a particular logic of sentimentality complicates the success of exposure and limits the power of enlightened vision.

When he sees Falkland in court, Caleb predictably confronts not the savage master but the weak father. The court scene leads to a moment of mutual penetration in which antagonists experience a final moment of loving intimacy. Caleb begins his speech in court by describing an imaginary scene of perfect intimacy, a lost opportunity between master and servant. He now wishes that he "had opened my heart to Mr. Falkland" and knowing that his master was at his "mercy" to have won from him "conciliation" rather than "inexorable cruelty." He accuses himself of lacking faith because if he had "told [Falkland] privately the tale that I have now been telling," Falkland would not have "resisted a frank and fervent expostulation, the frankness and the fervor in which the whole soul was poured out." Instead, by refusing to confide, Caleb's "despair" has become "criminal" and is "treason against the sovereignty of truth" (323). He declares that he is himself "a murderer" now (323). Having committed "treason" as if his attack on Falkland were a matter of state, Caleb regrets the loss of an enduring intimacy.

Monika Fludernik claims that this desire for honest dialogue is the novel's central moral claim: "The true justice that is rendered to Falkland by Caleb in the final scene of the novel is an ideal justice since it balances the merited regard for Falkland's virtues with sympathy and pity for his fall" (887). Sympathy, for Fludernik, "*reinstates* the sublime as an ideal of benevolence and unqualified affection for others, as divine love (*agape*), and it thereby cancels out the aesthetics and politics of terror" (886).[23]

However, the final moments of the novel suggest that sympathy is deeply problematic because sympathy for Falkland ultimately enslaves Caleb.[24] As many critics have noted, Caleb's sympathy for Falkland allows him to identify with the master to the point of exchanging places with him at the end of the novel.[25] Gary Handwerk has pointed out that the end only appears to "reiterate the political prescription of *Political Justice*: personal dialogue can transcend social differences and restore a genuinely impartial justice. The text seems to claim that knowledge of history allows us to erase its effects, to step outside relations of power" (947). However, this reading "resolves the narrative in essentially sentimental terms, ones that fit neatly with *Political Justice*'s faith in the power of sincerity, but elide certain problematic features of the novel. For Godwin's revised ending produces a countermovement against its own ethical prescriptions, a contrary interpretive force marked by Caleb's excessive feeling of guilt" (947–48).

The imaginary scene Caleb describes, this missed opportunity for closeness, becomes the actual scene realized in the court, which leads to Caleb's state of crippling guilt. Caleb claims that his "heart was pierced" by his master's suffering. In turn, Falkland is also penetrated by Caleb's remorse: "as I went on, he could no longer resist. He saw my sincerity; he was penetrated with my grief and compunction" and "threw himself into my arms!"

(324). Intimacy achieved, Falkland declares that Caleb has "conquered! I see too late the greatness and elevation of your mind" (324). In claiming that Caleb has "inflicted on me the most fatal of all mischiefs," he gives up all hostility and blesses "the hand that wounds me" (324).

The moment of penetration, in which master and servant are overcome by sympathy, leads to no real alteration of things as they are. Overwhelmed by guilt, Caleb becomes enslaved to Falkland's memory: "His figure is ever in imagination before me. Waking or sleeping I still behold him. He seems mildly to expostulate with me for my unfeeling behavior. I live the devoted victim of conscious reproach" (325). Consecrating himself to his master's memory, Caleb promises, "Falkland, I will think only of thee, and from that thought will draw ever fresh nourishment for my sorrows!" (325). By the end, Caleb sees Falkland as a victim of power. If, for much of the novel, Falkland embodies the "other of the other," the obscene shadow of the public law, by the end, the murder of Tyrrel becomes evidence of a greater power that victimizes Falkland. Caleb is no longer Falkland's victim but, rather the agent of power who persecutes the wounded master, underscoring the law's pervasive hold.

Gary Handwerk sees Caleb's description of Falkland as the victim of a political system as a moment of awareness in which Caleb offers a "historical explanation of events" (949). This awareness is only partial because Caleb cannot locate himself in "the historical narrative he has constructed to vindicate Falkland" (950). I claim, however, that Caleb's need to see Falkland as a victim of larger forces is part of his desire to reconnect with the master and become his loving subordinate as well as a means of safeguarding the law's weakness. Enlightened understanding of social forces in the novel produces the very attachment to the master that it should have destroyed as well as a fantasy of the overwhelming hold of the law.[26] For Handwerk, Caleb does not go far enough in his historical understanding. In my interpretation, the very historical reading of Falkland as victim licenses Caleb's fatal identification with the master and his inability to perceive the law's weakness. The novel reveals an illusion about power. Caleb's sympathy for the master produces what looks like an analysis of the social dimension of their power struggle. The nightmarish implication of the ending, however, is that seeing the larger picture, engaging in social analysis, can sometimes license a return to a more powerful identification with and attachment to the master. Caleb's tendency to see power as either embodied in the obscene master or in some larger inescapable structure that compels both master and servant does nothing to dissuade him from the master's hold or from the coherence of the law. Caleb fails to understand that Falkland is not a victim of the code of chivalry that compels his actions. Instead, Falkland's story reveals that the law of chivalry is flawed; it fails him in the most crucial moment of his life, in his confrontation with Tyrrel. Far from the victim of an overwhelming power, Falkland is the defender of a flawed law that is maintained only by the supplement of his illegal violence. Because it is not really as powerful as Caleb imagines, the law requires another support and Falkland in all of his various manifestations as benevolent leader, obscene tyrant, and wounded father ably protects and hides its insufficiencies, producing in Caleb a terrifying sense of its power.

The clearest sign of Caleb's failure to unmask power is his inability to distance himself from Falkland at the end. Like the brothers who murder their father in Freud's primitive horde in *Totem and Taboo*, Caleb's murder of the father leads to no liberation. Ultimately, in Godwin's time, a period overrun by sentimental discourse, what stimulates a lasting guilt is not the destruction of the tyrant, the obscene father, but the death of the vulnerable, victim father. Paternal weakness is not the occasion for revolution but for a more thorough submission to the powers that be.

Godwin's novel offers a cautionary tale for our all-too-frequent tendency to celebrate manifestations of male weakness, incoherence, and vulnerability. As chapter 1 argued, today's familiar narrative of beset masculinity in gender and literary studies claims that modern masculinity is experienced as inauthentic, vulnerable, and flaccid. Scholars have celebrated this masculine disempowerment as evidence of cracks in the patriarchal edifice. However, the novel suggests that weakness is a particularly powerful means of subduing others in modern times. For Godwin, nothing is more dangerous than a vulnerable man compelled to recognize the failures of his virtue and virility. The spectacle of manly ruin maintains things as they are. Godwin's narrative of modern power reveals the left-handed ways subjects refuse to be free.

Chapter 3

Political Seductions

The Show of War in Lord Byron's *Sardanapalus*

*O*f the canonical Romantic poets, Byron has often been read as the most masculinist, with the possible exception of Wordsworth. Sonia Hofkosh sees Byron as aggressively struggling to "design his own image" in a marketplace threatened by a female readership who may undermine his control.[1] When critics attempt to find a canonical Romantic writer less insistent about his masculine prerogative they often turn to John Keats, feminized by his class, his illness, and his politics.[2] But several critics have complicated Byron's investment in masculine power despite his many attacks on bluestockings and on his female readership. Some have pointed to Byron's homoerotic desire as one way Byron threatened acceptable definitions of manhood,[3] while others have shown how, for example, Byron's *Don Juan* enacts "the male revolt against the social conventions of nationalistic domestic manhood" and examines "the trouble with heroism."[4]

This chapter considers Byron's late play, *Sardanapalus* (1822), as a particularly important example of Byron's criticism of nationalistic manhood. The most popular writer of his day, a celebrity who inspired erotic fantasies in a public that could not separate Byronic heroes from the poet himself, Lord Byron was frequently described as a literary tyrant whose sway over the market was unchallenged. His seductive heroes made his fame and Byron sought to undermine their seductive powers in his later works. William Hazlitt wrote about Byron, "He hallows in order to desecrate; takes a pleasure in defacing the images of beauty his hands have wrought."[5] *Sardanapalus* performs this desecration of the thing of beauty Byron created to dramatize the political consequences of hero worship.

Although Byron's late dramatic works have been often ignored as deviations from central Romantic concerns,[6] recent interest in Byron's drama has found that his plays importantly comment on gender, the performance of political action, on the French Revolution, apostasy, and on political economy to mention only a few themes. This interest has led to a reconsideration of the importance of *Sardanapalus* in Byron's canon.[7] The play is particularly interesting because it promises a heroic apotheosis only to frustrate that desire. Byron's play repeats the scene of fascination in which followers in his earlier eastern tales imagine the impending emergence of a promised virility in their leader.[8] But, deliberately provocative, the play reveals the illusion inherent in this form of seduction. The king seems to promise but has nothing to deliver. His effeminacy becomes not a sign of martial cowardice but of a profound inability to believe in the theatrical illusion that transforms the merely human body into a sign of national strength. Sensual, sybaritic, the king is nonetheless a failed seducer. Having turned his back on the Byronic prescription for sexual and military conquest, the king leaves his subjects cold.

The Benevolent but Manly Nation

In Byron's play *Sardanapalus* the people are troubled by their king's refusal to appear effectively seductive, a seduction that requires "the show of war" (I.ii.532).[9] But the king is committed to luxury consumption and to pacifism, which puts him in conflict with the martial desires of his subjects. The king enjoys the fruits of empire while maintaining an apparent commitment to benevolence. He refuses to expand his empire and conquer new territory. A people, committed to a program of empire, who ascribe to republican ideals of a martial culture, call on their king to abjure his effeminate pacifism and exercise the nation's virility. The play represents a clash between the king's desire to consume luxury without accounting for its cost and the civic republican values of his people. However, beneath this apparent incompatibility, lies a fantasy, which most of the characters in the play share, that a moment may come in which the king will reveal the virility that lies dormant beneath his effeminate exterior.

Several characters testify to the belief that beneath the king's effeminacy beats a manly heart that can be roused to renewed manhood. This belief is so pervasive and so persuasive that the king himself shares it at certain points in the play. The play alludes to a reaction, described in chapter 1, taking place in Great Britain during the Napoleonic wars and during the reign of George III. Confronted by the Gallic threat, many Britons feared that the nation had become enervated by commerce and luxury and would be unable to defend itself. For many Britons some of the concerns that had motivated eighteenth-century civic republicans persisted into the nineteenth century. In the play, Byron represents a people who wish to see the nation's virility manifest in war, to prove that commerce and luxury have not vitiated the empire's power.

At the same time, chapter 1 argued, Britons wished to claim a superior liberality and benevolence in difference from the tyranny of Napoleonic France. In Byron's play the king assumes the British desire to appear benevolent, to assert that barbarism is a thing of the past, and that conquerors such as Napoleon are only an anachronism in a civilized modern world. As Jerome Christensen has pointed out, the king appears to ascribe to a liberal philosophy similar to that espoused by Benjamin Constant. In his "The Spirit of Conquest and Usurpation and Their Relation to European Civilization" (1814), "one of the founding documents of nineteenth-century liberalism,"[10] Constant defines Napoleonic despotism and violence as a "disastrous anachronism."[11] For Constant the progress of history leads to "peaceful commercial exchange" (277) so that Napoleon appears to be a "detour from the westering progress of enlightenment" (277). J. W. Burrow sees this emphasis on a progressive nation as a liberal inheritance from a Scottish Whig effort to "revise the historical pessimism of the neo-classical, constitutionalist preoccupation with balance and the corrupting effects of luxury."[12] Since the eighteenth century, then, imagining that commerce could lead not to cultural corruption, but to a more peaceful and civilized modernity, was possible. Sardanapalus recalls this optimism about commercial society at the same time that he rings all the civic republican warning bells about effeminacy. He recalls the British claims of moral superiority to the bellicose France, while, at the same time, encouraging a desire for a return to martial values coupled with commercial ones to safeguard the empire in a time of threat.

Byron, however, represents a king who, in the end, refuses to condone how commerce must be underwritten by imperial power, who refuses to perpetuate the empire, and who disrupts the gender fantasy of a slumbering virility beneath the liberal façade of a benevolent commercial nation. This chapter begins by examining British patriotic self-representations during the Napoleonic wars and how they accommodated the martial values of republicanism with a liberal view of commercial society. The second part of the chapter considers how the play seems poised to replicate this reconciliation and how Sardanapalus, in an ethical refusal, disrupts this accommodation to expose and reject the hypocrisy that has allowed him to rule over an empire.

Soft Kings and Hard Warriors

For Byron the appearance of national benevolence and liberality is a lie Britons tell themselves, an alibi under cover of which they wage imperialist wars. In Great Britain, the representation of monarchy under George III allowed Britons to perpetuate the myth of British moral superiority and benevolence. The insistence on an apolitical king served as a counterpoint to French Revolutionary and imperialist politics. Linda Colley writes, "One of the most powerful arguments employed by royal apologists at this time was that, whereas republican experiments in Continental Europe had led inexorably to anarchy, military despotism, mass conscription, and the despoliation of property, in Great Britain...things were blessedly different."[13] While a military despot overtook France, England remained true to its king. English kings made England free whereas French leaders only subjected the nation to escalating war.[14]

As Colley argues, "Great Britain" was "an invention forged above all by war. Time and time again, war with France brought Britons, whether they hailed from Wales, Scotland, or England, into confrontation with an obviously hostile Other and encouraged them to define themselves collectively against it" (5). Great Britain sought to define itself in difference from both "revolutionary and Napoleonic France," regimes whose ceremonial forms offered a "nationalist and militarist emphasis." In safeguarding the value of the monarch, in opposition to the leadership of the Jacobins and Napoleon, Britons did not intend to minimize British freedoms but, rather, to insist that monarchy was compatible with liberty.

To emphasize the British opposition to Napoleonic militarism, state-organized spectacle focused most heavily on the monarch and only secondly on the war and on the nation. This renewed interest in the monarch endeared the people to an individual with whom they could identify, someone who would replace political scrutiny with tabloid prurience, state violence with personal empathy and kindness. According to Colley, in reaction to Revolutionary and Napoleonic threats to monarchy, George III reinvented legitimacy by replacing the suspect notion of divine right with a new understanding of the king as both glorious and merely ordinary: a king and yet also "a husband, a father, a mortal man subject to illness, age and every mundane kind of vulnerability" (232). Part of this effort to "domesticate" the king required that he appear above both, politics and war, a figure of the nation, a father of his people. The people were to imagine the king as "essentially the same as his subjects" (232). Byron's Assyrian king also strives to remain above politics and war and declares the universal sameness of all people. But Sardanapalus's and George III's liberal benevolence only belies both the kings' own coercive power and the overtly bellicose desires of the people.

Although, as Linda Colley argues, monarchical spectacle during the war sought to emphasize the person of the king above politics and war, the importance of the army necessarily grew during the extended war with France.[15] During the war years, military heroes such as Nelson accrued a cult following that rivaled the public's interest in the king.[16] Recent work on the representations and symbolic manifestations of war shows a British public deeply fascinated by the virile culture of the army, clamoring like Byron's Assyrian public for the "show of war."

The British war effort was insistently accompanied by the public theatricalization of military might. The inescapable conjunction of theater and war characterized a political period in which power became spectacle, in which pageantry was vital, and in which war was simulated in countless reenactments. As Scott Hughes Myerly writes in *British Military Spectacle*, "Military spectacles took place regularly during the French wars and in 1798, 1803, and 1815, when war excitement was at a fever pitch, some martial ceremony took place almost every week. The spectacle of war was a craze."[17]

This desire to make war manifest in the theater was accompanied by a desire to make theater manifest in war. A crucial part of the war effort was expended on creating an army of men who looked heroic, larger than life, and capable of showing forth the nation's virile strength. Myerly concludes that in the army "looks superseded the fundamental task of wielding armed force" (1). The health, well-being, and life of army men were subordinate to the constant imperative to *look* like a warrior. In a lengthy account of the horrors of military life, Myerly contends that as deadly as actual war could be, the common soldier was as likely to be crippled or killed by the demands and inadequacies of his uniform. The varnishes, headdresses, hair powders, and the tight, heavy uniforms required to enhance a manly, powerful appearance drastically curtailed the freedom of bodily movement to the point of rendering soldiers less adequate in battle. These dangers to the health and life of soldiers created "one of the best military shows in Europe" (19). Costume allowed the army to create itself in the simulated image of an ideal, theatrical army. This image displayed a fantasy of a superior warrior caste, responsive to the demands of theater. That war became theater and that theater became obsessed with war does not mean that simulation destroyed the "reality" effect of war. Soldiers appearing on the battlefield in costumes that artificially enhanced their height and manly appearance did not appear to be mere actors performing in a false show. The spectacle of war needed a theatrical technology that would offer the experience of seeing a believable enactment of martial prowess so that the artificial, the costume and prop, could appear not as mere theatrical paraphernalia but as manifestations of a true virility representative of national prowess.

In *The Theaters of War: Performance, Publics and Society, 1793–1815*, Gillian Russell claims that the interest in war during the Napoleonic years called for a theatrical technology that was increasingly more realistic. Russell argues that theater and war did not become connected for the first time during the wars with France, but that connection reached a new level of intensity, which, as a result, changed the nature of both war and theater. Russell stresses the differences between the army's self-presentation in the eighteenth century and the changes that followed from the war with France in the nineteenth century. The construction of the soldier as a kind of sportsman was particularly important in the eighteenth century when warfare was represented "in terms which stressed its aristocratic, even festive *élan*" (26). War was a "gentleman's game" (27) in which the gentleman assumed a role he could also shed; he was capable of moving from the military camp to an elegant dinner party by merely changing his clothes. This aristocrat who approaches war like a game or a performance in a play is evoked by Byron's Assyrian king when he appears in battle. But the aristocrat's deliberate theatricality is no longer acceptable at a time in which war has become a serious occupation, not the pastime of the idle nobleman.

The challenge to the patently artificial theatricality of this kind of warfare came in large part as a response to the war with France and the French Revolution. "During the period 1793–1815 there was an increasing dissociation of the military from civilian society" so that the army began to be associated not with the camp but with the barracks, an exclusively male space removed from society. The extended war turned the aristocratic play into a much "more serious affair" in which all classes needed to feel involved and represented (49). In becoming a serious affair, war required soldiers who "had to be rather than act the soldier." The French wars "divest the army as a whole of its amateurism by creating a professional fighting force attached not to a local community or to civilian rank, but to king and country, and, above all, to one's fellow soldiers" (51). What became necessary, then, was a fighting force whose performance was so perfect that it seemed natural. The spectacle of war became increasingly popular but its tone changed to reflect the manliness of the soldier and his deadly seriousness.

The new emphasis in war, then, was not on the officer's ability to move seamlessly between the camp and the salon, but on the soldier's performance of his true, immutable warrior nature. That the soldier lived separately from the rest of society in the barracks, that his code of dress, behavior, and speech, differed radically from civilian society marked him as a being that had become the role he had assumed. The professional replaced the amateur; the actor became the role and remained the same, unchanging in all theaters. The costume made the man so that costume became the charged metonymic signifier of an interiority, a self, which was only produced in the first place by a uniform and required props.[18] An interiority that makes the man a true soldier or warrior rather than a mere performer can only, of course, be validated by the soldier's performance. But this performance must convincingly appear to offer evidence of the warrior's ability, his manly prowess. Costume made the man or the soldier, so fully enforcing his new role on him that his former self ceased to exist. For Russell, "war and theater were mutually sustaining" (179); theater overrode nature and turned performance into reality.

This desire for a performance that revealed a true manly interiority and the desire to separate the monarchy from war suggest how Sardanapalus might recall an actual leader who singularly failed to appeal to the public's imagination about war and leadership. If the times required good actors, in George IV the British public found a very poor actor who both failed to naturalize war and warriors and to make kings avatars of British benevolence. Critics have frequently compared the Assyrian king to the effeminate George IV. The marital discord, the revels in a palace of pleasure, and the effeminate relation to war, characterize both England's regent and Byron's Assyrian despot. Assyria's ruler, whose effeminate decadence seems to locate him within the most familiar Oriental stereotypes, is "no less effeminate than" England's own George IV.[19]

However, as prince regent, George yearned to abandon the nonmartial character of the monarchy and become a warrior in his own right. A notoriously effeminate figure, the regent earned his effeminacy not only because of his sensuous excesses but also because of his inappropriate relation to war. George desperately wanted to join the army, but when denied a post by his father he turned his fascination with war into a lifelong interest in the fashions of the army. According to Scott Hughes Myerly, the "regent's obsession with military display was not limited to his own dress; his great interest in designing militaria became symbolic of his reign and made him a laughingstock of the nation. In 1819, a caricature entitled "'The Dandy Taylor planning a new Hungary Dress. Pity that a good Taylor should be spoiled' ridiculed his hobby" (33). Remarkably adept at striking the wrong key, George's fascination with all things military amounted to an effeminate interest in the trivial details of costuming. Although this interest in military uniforms was part of the crown's "need to manifest [its] military power and glory," which was "closely linked with a monarch's personal prestige"(38), George IV's investment in the army uniform was so excessive that in fetishizing the uniform as an end in itself, he betrayed the seriousness of war.[20] The dandy's interest in props and costume marked the regent as a failed soldier, one who focused on the becoming qualities of the uniform without becoming the uniform. Essentially, the regent failed to perform his role believably. He always reminded his audience that he was an inadequate actor wearing clothes that did not fit him. The king's commitment to war was patently artificial, the interest of a dandy in the latest fashion or toy.

If the regent and the Assyrian king recall the eighteenth-century aristocrat, they, nonetheless, differ in crucial ways both from each other and from that outdated figure. Although the British public saw George IV as guilty of bad theater, the king himself was deeply invested in his warrior fantasy: later in life, George IV "came to believe that he had fought in person on the blood-soaked fields of Waterloo."[21] As obsessed with war as his public, George IV is merely a failure who cannot become what he ardently wishes to be. But Sardanapalus is a critic of war fever who insists on the benevolence of monarchical power. Unlike the eighteenth-century aristocrat who sees war as merely one aspect of his aristocratic self-display, the Assyrian king maintains an ethical commitment that is at least superficially reminiscent of the other British monarch in the period. But if George III studiously avoided any direct connection to the army or to war, maintaining an appearance of paternal benevolence, men such as Nelson and Wellington fulfilled the fantasy of national virility that the king could not assume in his person. If connections to the regent remind English audiences of an overeager fascination with war, the comparison to George III exposes the limitations of a British ideology of benevolent government. The play recalls both monarchs to underscore how an enthusiasm for war and empire undermines the illusion of British benevolence.

Warriors and Effeminati: Parts a King Might Play

In the play, the Assyrian people desire the kind of theater Russell describes in which war is a stage where latent virility becomes manifest. The people of Assyria call on their king to reveal that he, too, possesses this inherent affinity for war, this warrior nature. They want not an aristocratic dandy but a king who proves his right to rule because he is naturally a man of power, inherently a man of war. Called on to embody the martial allure of Wellington, Sardanapalus thwarts his people's desires by playing the effeminate dandy. Sardanapalus's refusal to go to war and his preoccupation with luxuries recalls the effeminati of civic republican discourse. For much of the play, Sardanapalus acts like a republican stereotype who, addicted to consumption and pleasure, creates only a degenerate nation. But when the people demand that their king give up his effeminate attachment to consumption and become the sober warrior who lays down his life for the people, his refusal becomes not merely effeminate but ethical. Much more than an embodiment of a stereotype, the king stands for a committed refusal to envision a politics in which a king in benevolent drag can become a warrior. By the end of the play, the king refuses to underwrite commercial culture with the necessary violence. The play exposes the fantasy of liberal benevolence by showing that commerce must necessarily be underwritten by imperial violence. British benevolence only masks the realities of modern commercial empires.[22]

Initially, the play establishes the republican binary of effeminatus and virile warrior. In defining the role of the effeminatus in eighteenth-century classical republican discourse, Linda Dowling argues that contempt for the effeminate male did not address "modern gender categories" but, rather, "a vanished archaic past in which the survival of a community was sustained in an almost metaphysical as well as wholly practical sense by the valor of its citizen soldiers."[23] Effeminacy was a failure to fulfill one's civic duty to the state and it harked back to an ancient Greek view of citizenship "in which the good of the citizen and that of the polity are always understood as wholly interdependent and reciprocal" (6–7). Borrowing from a Greek martial ethos, classical republicanism imagined that "the life of the entire community is reduced in moments of dire extremity to the body of the single warrior as he is willing to have his throat cut by a sword or his chest pierced by a spear in the name of the community not present on the battlefield" (7). The virile male offers his body and his life to the state in war. Effeminacy, then, "has to do not with femaleness in any modern sense but with an absence or privation of value. The root of *virtus* in Latin is indeed *vir*, signifying male" (8). The nonwarrior is effeminate, a figure of selfishness, of "monstrous self-absorption" (8).

Salemenes , the king's brother-in-law, repeatedly articulates this ethic of heroism. According to Salemenes, one great difference separates the sensual toil of the king in the harem and his toil on the battlefield. He describes an economy of energy in which the pleasures of the harem expend the same energy as those of the battlefield but without invigorating the reveler. Salemenes asks,

> Were it less toil
> To sway his nations than consume his life?
> To head an army than to rule a harem?
> He sweats in palling pleasures, dulls his soul,
> And saps his goodly strength, in toils which yield not
> Health like the chase, nor glory like the war (I.i.21–26).

Salemenes evokes a model of degeneracy in which luxury saps the vigor and health of the warrior. Manly pursuits yield health and glory not only for the individual but also for the nation. Without a healthy, manly king, the nation, too, becomes diseased and effeminate. He claims that the

> weakness and wickedness of luxury,
> The negligence, the apathy, the evils
> Of sensual sloth—produce ten thousand tyrants,
> Whose delegated cruelty surpasses
> The worst acts of one energetic master (I.ii.68–72).

Effeminacy only leads to a fracturing of power so that the empire is now run by a thousand petty despots rather than one king who controls and unifies the empire. Both Salemenes and his slave, Myrrha, a Greek appropriately wedded to a martial tradition, repeatedly attempt to rouse the king to military action. Salemenes urges the king,

Keep thou awake that energy
Which sleeps at times, but is not dead within thee,
And thou may'st yet be glorious in thy reign,
As powerful in thy realm (I.i.382–385).[24]

This effort of arousal on the part of loyal servants responds to the people's own desire to see their king at war. Salemenes declares that as "the mouthpiece of the people" (I.ii.82), he hears the "echoes of the nation's voice" (I.ii.95), which calls for a king (102). He claims to "echo thee the voice of empires" (I.ii.224). The voice of the nation and the voice of empires seem to be the same voice because both call for the restoration of an aggressive imperial power and the wars that allow empires to expand. The events of the play, the uprising, and the civil war suggest that Salemenes has heard the people well.[25] But the people do not want simply war and its spoils. As Myrrha, the king's concubine, puts it, the people require "the show of war" (I.ii.532), a spectacle in which the leader's prowess functions as the point of identification for them.[26] The people of Assyria clamor for a return to centralized power and a theatricality of state that offers the visual pleasure of concentrated power, of power that is all the more extraordinary for belonging to the single individual leader, rather than to a multiplicity of competing individuals.

Sardanapalus often echoed this fantasy, that the people may rouse their leader to a renewed martial vigor, himself. Whereas past critics understood Sardanapalus's pacifist commitment as simply a humane rejection of militarism, recent critics have pointed out how his pacifism allows him to preside over an imperial and violent state.[27] Those moments in which the king attempts to minimize his own power, to declare universal equality, and to represent himself as thoroughly benevolent never escape the taint of potential violence that simmers below the surface. In this respect, as chapter 2 argued, the king recalls the efforts of British Hanovarians to find new means of legitimation after the Glorious Revolution and the civil war damaged the case for divine right. Vincent Carretta argues, by the late seventeenth century, "Englishmen increasingly came to accept the monarchy to be 'though a wise institution...clearly a human institution.'"[28] The Glorious Revolution, even more than the Restoration, "enabled satirists to exploit the separation of the king's two bodies by more firmly establishing the king's right to power as positive rather than divine in origin" (38).

However, according to John Barrell, this effort to minimize the differences between king and subject is really only a ruse. Barrell argues that sentimental discourse about George III and Louis XVI in the eighteenth century, on the one hand, represented weak and vulnerable kings, feminized mortals, dependent on the protection of the people. On the other, however, this representation of benevolent monarchy only barely covered an underlying promise of danger: for Barrell, monarchical benevolence is only a mask, which, "like the stocking pulled down over the features of the bank robber...makes the face beneath still more frightening than it would be without the disguise."[29] This image of the tender father, then, depends on the very violence it claims to disavow.

As critics such as Michael Simpson and Susan Wolfson argue, the representation of Sardanapalus speaks to this problem of disavowed but nonetheless always threatened violence.[30] The king asks that his subjects "make me not remember/ I am a monarch" (I.ii.51–52), but this desire to forget is only superficially a sign of egalitarian politics. The king, at times, echoes Myrrha and Salemenes's fantasy that when pushed, he will revert to the manliness of his ancestors. Anticipating Barrell's account of a king "as a kind of drag queen,"[31] Sardanapalus describes himself as "softer clay, impregnated with flowers" (II.i.522). But when his loyal subjects warn the king that his people are displeased with him, the king declares,

> If [the rebellious people] rouse me, better
> They had conjured up stern Nimrod from his ashes,
> "The mighty hunter." I will turn these realms
> To one wide desert chase of brutes, who *were*
> But *would* no more, by their own choice, be human. (I.ii.372–76)

Violence remains a potential threat beneath the appearance of feminine softness and the protestations of peace and benevolence.

At one point in the play, Sardanapalus seems at least momentarily swayed to move from the harem to the battlefield. What the benevolent king hides, the warrior must reveal. Whereas George III denies British imperial power with his homely, fatherly appearance, Nelson and Wellington reveal the nation's manly power. In the Assyrian state, the king himself is called on to become Wellington, a call that George IV believed he too had received and answered on the fields of Waterloo. The Assyrian public calls the king's bluff and demands to see his latent capacity for violence. Without pretense of kindness, this public admires overt displays of power and understands its leader's martial virility as the barometer of the nation's health.

The Performance of Heroism in Sardanapalus

Because the theatricality of war is as vital to the king's power as is the actual might of his troops, Salemenes and Myrrha must rouse the king not only to fight but also to display himself before the people. When the revolt begins, Salemenes urges the king,

> To arm himself, altho but for a moment
> And show himself unto the soldiers: his
> Sole presence in this instant might do more
> Than hosts can do in his behalf. (III.i.95–98)

But with rebel armies threatening destruction, the king takes time to quibble about his attire. Refusing the battle helmet offered him, he calls for one adorned with gems. Warned that "all men will recognize you" (141) with so conspicuous an ornament, he cries, "I go forth to be recognized" (III.i.143). Before stepping onto the battlefield, Sardanapalus calls for a mirror and wastes precious time admiring his military attire:

> This cuirass fits me well, the baldric better,
> And the helm not at all. Methinks I seem
> Passing well in these toys. (III.i.163–165)

On the one hand, the king understands the role he must play and offers his rebel people what they have clamored for— a sight of their king in battle. On the other hand, this overinvestment in his appearance, like George IV's hobby, marks the king's continuing effeminacy.

Although to others he seems transformed (Myrrha declares her love for him because "now I know thee" [108]), this call to arms does not mark a profound manifestation of a true self previously latent. The king whose manliness lies dormant and must be roused is a fantasy of the king's subjects and does not really explain Sardanapalus's actions at the end of the play. The king removes one costume to take on another. His carelessness about appearing on the battlefield and his attention to details of costume suggest not a latent courage made manifest but, rather, the actor's preparation for a performance. Sardanapalus maintains a distance from his martial role that both Myrrha and Salemenes fail to see. Unlike Salemenes and Myrrha's account of the king's transformation from harem ruler to warrior, Sardanapalus enacts yet another performance in which the man who should be king discovers the "falsehood of this my station" (I.ii.448–449).

It is no great leap for the man who has played at being king for so long to ascend a new stage and play the warrior. Whether in the harem or on the battlefield, however, the performances are similar; as one soldier comments, the king "fights as he revels!" (III.i.213). And Myrrha concurs that he "rushes from the banquet to battle. As though it were a bed of love" (III.i.223–24).

Unnoticed by his followers, the king experiences a continuing effeminacy that keeps all his self-representations external, distanced, never truly
self-coincident. Effeminacy, in the play, is the king's perpetual awareness
of this divide between the self and the identities offered to it. Unlike
George IV, merely a failure who nonetheless desperately wished to assume
his martial role, a bad actor, who does not even know he is acting,
Sardanapalus can skillfully play the soldier but he can never become him.
Remaining a perpetual amateur, Sardanapalus acts the part of a soldier but
refuses to be professionalized, to become the part he plays. Like the aristocratic dandy Russell describes who makes a show of his refusal to take any
role seriously, the king can move from the harem to the battlefield and
back without ever fully becoming either soldier or king. Refusing to conflate his body at war with the nation's power, the aristocrat makes a game
of war and flaunts his skill to accentuate the carelessness with which he
abandons one theater to act in another.

By claiming that Sardanapalus ultimately refuses to assume the martial
image he is supposed to embody, I deviate from some of the most important
criticism on the play. Susan Wolfson avers that Byron reserves a certain sympathy for the king by suggesting that his effeminacy is not really the symptom of a coward but rather of a character with a certain flexibility. His
effeminacy can encompass both a latent masculinity and a humane kindness
because "beneath the surface of Sardanapalus's pleasure-seeking, he leaves
signs of 'latent energies' (1.1.11) pointed towards a plot of masculine emergence."[32] Although this emergence cannot cover the "the problem of effeminate character" that "retains its daring and conflicting strains of definition"
(894), for Wolfson, the king makes his peace to some degree with the image
of manhood he is supposed to embody. Likewise, Jerome Christensen sees
Sardanapalus as interpolated by his "Myrrha-ed image of himself" as warrior
(280). Playing on the name of the king's Greek slave, Christensen sees
Sardanapalus as seduced by "that *ideal* Sardanapalus who, having become as
kingly as his state, would be a self worthy of his own love" (280). My reading
of this play stresses, instead, the king's inability to recognize the mirrored
image as his own reflection. He cannot find in the warrior image held forth
for him any similitude to a self that is a "nothing," that, as he claims by the
end of the play, is characterized by a refusal to become the roles he plays.

The illusion of "masculine emergence," however, does take hold of the
Assyrian people. Sardanapalus stumbles on a theatrical moment in which his
playacting is mistaken for the real thing. For a moment, the effeminate king,
donning a new costume, is mistaken by his people for a warrior who can
embody national strength. However, when Byron's Assyrian spectacle was
presented on the British stage in the mid-nineteenth century, the play was
edited in such a way that the king could appear to have actually recovered his

virility, thus hiding his failure fully to assume his role from the British public as well. The masculinization of the nineteenth-century staged *Sardanapalus* required that no sign of the king's effeminacy remain after he decides to fight in battle. Victorian stage productions in England even edited out the mirror scene altogether.[33] An appalled nineteenth-century theater critic commented on the absurd lengths to which productions of the play went to deny the king's effeminacy:

> The impression Charles Kean is likely to leave is one of astonishment that any man accustomed to the stage could speak verse so ignorantly, and evade expression so successfully.... Thus, when the sword is placed in his hands, he gives it back, with the remark that it is too heavy, and this remark, instead of expressing effeminacy, he utters as if it were a stolid assertion of a matter of fact! How Byron would have fumed could he have heard his intention thus rendered![34]

If, as Byron writes the play, British audiences ought to remain aware of the king's continuing effeminacy, the Assyrian audience in the play is fooled. Sardanapalus's performance is remarkably successful because, unlike George IV's effeminate interest in costume, the Assyrian king's performance appears to be the realization of his latent warrior nature. On the point of losing everything to the rebels, the king's triumphant emergence in the theater of war helps push back the enemy and offers a possibility of victory. The power of theater is never more ironically evident than when the effeminate king, wearing his new "toys," succeeds in embodying the warrior ideal. The troops are mesmerized and revitalized by Sardanapalus's appearance before them; the rebels are pushed back and matched for a time if not defeated; Salemenes and Myrrha are won over by the show and see Sardanapalus's transformation as the sudden emergence of the king's latent virility. The irony is that the spectacle of military prowess can amount to little more than the performance of a dandy. It was the absurdity of this power of belief that the nineteenth-century stage productions of *Sardanapalus* tried to hide from their audiences. The play ridicules British audiences who, like their Assyrian counterparts, may have consumed the spectacle of war and the spectacle of heroism wholesale.[35]

The Feminine Warrior and the Effeminate King

If careful editing prevented nineteenth-century English audiences from perceiving the scandal of theater, one theatergoer does see the scandal and does not recover from it. Sardanapalus maintains a distance from his performance, an attachment to his effeminacy. This final section of the chapter addresses the king's attempts to redefine gender categories by refusing to conflate liberal benevolence and martial virility in a unity reminiscent of imperial Britain.

Throughout the play, characters such as Salemenes claim that manliness is defined by a certain disposition to war. Biological women, it seems, can become men by engaging in war. Sardanapalus's foremother, Semiramis, is a woman who has become a man by going to war. Undisturbed by biological sex, characters in the play simply understand Semiramis as a man. Salemenes refers to her as "Semiramis, the man-queen" (I.i.43) and "Like a *man*" (I.ii.129). Conversely, Sardanapalus, the reticent warrior, is "The she-king, / That less than woman" (II.i.48–49). In the last scenes of the play, this unproblematic commitment to war, this willingness to become a warrior, comes to mark, for Sardanapalus, not a manly disposition but a feminine one.

After stepping off the battlefield, Sardanapalus confronts the nightmare of his successful performance. He discovers that he has condemned himself to the perpetuation of his ancestors' reign, to the repeated enactment of a role that he cannot really inhabit. In a nightmare about Semiramis, following his performance on the battlefield, Sardanapalus relives the decay of his ancestors' aura and the concomitant rise of Semiramis's perversity and violence. In his dream, Sardanapalus attempts to make contact with his male ancestors who seem turned to stone until Nimrod

> laid his hand on mine: I took it,
> And grasp'd it— but it melted from my own;
> While he too vanish'd, and left nothing but
> The memory of a hero, for he look'd so. (IV.i.143–146)

The hero disappears, a mere shadow, a phantom that only lives in memory. Only Semiramis comes nightmarishly to life when she flies

> upon me,
> And burnt my lips with her noisome kisses
> Still she clung;
> The other phantoms, like a row of statues,
> Stood dull as in our temples. (149–55)

Between stone and air, his male ancestors are petrified idols who, paradoxically, vanish to the touch. For the king, male power has petrified itself away into nothing so that his forefathers have become insubstantial ghosts. The failure to concretize the reality and coherence of the father's power gives body to the obscenely sexualized mother.

Sardanapalus, at this point in the play, begins to formulate a new understanding of martial heroism inextricably connected to the female body. As
Susan Wolfson has pointed out, in the dream scene, Sardanapalus appears to
discover the similarities between his lover Myrrha and his foremother:

> I sought thy sweet face in the circle—but
> Instead—a grey-hair'd, wither'd bloody-eyed,
> And bloody-handed, ghastly, ghostly thing,
> Female in garb. (IV.i.103–106)[36]

Instead of his lover, the king discovers his ancestor who assaults him with
"her noisome kisses" (IV.i.150). This confusion between his violent foremother and his concubine occurs after Myrrha has stepped out onto the battlefield and has fought like a warrior. The king describes her in battle:

> like the dam of the young lion, femininely raging
> (And femininely meaneth furiously,
> Because all passions in excess are female)
> Against the hunter flying with her cub,
> She urged on with her voice. (III.i.379–83)

By connecting her violence to her maternal feelings, Sardanapalus sees
Myrrha's capacity to fight as the natural expression of her gender. After all,
"all passions in excess are female" and a woman's emergence on the battlefield is merely a new outlet for her excess.[37] Violence is also an expression of
sexual desire in women because Semiramis unites bloodthirsty violence with
"lust" (IV.i.108). Both figured as mothers, Myrrha and Semiramis become
examples of warriors who fight as though violence were a part of their nature.
Like the professional soldier that Russell describes, they become the part
they play. But by making violence the natural expression of the maternal and
sexualized female body, Sardanapalus turns violence into a feature of uncontrollable feminine excess. For Sardanapalus, then, femininity functions as the
obverse of effeminacy. If effeminacy is the refusal to really inhabit any role,
to assume the performance as an expression of the king's interiority, femininity marks the total immersion in the role, its naturalization.[38] When
Semiramis and Myrrha fight in battle they are not actors playing a part. They
fight because it is their nature to do so, because they are unable to achieve
distance between bodies and performances.[39]

This misogynist fantasy recalls to Sardanapalus the obscenity of war and
breaks his momentary desire to be reunited with the glory of the past. In her
violent frenzy, Semiramis, the queen, brings together the familiar figure of
the female revolutionary (such as Edmund Burke's furies in the *Reflections*)
with the figure of the warrior leader. The play appropriates the image of the
violent revolutionary woman to make her the excess symbolic of imperial

power rather than of revolutionary force. Far from critiquing the revolutionary woman, however, the misogynist aspects of this image undercut the imperialism of the established state. Sardanapalus imagines her "manly" violence as a sign of a feminine excess that contaminates every aspect of her life making sexuality, violence, and motherhood the signs of an uncontrollable and obscene femininity.

By the end of the play, Sardanapalus refuses the call to violence. When the last chance of victory depends on waiting for reinforcements as Salemenes recommends, Sardanapalus "over-rule[s] him" (V.i.147). If the rebels succeed it is because the king removes every obstacle to their coup. A successful revolt answers his purposes in a way that his own success never can. To defeat the rebels is to accept tyranny and the value of Semiramis's bloodthirsty reign. By configuring a certain relation to power as feminine, the king can finally abandon his claims to empire. If according to Salemenes a warrior woman becomes a man, now, according to Sardanapalus's logic, a warrior man becomes a woman. The king can say,

I am no soldier, but a man: speak not
Of soldiership, I loathe the word, and those
Who pride themselves upon it. (IV.i.565–68)

Having distinguished between manhood and soldiership, the king now seems poised to define a new manliness.

However, the attempt to bankrupt the traditional notion of martial virility by feminizing it may not offer a new political position. The play critiques British hypocrisy, which sees Napoleon as barbaric for expanding his empire while celebrating Britain's own imperial conquests. But in the person of the Assyrian king it does not appear to offer a clear alternative to British hypocrisy and imperialism. The king can debunk the assumptions of his culture but, in the end, he appears to commit an act of spectacular feminine self-destruction. His last act is an attempt to replace his ancestor's failed monuments with a monument of his own. This monument is a funeral pyre on which the king burns all his possessions, his slave, and himself.

Myrrha reads the king's desire to burn himself on the pyre as an example of the king's true manly courage that recalls the sacrifice of Indian widows. Eager to die herself, Myrrha declares,

dost thou think
A Greek girl dare not do for love, that which
An Indian widow braves for custom? (465–67)

Myrrha reminds Sardanapalus that she is a "Greek girl." Both her heritage, which links her to the martial culture par excellence, the model for and source of British manhood, and her gender make her fit for total commitment to an act of violence, even self-violence. The Indian widow here becomes one more example of women who truly commit to a role or action. Myrrha's willingness to "truly follow [Sardanapalus], freely and fearlessly" (463–64).

suggests that she has read this act of self-destruction as another example of devoted commitment— as she did when he assumed his martial costume and props and entered the field of battle. But if she could misread him once before, it may be that she misreads him again.

Myrrha's interpretation of the king's final act fails to account for how Sardanapalus refuses the identities offered to him. The king sets about creating a spectacular theatrical coup:

> In this blazing palace,
> And its enormous walls of reeking ruin,
> We leave a nobler monument than Egypt
> Hath piled in her brick mountains. (480–83)

If he has failed throughout the play to find the role that can truly become him, the king imagines that in death he will at least leave behind a monument that will "lesson ages." But, after the conflagration, of course, this monument will be a pile of ashes; it can only be memorable in the act of burning, as a spectacle in a play. Like his ancestors' monument that would be stone, this last "nobler monument" is as evanescent as smoke. By claiming to monumentalize himself and his reign, he appears to fall into the feminine he has wished to deny. However, his death offers potentially different meanings suggested by the king's final claims about his suicide.

By destroying everything that belongs to him, by leaving behind a monument that is a "reeking ruin" (V.i.481), the king literalizes the nothing he feels himself to be. He negates the value of martial virility but offers no clear alternative other than an abdication of all public power. If between the violence of empire and the hypocrisy of benevolence, the king finds no new politics, the king's monument perhaps does, nonetheless, "lessons ages" as a reminder of the scandalous link between British claims to liberty and benevolence and British imperialism. This link allows benevolence to mask a dependence on various forms of unacknowledged coercion. Sardanapalus's total destruction of his rule dramatizes a razing to the ground of an empire and, as an event, rather than a monument, it promises, like the French Revolution, to live on in historical memory as a "leap through flame into the future" (V.i.415), an as yet unrealized possibility for a future beyond empires and a liberalism that perpetuates them.

Chapter 4

Sublime Democracy and the Theater of Violence

Authoritarianism in William Hazlitt's *The Life of Napoleon Buonaparte*

*W*here Byron offers a pointed critique of how a liberal commitment to benevolence and commodity consumption relies on the thrilling presence of the martial leader, William Hazlitt explicitly champions violent leadership as the only means of creating unity in a modern commercial and political culture. This chapter considers the scandalous nature of Hazlitt's monomania for Napoleon by placing it within Hazlitt's critique of modernity as enervated and effeminate, requiring the supplement of a fanatical leader. For Hazlitt, political unity can take place only as a result of terror, a politics of committed violence against an enemy who allows the people to come together against a common foe. Of the writers this book examines, Hazlitt is the most explicit about the importance of violence in modern, enlightened times.

Although Hazlitt's readers and commentators have often tried to minimize Hazlitt's interest in Napoleon and to see his support of a tyrant as a miscalculation in a career long opposition to monarchy, evidence suggests that, even before Hazlitt dedicated his last years to the biography of Napoleon, he saw the need to arrest democratic plurality and to acclaim the strongman. In an 1821 essay, "Guy Faux," Hazlitt offers a long critique of the effeminate modern temperament, emasculated by a commercial culture. Central in much of Hazlitt's criticism of the present is the modern citizen's refusal to commit to a great cause. The capacity to remain imaginatively committed to a cause or individual is hampered by a culture of mass publicity that undermines any stable source of value or authority. Hazlitt claims that fanaticism belongs only to the past when people so thoroughly believed in an idea or object that they are ready to give up their lives for it. Far from abhorring fanaticism, Hazlitt makes the odd argument that to be a fanatic is to be free: "He who can prevail upon himself to devote his life to a cause, however we may condemn his opinions or abhor his actions, vouches at least for the honesty of his principles and the disinterestedness of his motives. He may be guilty of the worst practices, but he is capable of the greatest. He is no longer a slave, but free."[1] Freedom, here, means the ability to dedicate oneself to a cause in which one truly believes without being enslaved by fear for one's life. In the present, "We have no Guy Fauxes now" because self-sacrifice "does not suit the *radical* scepticism [*sic*] of the age!"(20:99) In modern times "fanaticism expires with philosophy, and heroism with refinement. There can be no mixture of scepticism [*sic*] in the one, nor any distraction of interest in the other. That blind attachment to individuals or principles, which is necessary to make us stake our all upon a single die, wears out with the progress of society" (20:100). Hazlitt mourns this past faith because "it shews that in the public mind and feeling there is something better than life; that there is a belief of something in the universe and the order of nature, to which it is worth while to sacrifice this poor brief span of existence" (20:99).

Hazlitt claims that without faith in an object greater than himself, Guy Faux would be:

> Like the wretched straw-figure, the automaton we see representing him, "disembowelled of his natural entrails, without a real heart of flesh and blood beating in his bosom," a modern time-server, an unimpassioned slave, a canting Jesuit, a petty, cautious, cringing sycophant, promoting his own interest by taking the bread out of honest mouths, a mercenary malignant coward, a Clerical Magistrate, a Quarterly Reviewer, a Member of the Constitutional Association, the concealed Editor of Blackwood's Magazine! (20:101)

On the face of it, the language of slavery in this passage might suggest that Hazlitt blames modern men for not freeing themselves from the powers that subject them. These men are, after all, "cringing sycophants." But the problem seems otherwise. Hazlitt describes "unimpassioned" slaves who submit without any real commitment to the powers they serve. In fact, the sycophant only subjects himself to serve his own interest. He is a coward, but a "mercenary" one. The modern man's subjection is a false pose of submission in which he pretends to submit to another while really only serving himself.[2] The types Hazlitt lists—the magistrate, the reviewer, the editor, the assemblyman—hold public offices but they perversely promote the self over the public good. The politician, like the man of letters, serves no larger cause than self-promotion. Guy Faux may be represented in effigy as a straw figure but the real straw man is the modern, living man. Like Burke's French revolutionaries, modern men are disembowelled of all feeling; the straw man represents the modern failure to believe in the servile poses one assumes.

Hazlitt's essay also considers the fanaticism of another historical figure, Margaret of Lambrun. Particularly interesting is that Hazlitt pairs an example of male heroism and true devotion with a woman. In this essay, the virility expressed by true commitment is not a feature of men but of certain historical subjects living in a world that permits fanatical commitment. Margaret is a fanatical devotee of Mary Queen of Scots. Dressed as a man, Margaret attempts to assassinate Queen Elizabeth to avenge Mary's execution. That the patriarchal structure is replicated in a matriarchal context seems to offer no obstacle to fanatical attachment in this essay. In this older culture, virility extends to both sexes.[3]

In his discussion of Lambrun, Hazlitt makes clear that the obstacle to modern fanaticism is commodity culture. He writes, once, "Novels, plays, magazines, treatises of philosophy, Monthly Museums, and *Belles Assemblees*, did not fly in numbers about the country and 'through the airy region stream so bright,' as to blot out the impression of all real forms" (20:103). In the past "the heart made its election once, and was fixed till death" (20:103). But now:

> A devoted and incorrigible attachment to individuals, as well as to doctrines, is weakened by the progress of knowledge and civilization. A spirit of scepticism [*sic*], of inquiry, of comparison, is introduced too, by the course of reading, observation, and reflection which strikes at the root of our disproportionate idolatry. Margaret Lambrun did not think there was such another woman in the world as her mistress, Queen Mary; nor could she, after her death, see any thing in it worth living for. Had she had access to a modern circulating library, she would have read of a hundred such heroines, all peerless alike; and would have consoled herself for the death of them all, one after another, pretty much in the same manner. (20:103)

Margaret's devotion depends on her limited exposure to publicity because the "truth is, she had never seen such another woman as her mistress, and she had no means, by books or otherwise, of forming an idea of any thing but what she saw" (20:103). In a society lacking publicity, "people grew together like trees, and clung around the strongest for support.... They became devoted to others with the same violence of attachment as they were to themselves" (20:103). To lose one's leader meant "the loss of another self" (20:104). This capacity for total self-identification with another and for total submission in the service of a leader thought to be greater than one-self is no longer possible. Modern publicity or publication creates a culture in which the "respect of persons" is lost and in which the real attachment to the individual is destroyed by the insistent representation of like individuals that replace the original. Once the circulating libraries, particularly reviled sites of fashion making, offer infinite objects of idolatry, Margaret fails to be a devoted fanatic and becomes instead a vacuous reader of fashionable novels.[4] Content with the "airy region," she need not look for "real forms."

Part of the problem is that nothing in modern times is worth dying for. In the present:

> We are [ordinarily] placed out of the reach of "the shot of accident and the dart of chance"; and grow indolent, tender, and effeminate in our notions and habits. Books do not make men valiant,— not even reading the chronicle of the Cid. The police look after all breaches of the peace and resorts of suspicious characters, so that we need not buckle on our armour to go to the succour of distressed damsels, or to give battle to giants and enchanters. Instead of killing some fourteen before breakfast, like Hotspur, we are contented to read of these things in the newspapers, or to see them performed on the stage. We enjoy all the dramatic interest of such scenes, without the tragic results.... We love fight and are slain by proxy—live over the adventures of a hundred heroes and die their deaths—and the next day are as well as ever, and ready to begin again. (20:112)

Modern people are effeminate because they live "by proxy." Like the effeminati of republican discourse, they no longer fight their own wars and defend their own communities. They become the consumers of commodity culture, who give up their manly independence for the pleasures of culture. For Hazlitt, "Men, the more they cultivate their intellect, become more careful of their persons.... Their existence has been chiefly theatrical, ideal, a tragedy rehearsed in print—why should it receive its *denouement* in their proper persons, in *corpore vili?*" (20:112). A culture of warriors disappears to be replaced by a culture of theatergoers and novel readers. Modern people are effeminate because they live in and with the literary and theatrical spectacles of their age, rather than placing their actual bodies at risk.

Here, Hazlitt's tone is lighthearted and amused. He seems to view the martial failures of his culture and its obsession with theater with a certain indulgence. After all, when Hazlitt writes, "we are contented to read of these things in the newspapers, or to see them performed on the stage," the theater critic implicates his own desire in this modern culture of spectatorship. This essay offers both a humorous understanding of modern effeminacy and suggests the impossibility of a return to older forms of fanaticism.

In modernity, Hazlitt claims, echoing Burke, people have lost their "prejudices," which are "honest, hearty, wholesome things" (20:102). Burke's point about enlightened thought, of course, is that it is not simply wrong but that it strips the decent drapery from the most cherished illusions, revealing that the king is merely a man beneath the regalia of his office. For Burke, then, illusions serve the English better than naked nature. The monarch must be covered by "pleasing illusions" because he requires the supplement of "super-added ideas . . . necessary to cover the defects of our naked shivering nature."[5] As a fanatic, Guy Faux is perhaps merely someone who believes in illusions, unlike enlightened modern men. And Margaret is the victim of a "disproportionate idolatry" (20:103). Faux's idol is Catholicism and Lambrun's idol is a monarch and a woman, doubly illegitimate. Also Faux and Lambrun seem, themselves, mired in error and obfuscation. Guy Faux's name suggests his falseness or that of his cause. Margaret must dissemble her sex because to commit murder "she put on a man's habit" (100). The image of Margaret putting on a habit that is not her own is perhaps the most suggestive image of the problem in which Hazlitt finds himself embroiled. Every habit may be put on—the priest's as well as the man's. Guy Faux, as priest and man, is doubly put upon by Margaret's "put on." Hazlitt's interest in fanaticism confronts the problem of authenticity. From the perspective of the nineteenth-century essayist who attempts to recover some value in Faux's and Lambrun's fanaticism, their commitment appears if not altogether false, at least, idiotically deluded. Hazlitt's essay explores the desire for a cause but finds only failure. The essay speaks to a desire without satisfaction in a modern political culture dedicated to self-interest rather than the public good and a commodity culture in which all objects lose their value and are replaced with every new fashion.

If Faux and Lambrun are anachronistic failures, in Napoleon, Hazlitt attempts to find a genuine modern fanatic to whom modern people can commit. The *Life of Napoleon Buonaparte* reveals that Hazlitt is profoundly concerned about the chaotic multiplicity of the people's desires and about the dullness of modern political and commercial culture that cannot unify the people in support of a worthy cause. Hazlitt's support for Napoleon reveals a desire for a unified public untroubled by democratic plurality.

Authoritarian Democracy

Between 1828 and 1830 Hazlitt's *The Life of Napoleon Buonaparte* appeared in print, a work of four volumes that was "the most ambitious task Hazlitt had ever undertaken" and that he "confidently hoped would outlast all his work for the periodicals."[6] Hazlitt wrote the biography as an answer to Sir Walter

Scott's attack on Napoleon in his *Life of Napoleon* (1827). Spanning Napoleon's life from his birth in Corsica to his death on St. Helena, Hazlitt's biography was intended as a work that would redeem Napoleon in the eyes of his detractors and justify Hazlitt's championing of him.

Hazlitt's critics have long tried to minimize the scandalous nature of Hazlitt's defense. One often-repeated argument is that Hazlitt admired Napoleon only because, despite his faults he at least, represented the ascendancy of democratic merit over aristocratic inheritance. Henry Crabb Robinson, Hazlitt's contemporary, offers a typical account of Hazlitt's interest in Napoleon:

> Hazlitt retains all his hatred of kings and bad governments, and believing them to be incorrigible, he from principle of revenge, rejoices that they are punished.... Hazlitt is angry with the friends of liberty for weakening their strength by going with the common foe against Buonaparte, by which the old governors are so much assisted, even in their attempts against the general liberty.... Hazlitt says: "Let the enemy of the old tyrannical governments triumph, I am glad, and I do not much care how the new government turns out."[7]

For Robinson, Hazlitt's interest in Napoleon is purely negative. Who or what he is matters little as long as Napoleon triumphs against the old tyrannical governments. Likewise, a modern critic of Hazlitt, John Kinnaird, claims, "when we examine Hazlitt's 'idolatry' in the context of English liberal attitudes...we soon discover that Napoleon's regime was often seen and judged...as perhaps the only 'enlightened' alternative to the hoary anachronisms that opposed his power."[8] According to David Bromwich, Napoleon represents, for Hazlitt, "the idea of individual power" as opposed to "the idea of aggregate power as embodied in an individual, 'The right divine of kings to govern wrong.'"[9] In one of the few extended analyses of the biography, Simon Bainbridge has argued, "Hazlitt's writing on Napoleon Bonaparte...was no simple indulgence of his own idolatry, but a calculated campaign of imaginative terrorism undertaken by a 'political partisan.' His Bonapartism was less an embarrassing personal flaw than a powerful and controversial expression of his unyielding radicalism."[10] Championing Napoleon is not an embarrassing indulgence but an imaginative strategy in Hazlitt's war against reactionary forces: "Napoleon was a figure for whom he developed 'a passionate attachment founded on an abstract idea' (XVII, 34)—namely opposition to the arbitrary power of legitimacy" (188). For these critics, Hazlitt's entire sense of Napoleon's merits stems from Hazlitt's hatred of kings; Napoleon appeals to Hazlitt because, whatever his personal defects, he ridicules the claims of divine-right rulers.[11] By these accounts, Hazlitt supports the claims of liberal individualism and merit against the tyranny of absolutism.

This chapter claims, however, that Hazlitt's interest in Napoleon goes far beyond a critique of absolutism. Hazlitt offers an extended argument against the dangers of democracy by calling for a strong man who can control democratic plurality. Hazlitt's biography makes clear that the temptation to resolve the problems of democratic plurality by turning to despotism was not limited to reactionaries.

Spectacles of Power: From the Terror to Napoleon

If Faux and Lambrun are hopeless anachronisms, Napoleon, Hazlitt argues in his biography, can arrest the wandering attention of a commodity-addicted public by replacing theatrical spectacles with the theater of war. To the political problems of modernity, Hazlitt offers the solution of violence, of protracted terror. Like Wordsworth in his *Convention of Cintra* and the Assyrian people in Byron's play, Hazlitt imagines war as the means of unifying a modern people. The first volume of the biography, which describes Napoleon's early years, offers a long digression on the Revolution and focuses on the battles and events of Napoleon's early career, Hazlitt explains why violence is central to any committed politics in modern times.

The first chapters of the biography offer a historical narrative leading up to the French revolution in which Hazlitt claims that, whereas the past was marked by ignorance, superstition, and barbarity, the present is marked by knowledge and a refusal of false idols, including kings. Echoing a view people on both the left and the right of the political spectrum held, Hazlitt writes the "French Revolution might be described as a remote but inevitable result of the invention of the art of printing"(13:38). Books "render the knowledge possessed by everyone in the community accessible to all" (13:38). In the present, Hazlitt argues, "opinion at last becomes a match for arbitrary power" (13:38). Sounding much like Jürgen Habermas's eighteenth-century public sphere, Hazlitt's enlightened public becomes united by "a body of opinion directly at variance with the selfish and servile code that before reigned paramount" (13:40).[12] The public gains "strength from being united in public opinion, and expressed by the public voice, are like the congregated roar of many waters, and quail the hearts of princes" (13:40). According to this account of the public and of publicity, knowledge allows the community to form a consensus of opinion that forwards progressive, antimonarchical goals and creates revolutionary change. Hazlitt writes, a "public sense is thus formed, free from slavish awe of the traditional assumption of insolent superiority, which the more it is exercised the more it becomes enlightened and enlarged, and more and more requires equal rights and equal laws" (13:41). The press creates a "public sense" that is free from "slavish awe," that is no longer bound by fear or "traditional assumption of insolent superiority." This enlightened freedom from former attachments impels the public to require a more democratic state comprising "equal rights and equal laws." In the face of tyranny "public opinion must become active, and break the moulds of pre-scription in which [the king's] right derived from his ancestors is cast, and this will be a Revolution" (13:42). Publicity in this context creates "the germ of a body of opinion" (13:40). The public is not an unintelligible mass but rather a unified entity with a "body," an "opinion," and a "voice" (13:40) that Hazlitt represents as the "congregated roar of many waters" (13:40). He argues, "books anticipate and conform the decision of the public...to that lofty and irrevocable standard, mould and fashion the heart...so that some-thing manly, liberal and generous grows out of the fever of passion and the palsy of base fear" (13:41). Manliness becomes the capacity to work for the public good, beyond selfish interest, so that enlightened people are "gener-ous" and able to match their actions to lofty standards.

However, this moment of Habermasian enlightened publicity is short lived for Hazlitt. Once enlightened understanding destroys the fear of the ancien regime, and a "king was no longer thought to be an image of Divinity," (13:43) then "the ancient *regime* ceased to be supported by that system of faith and manners" and "the whole order of the state became warped and disunited, a wretched jumble of claims that were neither enforced nor relinquished" (13:45). This government, "effete in all its branches," was no longer capable of uniting the people in servile terror and "fell to the ground as a useless encumbrance" (13:46).

If the Revolution can be said to have one particular meaning for its con-temporaries it was that the present broke ties with the patriarchal past, a break symbolized most dramatically in the beheading of the king, the sever-ing of patriarchal and divine links. Kant, in an often-quoted footnote from *The Metaphysics of Morals*, claims that the public nature of the king's death transformed an act of regicide into an act of symbolic "suicide."[13] The murder of the king in secret would have been merely an act of regicide but by offering a public execution, the revolutionaries struck beyond the merely "empirical body" and killed the king's divine body, that body which consti-tuted the community as such. In her reading of this footnote, Alenka Zupancic asks, "Why is it that for Kant this act of 'the people' has the struc-ture of suicide? Because the people are constituted as The People only in relation to this symbolic order. Outside it, they are nothing more than 'masses' with no proper status. It is the monarch (in his symbolic function) who gives the people their symbolic existence."[14] The beheading of the king destroys the community's capacity to see itself reflected in its representative and generates chaos.

In Hazlitt's account of the Revolution, however, the government avoids this chaos by creating a substitute image in which the people can find some, at least, temporary sense of unity. Unlike many "French accounts" of the Revolution that see it as "a succession of harebrained leaders and sanguinary factions, chasing one another round the arena," Hazlitt sees a focused purpose in the Reign of Terror (13:54). The French avoided dissolution and anarchy, ironically, by instituting the Terror. The public spectacle of violence saved the Revolution from enemies within and without the nation. In the biography and throughout his essays, Hazlitt insistently accuses women, the French, modern people, and humanity in general of a profound lack of constancy to higher principles or great causes. In *The Life*, in particular, he lambastes the French for an inability to steer the course of Revolution.[15] In the biography, this tendency is avoided because the French become obsessed with public violence:

> To rouse or keep alive any strong enthusiasm, there must be a dramatic effect added to the conviction of truth or justice. Liberty must have its festivals, its garlands, its altars; and when these fail or are soiled, its tragic stage, its scaffolds, its daggers, and the sliders of the guillotine. Otherwise the interest soon flags—they would be sick of it in a month. But give them excitement, and there is nothing they will stop at under its impulse...a bleeding head stuck upon a pole in honour of liberty, would do more to attach them to it than all the good it could to millions of men for ages to come. (13:120)

The way "to attach" the French to Revolutionary action is to stimulate their taste for theater. For Hazlitt, the "craving after excitement was pampered into a disease, a *mania*; and no matter who or what the subject, it was necessary to bring out new plots, new accusations, new horrors for the public entertainment, like a succession of new pieces at a theater" (13:135). Hazlitt adds, that the "habit of going to the place of execution resembled that of visiting the theater...[France] became one scene of wild disorder, and the Revolution a stage of blood!" (13:152–53). The French want a theater in which they can strike "at the spectre of power which haunted them like a filthy nightmare" (13:112). The French are neither brave nor manly, Hazlitt claims, so that, to build their courage "to adhere to certain fixed principles" (13:119), they must first meet their adversaries "by proxy. Having cut the throats of the royalists in prison, they looked upon them as poor wretches and themselves as heroes, and thus recovered spirit to face them in the field. A massacre was therefore a necessary prelude to a victory" (13:120). The theater of public execution offers the "stimulus to produce the customary sense of energy and self-complacency" (13:134) and compels an effeminate people to defend the Revolution. At the heart of this interest in execution is "the love of power" (13:164). The French can defeat their enemies in battle because they have already defeated them in the theater of execution.

The executions reflect both what the French have lost and what they wish to regain: an image of themselves, a focal point of self-representation that instills in them a sense of their power as people. This public of the Revolution cannot sustain an attachment to abstractions such as liberty or even to a conception of the people; it can only attach itself to images—bloody images. The severed head offers a perverse point of unity. If the king's headless body no longer represents the people, then his severed head can offer a macabre image of the masses united in power. Although Hazlitt is troubled by this violence, he writes, the "rabid and violent whirl of the political machine might be said for a wonder to have suspended the versatility of the national character" (13:169).

The real danger to the Revolution emerges only when the pressures of foreign attack and internal dissension abate and "within a few months the volatile genius of this people, impatient of liberty or repose, and eager for some new theatrical display, since the daily procession of the *guillotine* no longer kept them in a state of excitement or dismay, seemed anxious to get rid of the Revolution altogether" (13:184). Now that the terror is over, Hazlitt sees France caught up in "the shifting of the scenes of a pantomime, the oscillation from one dangerous extreme to another, without any motive but the love of change or contrast" (13:185). Hazlitt admits to a "disposition to excuse Robespierre and others for thinking that liberty and patriotism alone had not sufficient charms for the Parisians without the aid of terror, and that it was necessary to resort to extreme violence to compress their extreme versatility" (13:185).

Hazlitt claims this is the lesson Napoleon learns: "Buonaparte, who was in Paris at the time of this reaction...might then probably have come to the conclusion (on which he acted afterward) that a people so prone to vanity... were as unfit as possible for the enjoyment of a system of regulated and constitutional liberty" (13:185). For Hazlitt, Napoleon comes to substitute the spectacle of his own power and violence for that of the guillotine, thus reuniting the French and repressing "their extreme versatility." By the end of the biography, Hazlitt explains, "Men in a savage and rude society are slaves, because they do not know what liberty is: in a state of civilization and knowledge, they want the courage to defend it. Liberty and independence are also nearly another name for disunion and party-spirit" (15:233). Democracy threatens to become a state of complete "disunion" in which each individual pursues his or her own liberty, his or her own interests. The paradox of

Napoleon's reign is that he must impose a despotic unity to make the people strong enough to defend liberty.

This vision of a divided and fickle public that constantly threatens to destroy the Revolution is symptomatic of a democratic imaginary in which a successful democracy must be essentially constituted by a single voice. Claude Lefort's work on the emergence of totalitarianism from democracy makes explicit why Hazlitt's view of democracy lends itself to the seductions of Napoleonic rule. The need to imagine a unified people arises because "modern democratic society seems to me, in fact, like a society that has become the theater of an uncontrollable adventure."[16] For Lefort, a public desire to visualize power emerges because the "real" object is missing. The people cannot be visualized and power is both everywhere and nowhere. The totalitarian leader replaces the impossible realization of the social, the impossible experience of the people-as-one with his, own singular image. The belief in the reality or possibility of a unified voice engenders the desire to manifest that voice. "Napoleon" is Hazlitt's name for a public will in the postrevolutionary world, a will that can subsume the antagonisms of a desiring multitude. By replacing divine-right monarchy with despotic militarism, he becomes what Lefort calls an "Egocrat." If leaders in the past could claim, however tenuously, that their authority derived from divine authority, the modern leader's right to rule stems from his merit, strength, and charisma. Traditionally, Lefort writes, the prince "was *supposed* to obey a superior power; he declared himself to be both above the law and subjected to the law, to be both the father and the son of justice" (306). However, "The Egocrat coincides with himself, as society is supposed to coincide with itself" (306). The egocrat assumes full responsibility for his power and aura. It emanates only from him because he is not a representative of some other power located in some other place.

The Power of Terror

If Hazlitt might be said to predate many of Lefort's arguments about why egocrats emerge after the end of absolutism, he is far more interested than Lefort in the problems of publicity, in how the leader manifests himself before the people and how he protects himself against their fickle desires. The warnings of republican thinkers reappear in Hazlitt's writing about modern political and economic power. Because we cannot recreate the conditions of an ideal enlightened public, because modern people are easily seduced by the multiple spectacles of a mass culture and by the promises of liberal individualism, Napoleon must adapt to modern conditions. He must create a spectacle that is so thrilling it fascinates and fixes the public gaze to produce unity and loyalty.

On the one hand, Hazlitt wishes to represent a Napoleon who is above making theater of himself, who "passes shew." On the other, he understands the necessity of making war a spectacle for public consumption. In the first volume, Hazlitt offers an example of a Napoleon who resists publicity. A young hero, Napoleon declines an appearance at the theaters on his return from a successful campaign:

> This shyness was not, as it may be thought, affected or the result of policy, but natural. It was the coming forward that was forced or like assuming a part. His temper was in itself reserved, and all his habits plain and simple. Besides, true glory always shrinks from the public gaze and admiration, except on rare and appropriate occasions; it has "that within which passes shew"; and mere personal appearance or external homage can but ill correspond with and but imperfectly express the great things it has performed, or the greater which it meditates. (13:319)

Like the theater that the French attend, Napoleon's battles have been a distant theater that the public wishes to bring home, but Napoleon shrinks from the "public gaze" because he "has 'that within which passes shew.'" Quoting from *Hamlet*, Hazlitt insists on an interiority that is unavailable for representation. No "mere personal appearance or external homage" can "correspond" with Napoleon's "true glory" so that appearing in public necessarily implies a self-betrayal, "assuming a part."

This fear of Napoleon's exposure before the public gaze speaks to a tradition Romantic writers inherited that is suspicious of images, that sees them as potentially seductive and treacherous, that associates the visible with the feminine. W. J. T. Mitchell writes, "Burke's essay on the sublime and the beautiful...made quite unmistakable the connection between poetry, sublimity, and masculinity on the one hand, and painting, beauty, and femininity on the other." [17] Burke's dichotomies helped shape a tradition in which "paintings, like women, are ideally silent, beautiful creatures designed for the gratification of the eye, in contrast to the sublime eloquence proper to the manly art of poetry" (111). Romantic writers imagine the power of the sublime that registers the impossibility of images to capture the self. When Burke valorizes writing over painting, he does so because "words are the sublime medium precisely because they cannot provide clear images" (125). For Mitchell, Burke wants to disassociate word from image, and so "strong is this desire that he becomes uneasy with the notion that words have a connection with *ideas*, since an idea, in the theory Burke wants to correct, is invariably equated with an image" (137). In the Romantic period, the sublime subject marks a desire to escape the image, deemed irretrievably corrupt, and to emancipate the self from visual representation altogether.

According to Uttara Natarajan, Hazlitt's poetic theory resembles "the poetics of his favorite literary icon, Edmund Burke. Burke's *Enquiry into the Origins of Our Ideas of the Sublime and the Beautiful* (1759) argues persuasively against the strictly mimetic view of language and poetry. The pictorial quality of words, Burke contends, is limited and cannot account for the greatest part of their effect."[18] In the biography, Hazlitt also sometimes fashions his notions of power on this version of Burke's sublime as profoundly iconoclastic. Burke writes, "Despotic governments...keep their chief as much as may be from the public eye."[19] This avoidance of the "public eye" is necessary because it preserves the awe in which the public views its leader and allows for a stable hierarchical order: "we submit to what we admire."[20] Mitchell calls this preservation a "strategy of visual deprivation" (130).

Yet, if the sublime Napoleon, unavailable to the gaze is Hazlitt's ideal, he is an untenable figure. As the Revolution teaches both Napoleon and Hazlitt, the people need a spectacle of power. Hazlitt at times valorizes a different sublime, a visual sublime in which the great man awes the public with spectacles of his power. Simon Bainbridge claims Hazlitt performs acts of "imaginative terrorism" by creating a Napoleon who can "appeal to the 'imagination,' a faculty which, as he wrote in his 'Letter to William Gifford,' 'delights in power, in strong excitement, as well as in truth, in good, in right (IX, 37)" (188). For Bainbridge, to create this appeal, Hazlitt has to remake Napoleon's allure in the image of kings who alone, according to much of Hazlitt's writing, can create a delight "in power." For Bainbridge, in "*The Life* and elsewhere, Hazlitt conceives Napoleon, like Satan, in terms of the visual sublime" (203). This visual sublime involves representing Napoleon as both gigantic in stature and invested with a dazzling brightness (203). Bainbridge argues that the appeal of a sublime Napoleon is "not just terrifying in the tradition of the Burkean sublime, producing 'fear and personal awe,' but enchanting—it 'threw a spell over them,' and was 'full of the marvellous'" (204).

Bainbridge emphasizes the crucial importance of Napoleon's image in a democracy. For Bainbridge, Hazlitt calls for Napoleonic spectacle because of a crisis of representation. Democracy itself is fundamentally unrepresentable or, to gesture toward Mitchell, whom Bainbridge does not address, it is unbearably sublime, antivisual, because it cannot be represented by any image. Hazlitt claims, "the imagination can only be appealed to by individual objects and personal interests" (14: 274). Power is best manifested in Hazlitt's work, as Bainbridge argues, first by kings and then by Napoleon's "individuality and uniqueness."[21] For power to be seen and felt, it must be attributed to a single individual who can represent it in his own person.

Imagination cannot address democracy because, *The Life* claims, "politics treats of the public weal" but the public or the people "because they were millions could never be brought forward by the imaginative faculty" (14:274). Millions cannot earn the interest of an individual who can be seen, known, and admired. Whereas kings can comprise the "*dramatis personae*," the people cannot. Democracy is antitheatrical. It lacks a visual aesthetic and can only be "weighed in the balance of abstract truth and reason" (14:274). The conditions of democracy itself require that Napoleon abandon the sublime that Mitchell describes as fundamentally averse to all images and assume the visual sublime that Bainbridge describes in *The Life*.

At stake here is a problem of how to represent power in a democracy when the "public weal" is made up of millions. Bainbridge claims that Hazlitt does not really believe that most people can apply "abstract truth and reason" to politics and Hazlitt, therefore, compromises by making Napoleon an idol. Hazlitt knew that "he needed to satisfy the idolization of power...that he repeatedly argued were inherent in the human mind. He fought to convert Napoleon into a suitable object for popular idolatry" (201). Napoleon is supposed to combine "imaginative appeal" while still representing "the cause of the people" (201). Bainbridge reads the idol Napoleon, then, as a form of manipulation that helps the mentally lax. But Hazlitt's repeated claim in the biography is that this visual Napoleon is not simply a creation of the author; the seductive Napoleonic image actually existed in the realm of politics and functioned not only to put kings to shame but also as a means of offering an image of power in which the people could see themselves reflected. Hazlitt makes clear that Napoleon does not provide, as Bainbridge phrases it, only "imaginative terrorism" but actual terrorism that takes place against bodies political and human. If the unrepresentable people find themselves represented by Napoleon's singular image, they must pay for that sense of identity with blood. War arrests the public imagination so that it no longer wanders in search of a new object of interest. Napoleon is as necessary to calm the antagonisms of democratic modernity as he is to thwart ancient legitimacy. However, although Hazlitt sees the necessity of Napoleon's publicity, he also sees its dangers.

The Spectacle of Napoleonic Violence

Crucial to Napoleon's appeal in the biography is his almost savage violence that replaces the horrors of the guillotine with a new exhibition of violent public power. For Hazlitt, Napoleon's violence, like that of Robespierre, is not simply something to condemn. Hazlitt's insistence on Napoleon's difference from modern men, a commonplace of much contemporary writing on

Napoleon, indicates the leader's capacity to eschew modern benevolence and softness in favor of a directed, purposeful violence that awes the people and apparently keeps the Revolution on course.

What Hazlitt has to say about the revolutionaries applies in large measure to Napoleon's own reign: "in times of Revolution" leaders require "that *moral courage*, which uses a discretionary power and takes an awful responsibility on itself, going right forward to its object, and setting fastidious scruples, character, and consequences (all but principle and self-preservation) at defiance" (13:167). "Principle" refers to preserving the Revolution at all costs. Setting aside scruples was necessary to "give to the political machine the utmost possible *momentum* and energy of which it was capable" (13:167). A central theme, for Hazlitt, is that the Revolution would have been defeated, not only because all of Europe opposed it, but also because the "French character seems never to have been fixed, or directed steadily and effectually to a given purpose, except under the strong pressure and immediate control of Buonaparte's iron will" (14:53).[22] Napoleon brings "unity and vigour" (14:91) to a weak and debilitated state, saving the Revolution from destruction. He replaces multiplicity with unity:

> This is popularity; not when a thousand persons consult and deliver the result of their decisions formally and securely, but where each of the thousand does this (before that of the others can be known) from an uncontrollable impulse, and without ever thinking of the consequences. It was the greatest instance ever known of the power exerted by one man over opinion. (15:230)

Napoleon creates a universal will that, like "an uncontrollable impulse," compels everyone to think and act alike.

Part of this capacity to control "opinion," for Hazlitt, emerges from Napoleon's own almost fanatical strength of will. This commitment to a fixed purpose has, Hazlitt makes clear, profoundly antihumanitarian consequences: "No son of the Desert...could express a more determined disbelief in and contempt for all the decencies, charities, and professed courtesies of general philanthropy as mere names and shadows" (14:121).[23] Napoleon's contempt signifies a failure to be a part of enlightened modernity: "The tendency of civilization and intellectual intercourse has been to extend the circle of sympathy with the circle of knowledge, to burst the barriers of tribe, nation, and colour" (14:121). Anachronistically attached to particular local identities and ties, Napoleon eschews the liberal commitment to universal human rights in favor of the prejudices that modern people have presumably overcome. Objects retain uniqueness for Napoleon so that he cannot generalize his sympathies to all humanity and can only attach himself to the single tribe. Hazlitt's language is neither exactly castigating nor laudatory but leaves readers with the impression that a certain anachronistic violence and savagery are necessary for Napoleon's power.[24] Like Byron, Hazlitt understands the image of the Eastern despot as a way of figuring a certain attitude about power that contrasts with modern benevolence.

The representation of the anachronistic despot who can only extend his sympathies to the tribe and never to humanity recalls the Weimar legal theorist Carl Schmitt's claims about the fundamental nature of politics and of democracy. For Schmitt, a people cannot exist without a clear sense of who belongs to the polity and who is excluded. Schmitt believes that the nation, the state, democracy itself, depend on a crucial dividing line between who belongs to the people and who is foreign. Best known for his conception of real politics as a friend/enemy struggle, Schmitt argues that no people can really come to understand itself, can really gain a clear identity, unless it also defines its other: "The distinction of friend and enemy denotes the utmost degree of intensity of a union or separation, of an association or dissociation."[25] The enemy is "the other, the stranger; and it is sufficient for his nature that he is, in a specially intense way, existentially something different and alien" (27). The struggle with the enemy allows one to realize one's essential identity because the enemy "intends to negate his opponent's way of life" (27). This struggle with the enemy is a struggle to the death. It is a struggle in which allies agree to risk their lives to maintain the core of their identity and way of life. Liberalism insists on debate and competition and supports the idea of universal human sameness rather than local identity. But for Schmitt, politics and human existence only gain meaning in a real clash with the enemy who is considered radically other and with whom one does not discuss. Schmitt argues, combat "does not mean competition.... The friend, enemy, and combat concepts receive their real meaning precisely because they refer to the real possibility of physical killing" (33). In *The Crisis of Parliamentary Democracy*, Schmitt argues that this friend/enemy struggle creates the meaningful affect missing from modern politics. Schmitt admires both right- and left-wing thinkers who believe that "warlike and heroic conceptions that are bound up with battle and struggle" are "the true impulse of an intensive life."[26] He adds: "Bellicose, revolutionary excitement and the expectation of monstrous catastrophes belong to the intensity of life and move history" (71). Hazlitt's Napoleon instantiates Schmitt's concept of the political by insisting on the strict division of friend/enemy, by refusing the liberal acceptance of universal benevolence. Napoleon creates a people out of war, out of a friend/enemy politics that, for a time at least, makes the French into something more than just a viewing public.

Napoleon, whose power is violent, savage, and utterly focused, creates the kind of committed action in others that exists under the Terror. The army represents the most powerful example of this unity, creating the kind of homosocial community that becomes so important in Carlyle's work. Hazlitt describes Napoleon as a supernatural force that compels a following: in battle "wherever his presence was most wanted, thither he was attracted by the irresistible impulse of conscious power to contend with an occasion worthy of it; and his spirit flamed in every part of the theater of war, as the lightning illumines the thundercloud" (13:226). Napoleon's soldiers testify that all troubles "vanished at his sight; a single word repaid us for all our fatigues; our wishes were satisfied, we feared nothing from the moment that we saw him" (14:53–54). In the last volume of the biography, during the Russian campaign at the height of the army's despair, "Every man would rather have his arms against himself (which indeed many did) than against their leader" (15:101). In the worst times, the "sight of their Emperor sustained their courage" (15:101). The soldiers felt "of all their misfortunes, the greatest was that of displeasing him; so rooted was their trust in and their submission to the man who had made the world submit to them, and whose genius, till now always triumphant, always infallible, had taken the place of their own free-will!" (15:101). Hazlitt, here, describes a homosocial community bonded through the idolization of the leader. At the most extreme, the soldiers lose a sense of themselves and give up their "free-will" to the greater and more powerful will of Napoleon. Individual egos become absorbed in one great, overwhelming self "who had made the world submit to them." Hazlitt's representation of this unified community is actually removed from the larger public sphere and removed entirely from the presence of women. Unlike the fickle modern public, this community depends on the commitment of men to die for a cause. The theater of war, here, produces men who, like the fanatic Hazlitt admires, have found a cause to die for.

Napoleon, himself, in Hazlitt's biography comes to understand his battles as theatrical events that create unity. Hazlitt quotes Napoleon: "Former victories, seen at a distance, do not strike much...for the present, there is nothing that carries such a sound with it as military successes. This is my conviction; it is the misfortune of our situation. A new government, such as ours, requires, I repeat it, to dazzle and astonish in order to maintain itself" (14:180).[27] Military successes have both "sound" and visual effects but these effects can only "carr[y]" so far before they cease to "strike much." Like the theater of the Revolution, the theater of Napoleonic power must offer constantly new spectacles for the public. Napoleon offers a modern idolatry, appealing to a contemporary democratic audience that respects merit over traditional legitimacy.

Hazlitt reinforces Napoleon's conviction of the theatrical effect of his battles by claiming that his successes in war become a part of him, creating an aura of power that transforms his merely mortal physical presence. In the war with Russia, Napoleon finds that his greatest weapon is his own presence because "the very sight of the conqueror in so many fields of battle struck them with awe and terror.... [His many victories] seemed to rise up for his defense and assistance, and to interpose, as with some overmastering spell, between him and this immense body of Russians" (15:94). Napoleon's former battles function as a "spell," magically overwhelming the enemy at the mere sight of the emperor. Becoming a living embodiment of war, his body functions as a defense against the "immense body of Russians" because it magically encapsulates a history of victories, memorializing French power for the world to see.

Hazlitt demonstrates a new means of adapting republican ideals to nineteenth-century leadership. Like Pocock's republican man, the Napoleonic soldier willingly gives up his life. But, unlike his eighteenth-century predecessors, Hazlitt imagines that this willingness can only be inspired by a thorough submission to a great leader who controls his men body and mind. The republican's fear of tyranny seems forgotten here in Hazlitt's desire to imagine a unified, even fanatical polity.

Although Hazlitt in many ways admires this theater that takes place on the battlefield because, spectacular as it may be, it is a theater in which real men risk real lives, the fact that Napoleon must insistently repeat his performances suggests the larger problem of representation that will haunt Napoleon's career and the future of the Revolution. The real problem in the modern world, Hazlitt argues, is a problem of memory.

Napoleonic Souvenirs and the Limits of Political Memory

Napoleon's obsessive reenactment of his glory in the theater of war suggests a problem of political memory in a world in which viewers consume exciting spectacles that leave no lasting impression. The aura that elevates Napoleon above others creates only a short-term memory forgotten as soon as Napoleon can no longer prove his valor in battle. Hazlitt describes both the power of Napoleon's aura and its failure to ensure any lasting memory or commitment.

Hazlitt offers a particularly striking example of the problem when he considers the effect of a dead leader's monument on modern viewers. During Napoleon's campaign in Egypt, the French pointed telescopes at the pyramids. Hazlitt asks:

> But why at once [should the French] wish to bring them so close to the eye, to be familiar and in contact with them?... Wonder and fear should hold curiosity back, and gaze at a distance as at the giant phantom of the past. But no; the French think no object

sacred from vulgar or scientific impertinence . . . the world of imagination is lost upon them! Buonaparte might have foreseen in this how they would oneday turn round to look at him; pry into his foibles with their glasses, take his dimensions with a quadrant, and fortune having broken down the barrier between them, scan him with a critical eye, and wonder what it was they had ever found in him greater than themselves! (14:5)[28]

The French look at a memorial belonging to a country they have conquered. Their sense of their own power and of the weakness of the nation they would despoil authorizes this impertinent gaze. Hazlitt writes that fear should compel the French to gaze "at a distance as at the giant phantom of the past." The language here already suggests the disbelief that affects the French. The Frenchman must maintain a distance *as if* he were viewing the phantoms of the past. But the pyramids, for him, are suspiciously lacking in this ability to memorialize their history because no present political power animates these objects. The sublime effect of these monuments disappears before the scientific instruments that bring the object close, break it into pieces, and reduce it into a rubble heap of worthless stones. The "world of imagination" here indicates the capacity to preserve the sense of awe, the effect of sublimity, which familiarity dissipates. The vulgar gaze has no respect for the aura that preserves the object's power because the French must see power as immanent. Objects only appear magical by proximity to living power. Egypt's political glory, long dead, leaves behind only heaps of rubble. This mode of viewing foreshadows Napoleon's fate, according to Hazlitt. Once adversity destroys their leader's power, the French pry into his failings and discover that he is no different from themselves. The idol can only sustain itself with the terrorism of actual power. Once "fortune" breaks "down the barriers between" Napoleon and the public, he becomes a junk heap like the pyramids, worthless, unable to sustain a compelling memory of his past glory.[29]

Memory, Text, Iconoclasm

Hazlitt's biography can be read as an attempt to offer an alternative to this culture of spectacle in which commitment to a cause depends on the visual manifestation of political power. This alternative is suggested in the peculiarly plodding and unoriginal style of the work itself, which counteracts the allure of the image with textual memory. But the conclusion and the general effect of the biography suggest that Hazlitt's political disappointments run so deep that the text only repeats the exhaustion of the image and can offer no alternative affective memory. Furthermore, by relying on eyewitness accounts of Napoleon throughout the work and by concluding with a last sighting of the emperor, Hazlitt's work suggests that, however critical of the image he may be, Hazlitt mourns the loss of its power.

Hazlitt's apparent privileging of text over image recalls the reactions of radicals in England to Burke's *Reflections*. Mitchell argues that in the *Reflections*, Burke's "reliance on detailed analysis of the circumstances surrounding any political event gave way to the very sort of imaginative excess he deplored in the French."[30] Burke's "tendency to project and dwell upon 'spectacles' of the Revolution without regard to their antecedent causes or historical accuracy" (143) suggests, according to "the liberals and radicals of the 1790's," that Burke's imagination became corrupted by images. For Paine, Burke "outraged his own imagination."[31]

For Hazlitt, the French obsession with images, like Burke's own, has destroyed political memory and historical context. The biography attempts to counteract the effect of the image by placing it in context, by showing historical causes. Yet, if the biography is supposed to replace visual publicity, it offers a notoriously unappealing alternative. Hazlitt's contemporary critics were aware that the biography lacked the sparkle of originality that usually characterized Hazlitt's writing.[32] Lamb wrote that he "admired the 'speculative episodes,' but... 'skip[ped] the battles.'" Others found an apologia for Napoleon merely "wild-goose foolery."[33] But, as Ralph M. Wardle adumbrates:

> It remained for a twentieth-century scholar to disclose why the narrative passages were so dull—to reveal, in truth, some very damning facts about the book. After examining Hazlitt's sources Robert E. Robinson reported in 1959, with abundant documentation, that, of the 1049 pages in the Howe edition, "about 310 are verbatim translation or transcription, or a shortened form of the original in which condensation is accomplished mainly by omissions; about 435 pages are made up of summary, paraphrase, and reorganization of the source materials" and that "Hazlitt's transitional, interpretive, and analytical passages, including his 'characters' of a number of important personages, fill about 240 pages"—little more than a fifth of the completed four volumes. (448–49)

The biography comprises documents taken from historical texts, memoirs, and official documents.

This excessive borrowing from previously published texts might be a desire to recapture a moment of enlightened publicity that characterized the years before the Revolution. Instead of the dazzle of Napoleon's image, Hazlitt turns to details, facts, and labored descriptions of the events of

Napoleon's life and rule, interspersing paraphrases, and sometimes "verbatim translation[s]" with his own interpretation of facts. A tissue of publicity, offering the repetition and remarking of previous writing, the biography brings together historical research and the memories of individuals who witnessed Napoleon's career and recorded his words.[34] The biography claims that once Napoleon fails, his image loses its most widespread appeal. Textual memory replaces iconic memory to memorialize both Napoleon and the Revolutionary cause. As a compendium of public texts, histories, memoirs, documents, and Hazlitt's own commentaries, *The Life* resembles the kind of publicity that follows the invention of the press. Attempting to return to the founding moment of the Revolution by engaging textual rather than iconic publicity, the biography offers a history of struggle between idolatry and iconoclasm, moving from visual (ancien regime) to textual (the enlightened press) to visual (the Terror and Napoleon's battles) and back to the textual (Hazlitt's biography). By privileging textual publicity over visual publicity in the very form of the work, Hazlitt appears to retrieve memory and history from the tyranny of the image. If the image allows, at times, for some provisional headway toward liberty by creating a single idol for the people to rally toward, it must be supplemented by biography, by the writing of the life, the story that draws connections and embeds the image in the story of the Revolution, recalling for the reader the purpose and teleology of the Revolution.

Whereas the form of the work suggests a desire to liberate the reader from the hold of the image so that a new commitment or a better political memory can take hold, both the work's stylistic tedium and its conclusion suggest that this alternative is a failure. The exhaustion of the image's capacity to memorialize after Napoleon's fall is repeated rather than counteracted in textual memory.

Unlike Carlyle, whose writing eroticizes loss and death to create an attachment to hero worship, Hazlitt's imagination is exhausted by failure and cannot develop a poetics of loss. The work ends not with a final explanation of the larger goals of the Revolution but with a detailed description of Napoleon's funeral. After a meticulous list of the participants of the funeral procession and the details of the burial ceremony, Hazlitt writes:

> the crowd fell upon the willows, which the former presence of Napoleon, had already rendered objects of veneration. Every one was ambitious to possess a branch or some leaves of these trees, which were henceforth to shadow the tomb of this great man; and to preserve them as a precious relic of so memorable a scene. (15:363)

The willow branches underscore the continuing desire to represent, remember, and recollect Napoleon's glory. However, this effort seems all but futile.

The suggestion, here, is that, like the leaves of the willow, the leaves of the biography may offer nothing more than useless collectible objects rather than an alternative to visual memory.

Hazlitt concludes by writing about Antommarchi, one of the witnesses of Napoleon's final days. Having borrowed throughout his writing from him and other eyewitnesses, the end of the biography reminds the reader that these textual productions of memory originate in the actual presence of the emperor, in having sighted him. Perhaps the secret pleasure of these memorials for Hazlitt is their visual origin, a pleasure denied in Hazlitt's invectives against idols and in his interest in historical narrative.[35] But visual and textual memory suffer the same fate here. Like the ineffectual willow branches, Antommarchi's story has no audience. The last lackluster sentence of the biography is: "Antommarchi, on his return to the Continent, could not procure an interview with Maria-Louisa; but he saw the Princess Pauline at Rome, and gave his mother an account of all that her son had gone through" (15:363). Like the willow branches, stories of Napoleon memorialize him but only trivially. Rather than informing a world eager for news about the fallen idol, Antommarchi merely informs a mother. The male following has disappeared and the story of Napoleon's final days only matter now to a few female auditors. Within the frame of the biography's narrative, Antommarchi's story gains no significant circulation because the audience for Napoleon has dwindled to almost none—not even the former emperor's wife seems attentive any longer. This poor reception with which Hazlitt concludes his longest work anticipates the biography's own reception as a work that has lost its audience.[36]

Paul de Man writes about writing that it crucially depends on "Memorization," a faculty that "has to be sharply distinguished from recollection and imagination. It is entirely devoid of images."[37] Writing is a "hieroglyphic" (102) system, that depends on dead matter rather than on "the sounds and the images of the imagination" (102). This "mechanical" process of memory cannot really recollect a profound experience because it involves "the learning by rote of *names*, or of words considered as names, and it can therefore not be separated from notation, the inscription, of the writing down of these names" (102). The biography, too, reads like the work of memory laid bare. Rather than creating the illusion of recollection, *The Life* fails to capture life at all and reproduces only inscriptions, the notations of other writings.

If de Man makes an ahistorical claim about the nature of writing, Hazlitt's biography shows how a moment of profound historical disappointment brings this hieroglyphic quality of writing to light.[38] The failure of Napoleon and the Revolution destroy Hazlitt's capacity to create affective prose and the illusion of affective memory. One might say that his language fails him without Napoleon's virile presence. Writing as inscription appears in a moment of historical loss when manhood has failed. Remembering the early days of Napoleon's power, Hazlitt writes:

> Happy still was this period when every spark of enthusiasm was not dead, and there was at least one man in the world who could excite the least emotion in the public breast! The intoxicating draughts of liberty and of glory that mankind have swallowed in the last forty years seem to have exhausted the vital principle of the human mind, and have brought on premature old age and decay! (14:56)

Although, ideally, the biography should return the reader to that early moment of enlightened publicity that created a unified culture, Hazlitt's writing does not create a community of like-minded revolutionaries but a solitary voice unheard and dismissed, a voice too unseductive even to establish a myth like that of Byron, as fallen Prometheus, or disappointed revolutionary. Hazlitt finds that political seduction is all the more necessary in modern times but that modern conditions render seduction short-lived, dependent on the fickle desires of an inattentive public.

Chapter 5

Communities in Mourning

Making Capital Out of Loss in Thomas Carlyle's
Past and Present and *Heroes*

*I*f the radical William Hazlitt offers an apology for the necessity of
violence and authoritarianism in modern times, which critical work
has tended to ignore, the more conservative Thomas Carlyle's interest in
authority has been far more central to critical commentary. This chapter
moves beyond the period of the Napoleonic wars to a time of domestic instability manifested most importantly, for Carlyle, in the Chartist rebellion
against economic exploitation. Turning inward, away from France and
Europe, and responding to different historical conditions, Carlyle, nonetheless, addresses many of Hazlitt's own concerns. The defeat of Napoleon
destroys Hazlitt's ability to conceive of an effective leadership that can overcome the atomizing forces of the age. If Hazlitt, overcome by loss, could not
articulate a seductive poetics of hero worship, Carlyle creates this poetics out
of loss itself.

Thomas Carlyle is perhaps most famous for his commitment to hero worship.[1] Heroes, Carlyle hopes, will resolve the problems of democratic and
industrial modernity. Despite his strident insistence on the necessity of heroes,
Carlyle represents leaders perpetually marked by social failure. Notoriously
inarticulate and resistant to public exposure, Carlyle's heroes preserve their
manly integrity by apparently forfeiting their social effectiveness. With so
many expectations resting on a hero who refuses to make himself available to
the public, Carlyle chooses to represent not leadership but a remarkably consistent failure of responsibility. This chapter, however, explores how the failure to
become visible to the public actually constitutes a powerful form of charismatic
seduction that relies on invisibility, absence, and mourning.

95

Carlyle, in *Past and Present* (1843) and *Heroes, Hero Worship, and the Heroic in History* (1840), creates an erotics of death, which allows the hero to be both irretrievably absent from the social and, yet, hauntingly present. Carlyle's dead leaders eroticize relations among men, presumably replacing relations of monetary exchange with relations of love. This love of death becomes particularly clear in the second book of *Past and Present* in the narrative of the monk Samson in which Carlyle elaborates the coordinates of a fantasy of dead heroes and male communities. This narrative of a medieval monk functions, for Carlyle, not as a hopelessly anachronistic narrative of a lost world, but as a model for how the dead matter of capitalism can become vitalized by the dead matter of the hero's body.

Male Heroism and Feminine Modernity: Carlyle's Phallic Agon

Before turning to books two and three of *Past and Present* and to *Heroes* in which Carlyle elaborates his cult of death, I want to consider how the first book of *Past and Present* establishes certain false expectations about the nature of the hero and his relation to the modern world. By positing the hero as engaged in the conquest of a baffling and inchoate industrial modernity, Carlyle claims that the hero is an agent of visibility whose purpose is to shed light on mystery and to reestablish transparent relations among men.

Chris R. Vanden Bossche writes, "Carlyle's works represent an attempt to resolve dilemmas raised by what he and his contemporaries perceived as a revolutionary shift of authority in virtually all realms of discourse and institutions of power in Western Europe. From his vantage point, it appeared not only that authority had shifted but that the transcendental grounds for it had been undermined" (1).

As a critic of modern individualism who nonetheless champions industrial modernity, Carlyle claims that replacing hierarchy and authority with individual freedom actually creates more strenuous forms of oppression. Alluding to Sir Walter Scott's fictional serf in Ivanhoe, Carlyle claims that in modern times, "Gurth is now 'emancipated' long since; has what we call 'Liberty.'"[2] But he is more oppressed than ever in a world in which no one claims responsibility for that oppression because everyone is presumably free. In this world "our enemies are we know not who or what; our friends are we know not where! How shall we attack anyone, shoot or be shot by any one?" (21). Because social relations are no longer transparent, the agents of oppression have become invisible: "O, if the accursed invisible Nightmare, that is crushing out the life of us and ours, would take a shape; approach us like the Hyrcanian tiger, the Behemoth of Chaos, the Archfiend himself; in any shape that we could see, and fasten on!"(21).

The enemy is invisible because the liberal economic ideology of laissez-faire removes agency from the present condition and isolates people from any sense of community. The people of England live "isolated, unrelated, girt in with a cold universal Laissez-faire" (210).[3] Carlyle describes a state of social existence, which echoes Marx's famous claim that in a capitalist society the relations between things replace relations between people. The relation of master and slave, explicitly visible in the Middle Ages, has become invisible and has been replaced by wealth. Human relations are mediated by the "cash nexus," which alone determines social difference.

Carlyle seems particularly odd both to modern readers and to his contemporaries because he insists on the violence and oppression that characterize industrial society despite an often-held belief since the eighteenth century that Great Britain was engaged in a process of amelioration from barbarism to civilization. Whigs often defined a historical trajectory from "pastoralism through feudalism to commerce as the history of civil society was also the history of manners from rudeness and barbarism to politeness and refinement."[4] Carlyle pessimistically counters this progressive view of history away from violence toward civilized manners by describing a violent modernity. A "diabolical monster" (21) exists out in the world, but it has grown far more subtle and dangerous because it is invisible. The monsters, tigers, behemoths, and archfiends in *Past and Present* figure the hidden, unacknowledged side of industrial democracy in which the ownership of things differentiates people, not ancient caste systems, perpetuating, nonetheless, a state of extreme oppression.

Uncompromising about how the system of production creates a new, even more terrible despotism, Carlyle imagines that this invisible "monster" has one fundamental vulnerability. Its invisibility destroys the old mystified attachment to the leader that kept Gurth happy in his bondage. Without the master who energizes social relations, according to Carlyle, production and consumption become empty procedures in which people become aware only of objects and lose sight of any social unity. As Carlyle's description of England as a vast wasteland and of its working class as paralyzed by a debilitating enchantment suggests, naked capitalism reminds modern people that their lives have no value.

On the face of it, Carlyle reacts to the "condition of England" by simply calling for the reestablishment of a kind of feudal order in the present. Chapter 2 describes a change from effeminate egotism to a manly resurgence. Carlyle figures this project of making the nation virile as a sexual conquest:

Such a Sphinx is this life of ours, to all men and societies of men. Nature, like the Sphinx, is of womanly celestial loveliness and tenderness; the face and bosom of a goddess, but ending in claws and the body of a lioness. . . . And does she not propound her riddle to us? Of each man she asks daily, in mild voice, yet with a terrible significance, "Knowest thou the meaning of this Day? What thou canst do Today; wisely attempt to do?" Nature, Universe, Destiny, Existence, howsoever we name this grand unnamable Fact in the midst of which we live and struggle, is as a heavenly bride and conquest to the wise and brave, to them that can discern her behests and do them; a destroying fiend to them who cannot. Answer her riddle, it is well with thee. Answer it not, pass on regarding it not, it will answer itself; the solution for thee is a thing of teeth and claws; Nature is a dumb lioness, deaf to thy pleadings, fiercely devouring. Thou art now her victorious bridegroom; thou art her mangled victim, scattered on the precipices as a slave found treacherous, recreant ought to be and must. (13)

On the one hand, Carlyle writes about a problem of authenticity that persists throughout history; on the other hand, this philosophical problem also has a certain historical dimension that makes the persistent problem of authenticity and true authority particularly urgent in industrial modernity. The Sphinx is both a symbol of the eternal problem of meaning and a figure of the present state of England. To uncover the meaning of modernity is a chivalric quest in which the "wise and brave" can "answer her riddle." The chaotic world, that hides the true facts, must be revealed, freed from its prison where it exists "inarticulate . . . chaotic." The claim here is that the modern world can only function effectively under conditions of enlightenment. It is the mystery of "this Day" that keeps the people enchanted. The hero, according to a series of sexual metaphors, is supposed to penetrate this mystery and "answer her riddle." Not only is the individual made virile in his quest, but also "with Nations it is as with individuals: Can they rede the riddle of Destiny? This English Nation, will it get to know the meaning of its strange new Today?" (13).

Carlyle's story of the modern Sphinx figures the struggle for control over a recalcitrant and treacherous world as a phallic agon in which heroes conquer their bride and revitalize the present.[5] The object is to refuse to dwell "in the temporary Semblances" and to "penetrate into the eternal Substance" and thus to "answer the Sphinx-riddle of Today" (18). Sexual metaphors abound in chapter 2, casting all insight as inherently masculine. The rest of the book virtually ignores women and relegates the feminine as that which must be conquered and transformed by the captain of industry.[6]

Carlyle creates a plot of heterosexual conquest that writes women out of the picture as actors and agents of the struggle for national, political, and economic survival. Herbert Sussman argues Carlyle's work virtually occludes the presence of women from men's lives, not only within the workplace, but also within the very fabric of social and communal interaction. In *Past and Present*, for Sussman, Samson's monastery becomes a fantasy space in which middle-class Victorians "could express in covert form, or as an open secret, their attraction to a world of chaste masculine bonding from which the female has been magically eliminated."[7] However, crucial to this fantasy is that the all-male space be "safely distanced in time" (5) because that space generates anxiety about affective relations among men that must be displaced into the past for Victorian men to fit into the normative ideal of male heterosexuality. This argument is curious, however, because the entire purpose of Carlyle's *Past and Present* is to replicate male communities for industrial England.[8] If we are to imagine the possibility of homophobic anxiety in Carlyle, a writer who shamelessly promotes the ideal of all-male communities, the figure of the Sphinx might be read as a heteronormative alibi for the male community. Under the guidance of the leader, that community unites to create the penetrative power that will reveal the Sphinx's secrets and render modernity pliable to the expansionist and imperialist desires of English men. Carlyle's anxieties do not appear to lie in the necessity of closeting homosexual desire, of negotiating "the troubled boundary between the homosocial and the homosexual" (5). Rather, they lie in the very real possibility that these all-male communities might fail to realize themselves. The anxiety appears to be located more on the axis of manliness/effeminacy than on the axis of homosociality/homosexuality. When men come together to form communities, the nation becomes powerfully virile. It is when men become atomized, distanced from one another, however, that the nation becomes effeminate. In *Past and Present*, Carlyle writes, "Democracy means despair of finding any Heroes to govern you" (214). Without heroes, the present democratic culture produces no men and no community, only an effeminate nation. As Alan Sinfield persuasively argues, a fear of effeminacy in the nineteenth century had no necessary connection to a fear of homosexuality. The discourse of effeminacy was rich and varied and "up to the time of the Wilde trials—far later than is widely supposed—it is unsafe to interpret effeminacy as defining of, or as a signal of, same-sex passion."[9]

Indeed, Carlyle's language and concerns do not address a modern homophobia but rather look back to a republican ideal of manly virtue in which modernity stands for a dangerous new effeminacy that will undermine national strength. But, unlike accounts of republicanism that stress its antimodern tendencies, Carlyle's republicanism is easily reconciled with industrial production. If Carlyle, in many of his pronouncements, seems to be a determined enemy of economic liberalism, his support for capitalist modernity suggests a more complex picture of his political commitments. Carlyle is no opponent of modernity. Rather, his celebration of the hero is an effort to bring the chivalric glamour of the manly ideal into the present so that it may energize industrial modernity. In Carlyle's work, the current state of industrial society destroys the manliness of both workers and leaders. Like dead weight, commodities and the industrial system paralyze the lives of English men and destroy their virility. Only the return of a visible, flesh-and-blood hero can bring life to a capitalist culture pervaded by death (consider Carlyle's extended description of an enchanted England in his chapter on Midas where masters have lost all attachment to life in their pursuit of dead gold). The presence of the manly leader presumably replaces the inchoate world of invisible monsters with a clear, transparent social structure of stratified relations of power.

If in book one Carlyle seems to call for a living hero to become a crucial public figure, the emphasis on visibility and on the regenerative powers of the living hero is far less marked in books two and three of *Past and Present.* The initial call for visibility masks a fear of the hero's public exposure, a fear that books two and three address more explicitly. The desire for the visible presence of the hero develops into a more complex fantasy about how the erotic power of the hero depends on the endless deferral of the hero's actual presence and how, far from representing an opposition to the dead matter of capitalism, the hero mimics its operations and powers of fascination.

Publicity, Commerce and the Failure of Value

Although in Carlyle's work heroes uncover nature's veils and reveal the Sphinx's secrets, Carlyle's writing is deeply ambivalent about this process of unveiling when it threatens to reveal the leader to the gaze of his public. As commentators have often emphasized, exposure, for Carlyle, is inevitably demystifying and feminizing.

In *Heroes* the accurate representation of the hero's merit becomes virtually impossible. Carlyle offers hope at first: "Given the living man, there will be found clothes for him; he will find himself clothes." [10] However, Carlyle's most compelling hero in this book, Cromwell, fails to change other men because he cannot show them his own merit and the merit of his cause: "The wild rude Sincerity, direct from Nature, is not glib in answering from the witness-box...he is scouted as a counterfeit" (262). Because talent cannot put on a false, sleek appearance, the hero has no way to show that he is the correct choice. In fact, that very inability is itself a sign of his potential greatness. Carlyle differentiates between Cromwell and the politicians of his day: "Poor Cromwell,— great Cromwell! The inarticulate Prophet; Prophet who could not speak....He looked so strange, among the elegant

Euphemisms, dainty little Falklands, didactic Chillingworths, diplomatic Clarendons!" (264).

Unlike Hazlitt's Napoleon, the Carlylean hero refuses to become a subject of publicity. Carlyle writes in *Heroes*: "The great silent men! Looking around on the noisy inanity of the world...one loves to reflect on the empire of Silence. The noble silent men, scattered here and there...silently thinking, silently working whom no Morning Newspaper makes mention of!" (272). The inchoate hero reverses the sphinx narrative of unveiling and revealing by becoming himself an unnamable fact. Because the trajectory of exposing and naming is phallic for Carlyle, the object of mystery is necessarily feminine, vulnerable to the scrutiny of a penetrating gaze. It is precisely this gaze turned onto the hero that Carlyle wishes to block. Carlyle writes in *Heroes*, "Let us honour the great empire of Silence, once more! The boundless treasury which we do not jingle in our pockets, or count up and present before men!" (122–23). The hero is the very measure of value but his value is a "treasury" that cannot be counted.

Much of the strangeness of Carlyle's prose style, I think, can be attributed to his attempt to offer a representation of the hero that avoids the discourses of publicity, of the morning paper. The erotics of veiling and unveiling that pertain to the heroic quest also expose the hero's own partial visibility. Carlyle's lives of heroes offers a paucity of detail and focuses instead on the invisible, on the limits of insight into the hero. The language itself becomes dense, palpable, audible, and strident, so that the reader becomes aware of a voice both relishing and crying out against the limitations of what it can say. The style points to the limits of what can be known about the hero and the attendant frustration and pleasure of that limit. As Carlyle repeatedly emphasizes, his writing seeks to transform history into poetry, biography into epic.[11]

The real danger for the hero is not that he will be ignored, but that he will be exposed to the public gaze. Commercial culture makes this danger particularly urgent because it relies on advertising, which creates false images and desires. In *Past and Present*, Carlyle writes about a "Hatter" who advertises to the public. He asks his readers to "consider, for example, that great Hat seven-feet high, which now perambulates London Streets" (144). The problem for Carlyle is that the hatter forgets his primary duty to produce, to make "better felt-hats than another," and becomes an advertiser to appeal to the consumer:

The Hatter in the Strand of London...mounts a huge lath-and-plaster Hat, seven-feet high, upon wheels; sends a man to drive it through the streets; hoping to be saved thereby. He has not attempted to make better hats, as he was appointed by the

Universe to do, and as with this ingenuity of his he could very probably have done; but his whole industry is turned to persuade us that he has made such! He too knows that the Quack has become God. (144)

Instead of producing, this manufacturer is in the business of persuasion so that illusion becomes the commodity he sells rather than the actual hat made better "than another." The point is that the manufacturer finds that "falsity" can now "serve [his] purpose" (144). But Carlyle vehemently opposes this "falsity" in advertising: "Nature requires no man to make proclamation of his doings and hat-makings." Any producer who advertises "feels, at first, that he is degrading himself if he speak of his excellencies.... He feels that he is already a poor braggart; fast hastening to be a falsity and speaker of Untruth" (145).

This self-promotion will destroy the nation, Carlyle predicts. He writes, "Shew me a Nation fallen everywhere into this course, so that each expects it, permits it to others and himself, I will shew you a Nation travelling with one assent on the broad way" (145). The healthy nation goes to "Elysian fields...earned by silent Valour...nature has appointed happy fields, victorious laurel-crowns; but only to the brave and true. Unnature, what we call Chaos, holds nothing in it but vacuities, devouring gulfs" (145). To advertise one's product, to make a show of one's ability is to destroy fact, to counter nature, and to lead the nation toward "Chaos." Chaos here describes a culture in which each individual is licensed to make a show, to become "a poor braggart," and thus call "on a discerning public" (144). To replace fact with advertisement turns "every man into his own trumpeter" (144). If, for Marx, commodities have no real value other than in relation to each other, Carlyle desires a commodity whose value is intrinsic to itself, a commodity, free of fetishistic illusion, which, like the captain of industry himself, possesses a value independent of the market and of public opinion.

Carlyle finds himself in a strange bind in his desire to celebrate and strengthen industrial culture. On the one hand, he calls for the endless expansion of production and imperial conquest, associating this expansion with ancient warriors. On the other hand, he sees the conditions of the market in which the products of labor and industry must be sold as a threat to the leader's virility. As soon as industrial production becomes a matter of appealing to a "discerning public," as Carlyle states ironically, then the manufacturer loses his connection to fact and enters the world of sham appearances, Carlyle's trajectory for effeminacy. England, overcome by commercial culture, will lose its "brave and true" because it lacks "silent Valour." Essentially, the market stimulates false desires and, advertising both, manipulates and is manipulated by the public leaving the producer at the mercy of his consumers, called on to be theatrical rather than true to stimulate their interest.

If the sphere of production guided by the true leader avoids false appearances and advertisement, then the commercial side of industrialism is a falling away from the manly integrity of the leader. As soon as the captain of industry moves away from conquering the earth, from submitting raw materials to his will, he must enter the arena of the market. Carlyle's *Past and Present* attempts to write out the market, to minimize if not obliterate its importance. But what is repressed returns in absurd forms and all out of normal proportion. The merchant parades the streets with a giant hat that advertises less the hat than the grotesque quality of advertising itself. The need to appeal to the market means that the producer does not merely sell a product of his making but a presentation, an object that has been embellished to appeal to the consumer. The manly facts collapse before the demands of the market. Against this effeminizing condition, Carlyle posits an industrial leader who, like all of Carlyle's other heroes, remains inchoate, silent, and unmarketable.

James Eli Adams addresses Carlyle's fear of public exposure and of the market. The danger of "self-reflexion," Adams claims, is that the "hero who presents himself to the gaze of an audience is always liable to submit to its desires, and thereby subvert the integrity of his mission."[12] The goal of the hero is to "repress, ideally to destroy, an existing but adventitious and degraded self... to discover or release a more essential, ultimately transcendental selfhood animated by divine necessity" (29). Focusing mostly on *Sartor Resartus*, Adams claims that the dandy is Carlyle's figure for the man who displays himself, who is hyperconscious of his public and of the need to manipulate it. Against the figure of the dandy, Carlyle "evokes a heroism founded on superbly self-forgetful devotion to productive labor—an ideal most famously celebrated as the reign of the 'Captains of Industry' in *Past and Present*. This antagonism between the hero and the dandy not only organizes much of Carlyle's writing, but operates as one of the founding symbolic oppositions of Victorian discourse" (21). The dandy is essentially a "theatrical being" antithetical to the hero "whose essential selfhood is typically bodied forth in a 'savage' disregard for social decorum and the public gaze" (22).

Adams's account of the hero, which focuses on the prophet or the man of letters, reveals how Carlyle's notion of subjectivity speaks to a problem of consciousness itself, as well as to modern pressures on the author exposed to the public. By extending this predicament of the leader's performance before an audience to the captain of industry, how this general condition is acerbated by the particular historical moment of industrial modernity becomes clear. G. R. Searle writes, "Carlyle came up with one of the most ingenious attempts to purge capitalism of its morally obnoxious features. Carlyle's originality was that he combined contempt for political economy in all its utilitarian...manifestations with an often grudging admiration for the organizational skills and speculative daring of the major capitalists." Essentially, "what Carlyle was in fact doing was splitting the entrepreneurial aspects of capitalism from its financial base—divorcing the profit-maximizing and speculative elements from the creative and organizational ones."[13] The market, the place of profit and speculation, the necessary correlate of industrial production, haunts the captain of industry in the way that the public self, the self that can be seen and heard by an audience, haunts the prophet.[14]

Crucially, for Adams, this desire to hide the hero, reflected in both Carlyle's style and thematics, comes "at the expense of the social reciprocity on which Carlylean hero-worship is ostensibly founded" (38). Carlyle's heroes forfeit their effect on the public to salvage their manliness. In this way, Carlyle's heroes represent an ineffectual and failed masculinity that can have no real social relevance.

In what follows, I argue in difference from Adams, that a necrophiliac desire pervades Carlyle's work transforming the apparent failure of public visibility into a powerful means of public seduction. The social function of the hero succeeds precisely by refusing to be institutionalized. The unrealizable hero/father/king activates relations and hierarchies among men by remaining perpetually unavailable. The failed hero is, in fact, a highly successful one whose power over his public depends on the perception of his public failure, his refusal to participate in a culture of publicity. Carlyle's hero is, paradoxically, an eminently social figure that motivates crucially cathected homosocial relations precisely in his absence. The nineteenth-century hero who seems to eschew social and political power actually represents a particularly powerful form of masculinity that responds to modern conditions.

Fetishism, Phallic Economies, and Dead Heroes

To specify how missing leaders create community, I turn to the narrative of the Abbot Samson in book two of *Past and Present*. By attending to the means by which Carlyle presents this narrative to his modern audience, the biography of the medieval monk is clearly constructed to avoid the disfiguring conditions of publicity.

Carlyle crucially limits the reader's access to Samson by creating a series of mediations that frame the narrative. Carlyle promises the reader a portrait of the past that will reveal the present. But this portrait is of a "remote Century" seen through "confused Papers" (45). The "Centuries" as "lineal children" are in some ways mirrors of one another but one cannot look directly at the present to understand it. Carlyle's elucidation only emerges by looking at what is remote, "obscure" (46), in "fragments" (49), through "an altogether imperfect mirror" (49), and "through a glass darkly" (50). This circuitous route through which modern readers see only fragments, is an old text written by a monk, Jocelin of Brakelond. Through Jocelin's writing, and then through Carlyle's translation or interpretation of it, the modern reader is supposed to gain glances of Samson.

This indirection by which Carlyle chooses to describe the hero allows him to avoid the intimate scrutiny that destroys the hero's aura. Carlyle's account of the effects of publicity anticipates questions that Walter Benjamin addresses in "The Work of Art in the Age of Mechanical Reproduction." Focusing on works of art, rather than on men, Benjamin writes, "that which withers in the age of mechanical reproduction is the aura of the work of art....One might generalize by saying: the technique of reproduction detaches the reproduced object from tradition. By making many reproductions it substitutes a plurality of copies for a unique existence."[15] Carlyle sees this destruction of aura as a problem for the hero when his image is copied and disfigured. Whereas Benjamin celebrates the end of what he calls the "aura" of the originary art object, Carlyle mourns the loss of the leader's sacred nature. However, both Benjamin and Carlyle claim that when the authentic object or hero becomes suspect, the failure of aura itself produces a kind of compensatory desire to replace a tarnished authenticity with a new charisma. For Benjamin, this desire is evident in the popular obsession with the Hollywood film star, which he calls "the phony spell of a commodity" (581). For Carlyle, the failure of authority produces a fascination with virile leaders whose value must be safeguarded from the destructive unveiling of the modern press. In Carlyle's work, history becomes a narrative strategy to create a simulacrum of the sacred, a representation paradoxically so defaced by time that it cannot be defaced by public scrutiny.

Carlyle's purpose is to rectify modern vision, which is at present incapable of seeing heroism, that is, of maintaining the necessary distance from the object:[16]

> Brethren, have we no need of discovering true Governors, but will sham ones forever do for us?...We also have eyes, or ought to have; we have hustings, telescopes; we have lights, link-lights and rush-lights of an enlightened free-Press....Such telescopes, such enlightenment,—and such discovery! How comes it, I say; how comes it? (89)

Offering a new mode of seeing, Carlyle rejects "telescopes" that bring distant objects near and the "lights, link-lights and rush-lights of an enlightened free-Press" that scrutinize great men. In place of the politician whose every move earns the attention of the all-seeing press, Carlyle proffers the Abbot who can be seen only from a distance and can thus maintain his integrity. But a truly secure impenetrability to the public and the press, for Carlyle, can only be achieved through death.

The importance of death becomes clear when Carlyle reveals that Samson, in life, is not so much the exalted leader as he is his surrogate, the humble custodian of St. Edmund's memory and body. Samson begins his career as a lowly monk, subjected to the whims of his superiors, but the "harshest slave-apprenticeship to obeying" is the means by which Samson learns to govern (92). This apprenticeship to obeying begins when the little boy Samson has a dream about St. Edmund, the founder of the abbacy. Saved by the saint from "the Arch Enemy," Samson becomes a monk (74). The dream turns Samson into a follower dedicated to his protector and founding father.

Tellingly, Carlyle begins book two with a hagiography that is resumed at the end of the narrative of Samson's rule. St. Edmund's story is less a biography than a memorial, concerned primarily with the significance of Edmund's death. Once canonized, "His Life had become a poetic, nay a religious Mythus" (58). His death transforms the genre of his life story: "it was once a prose Fact, as our poor lives are; and even a ragged unmanageable one. This landlord Edmund did go about in leather shoes... and daily had his breakfast to procure" (58). The transformation of Edmund's story from a mere "prose Fact" about shoes and breakfast into a "poetic" or "religious Mythus" offers in localized and condensed form the effect of most of Carlyle's writing, which seeks to infuse the details of ordinary life with the power of a mythus. But poetry and myth are not merely fantasies separate from the daily facts of existence. Instead, this kind of narrative organizes and makes that daily existence possible.

Edmund's death has precisely this organizing power. Carlyle writes, "In one word, St. Edmund's Body has raised a monastery round it. To such length, in such manner, has the Spirit of the Time visibly taken body, and crystallized itself here" (61). The merely mortal body, tortured to death, becomes "the Spirit of the Time," "visibly" embodied in the monastery. Carlyle extends the effect of the dead body to encompass the entire town: "All that thou now seest, and namest Bury Town, is properly the Funeral Monument of Saint or Landlord Edmund" (62). The dead father, the father's death in itself, causes an entire town to exist. Its existence is a "Funeral Monument" to the dead saint, also known as the landlord, the true holder of the town's power and property. Carlyle extends this vision of towns as memorials to dead leaders to modernity itself:

> Certain times do crystallize themselves in a magnificent manner.... Richard Arkwright too will have his Monument, a

thousand years hence: all Lancashire and Yorkshire, and how many other shires and countries, with their machineries and industries for his monument! A true pyramid or "flame-mountain," flaming with steam fires and useful labor over wide continents, usefully towards the Stars, to a certain height;— how much grander than your foolish Cheops Pyramids or Sakhara clay ones! (62)

The father of modern industry will, like St. Edmund, be memorialized in his own "Funeral Monument," the factories across "wide continents." Like the pyramids and like the monastery, modern "shires and countries" will grow out of a cult of the dead, a worship of dead heroes. Arkwright will only really achieve his effect when long dead, "a thousand years hence," when the merely human life, the prose fact, has become legend.

Hero worship, for Carlyle, coheres around funeral monuments. If monuments participate in a project of imaging the object of worship as, for example, in a bust or public statue, if they raise the hero for public viewing, an object vulnerable to all the irreverent re-markings of the public and to the stultifying effects of habitual viewing, Carlyle's monuments are remarkably resistant to show.[17] In fact, they resemble the Sphinx, that feminine figure of mystery. A monument designed to mark an absence, the Sphinx cannot be defaced because it has no determinate face to show. Contrary to his stated purpose, Carlyle's text safeguards the hero's aura by collapsing the difference between him and the figure of modern capitalism. Carlyle's funeral monuments avoid scrutiny because they are monuments to what cannot be seen, to what inspires an impossible hermeneutic effort of reconstruction. The desire for full visibility, always frustrated, however, builds communities and creates the bonds among men. Victorian men become men by mourning the dead.

Samson, himself, exemplifies the proper relation to the dead. When he becomes a leader, his leadership is still a continued servitude to his dead patron saint. In the most affectively charged scene of Carlyle's narrative of Samson's life, the abbot visits the tomb of the founding saint of the abbacy. This moment is the "culminating point of [Samson's] existence" (127). When Samson finds St. Edmund's body wrapped in linen, he refuses to unwrap the body any further "saying he durst not proceed farther, or look at the sacred flesh naked" but:

Taking the head between his hands, he thus spake groaning: "Glorious Martyr, holy Edmund, blessed be the hour when thou wert born. Glorious Martyr, turn it not to my perdition that I have so dared to touch thee, I miserable and sinful; thou knowest my devout love, and the intention of my mind." And proceeding, he touched the eyes; and the nose, which was very massive and prominent... and then he touched the breast and arms; and raising the left arm he touched the fingers, and placed his own fingers between the sacred fingers. And proceeding he found the feet standing stiff up, like the feet of a man dead yesterday; and he touched the toes and counted them. (124)

Impervious to decay, the body of the saint can be traced with loving precision without betraying putrefaction. The supine, lifeless body appears, instead, in its parts as "very massive and prominent" and as "standing stiff." The corpse retains the saint's phallic power and the new leader interlaces his fingers with those of his predecessor in a moment of religious and erotic ecstasy in which one man unites with another, or, rather, a living man unites with his dead master.[18]

Describing the body of Saint Edmund, Carlyle writes:

who knows how to reverence the Body of Man? It is the most reverend phenomenon under the Sun. For the Highest God dwells visible in that mystical unfathomable Visibility, which calls itself "I" on Earth. "Bending before men," says Novalis, "is a reverence done to this Revelation in the Flesh. We touch Heaven when we lay our hands on a human Body." And the Body of one Dead;— a temple where the Hero-soul once was and now is not: Oh, all mystery, all pity, all mute awe and wonder; Supernaturalism brought home to the very dullest. (126)

Sacralizing the body, Carlyle claims that it makes "Visible" the "Highest God." But this visibility is a "mystical unfathomable Visibility." In other words, the hero and his body point to the limits of visibility, to a mystery that is unfathomable. The saint's body becomes like Christ's, a "Revelation in the Flesh" that connects other men to "Heaven." This connection through the body realizes itself by "bending before men." Submission to the power manifested by the body is salvation but that power belongs to "the Body of one Dead." The leader has already passed away, but his followers continue to bend before him, earning the right to rule other men and to create new passionate communities of followers. The homoerotic desire in *Past and Present* is also a necrophiliac desire for a dead man's body. The dead body is "a temple where the Hero-soul once was and now is not." The dead body, as the marker of absence, represents the most erotic object possible in *Past and Present*. It seems to promise the most intimate union, the coming together of flesh with flesh, but this flesh that is as hard as stone, is only an empty shell. In its emptiness lies its power of fascination, a true funeral monument stiffened into phallic prominence but devoid of life.

The solution to the modern problem of publicity, of the market, is to rely on a dead hero in whose name living men act. Dead leaders sacralize submission and offer an aura that cannot be tarnished in the morning paper. If during his life Samson functions in some ways as a follower, a living enactment of the leader's will, after centuries, and through the unclear lens of Jocelin's narrative, he becomes a dead leader in his own right.

Because the real leader is already missing when he comes into his own power, because whatever leader might appear to guide men in the present can only be a faint emblem of the dead leader, Carlyle's work emphasizes the crucial importance of hero worship over the actual existence of the hero. In *Heroes*, Carlyle writes:

> They are all as bank-notes, these social dignitaries, all representing gold;—and several of them, alas are forged notes. We can do with some forged notes; with a good many even; but not with all, or the most of them forged! No: there have to come revolutions then; cries of Democracy, Liberty, Equality, and I know not what. (15)

False leaders create the belief that "there is not gold, that there never was any!" But, Carlyle claims, "'Gold,' Hero-worship, is nevertheless, as it was always and everywhere, and cannot cease till man himself ceases" (15). Revolutions and democracies are then reactions to a failure of value in which the thing that stands in for the valuable object is a false representation.[19]

Carlyle's analogy in some respects anticipates Jean-Joseph Goux's work on symbolic economies. According to Goux, "modern ideology" refuses an "identity between the thing and its symbolic image" by widening "the gap between reference and its sign, between commodity and currency."[20] The loss of the gold standard, as one fundamental determinant of value, in 1915 in Great Britain is, for Goux, significant of this ever more drastic move from a culture of meaningful symbols to a culture of abstract operations deprived of meaning. But this move from gold to paper currency was already a scandalous part of the French Revolutionary regime, a move that earned the new government Edmund Burke's deepest scorn. For Burke, banknotes without gold to ensure them represented a devastating blow to tradition and to value itself. Not only did this move threaten the economy but patriarchal inheritance and national coherence as well. Cash could only offer "a fictitious representation."[21] Like Burke, Carlyle believes that "a fictitious representation" of value actually lies because nothing lies behind it. In more traditional cultures, for Goux, people believe that representations point to "something else."[22] When that "something else" begins to vanish and is replaced by what Carlyle obsessively refers to as a machine world, then "what is banished, completely excluded from capitalist sociality is the surplus of meaning arising from an unconscious identification with something else. As the predominant social relation becomes founded on economic surplus value, this relation suffers from a depreciation of meaning" (131). In his emphasis on the failure of meaning, on how "the sociality subsides to a merely abstract transsubjective relation that deerotizes social relations" (131), Goux's writing about late capitalism sounds much like Carlyle writing about value and meaning at the beginning of industrialization in Great Britain.

But Carlyle's emphasis on gold and false representation complicates Goux's account of value. The expectation Carlyle sets up, of course, is that gold is the true object of worship and that it is therefore a metaphor for the true leader or the genuine substance of the hero. Instead, gold becomes another word for hero worship. The object of value here is not the hero but rather the very act of worship ("'Gold,' Hero-worship"). This sentence that proclaims a return to the object of value, in fact, avoids that encounter by validating the process of seeking for and desiring the object. What Carlyle wishes to avoid here is how the failure of each representation, of each false banknote, threatens to destroy hero worship itself. After all, "I am well aware that in these days Hero-worship, the thing I call Hero-worship, professes to have gone out, and finally ceased" (15). Hero worship seems to be bankrupt, lost by the emergence of false heroes who have diluted the force of this desire. By stressing that the act of worship is itself the goal, Carlyle's language prioritizes the act of worship over the object, thus seeking to avoid the problematic of public representation. It is hero worship that matters, that must survive, not the hero. Carlyle's hero worship is an end in itself, which creates the circuit of desire that organizes the relations of living followers in thrall to a dead leader.[23]

Carlyle's conception of hero worship resembles the very procedures that create value in another form of dead matter—the commodity. In *Capital*, Marx writes, "the value of commodities has a purely social reality, and that they acquire this reality only insofar as they are expressions or embodiments of one identical social substance, viz., human labor."[24] Although "from the moment that men in any way work for one another, their labour assumes a social form," the "social character of men's labour appears to them as an objective character stamped upon the product of that labour" (321). In the ideal state of capitalism, for Carlyle, however, the "magic and necromancy that surround the products of labour"[25] become a property of the leader. The leader's powers of fascination depend on the same mechanisms that produce the fetishistic illusion in commodities.

Commodity fetishism, for Marx, depends on a misrecognition in which objects that have value only because of their place in a symbolic network or economy, appear, instead, "as independent beings endowed with life" (321). To understand this error "we must have recourse to the mist-enveloped regions of the religious world" (321). Fetishism endows an element in a system with value and meaning as though these properties belonged to it intrinsically, ignoring the fact that they emerge as the effect of a signifying network. In Carlyle's work, the same effect occurs in the production of the leader's seductive hold over men. His power depends on a network of relations but is felt to be the direct property of the individual hero. The recourse to a gendered model that can presumably return mystified social relations to the modern world, actually replicates the very structures of commodity fetishism to produce an illusion about power.[26]

Hero worship, funeral monuments, the Sphinx, and money are terms in Carlyle's work that repeat the same procedure by which value emerges. None depend on some actual anchor of value. Instead, like money, hero worship creates value from the circulation of desire for an absent object. Value emerges, here from a network of signification, not from a reified object. But like money, hero worship is subject to a fetishistic illusion. Although everyone knows that money is just paper, this completely corruptible object seems invested with a kind of other magical body, a sublime body.[27] The illusory object, this effect of a network of exchanges, appears to be the very cause of that exchange. This strange body, this ghost that animates dead matter, is none other than Carlyle's hero, the thing that emerges from hero worship, the effect that passes for the cause. The fetishization of the dead in Carlyle makes the similitude between capitalism and hero worship clear. Instead of escaping a system lacking a source of authority and value, Carlyle replicates its very procedures to phallicize a nascent industrial culture.

For Carlyle, gender is crucial for effective modernization. With the operations of capitalism obscured by hero worship, Carlyle can replace a meaningless system with one charged with almost religious fervor. A phallic economy is necessary for Carlyle because without it capitalism lacks the necessary erotic power to motivate production and consumption. The mechanisms of commodity fetishism, replicated in Carlyle's account of hero worship suggest that this gendered form of seduction offers repetition with a difference. If hero worship, like fetishism engages a desire that navigates around a central absence, it also offers the allure of masculinity to strengthen the appeal of capitalism. Whereas Marx virtually ignores gender in this context, Carlyle emphasizes the crucial importance of gender in cementing not only the legitimacy of industrial modernity but also its powers of fascination.

Chapter 6

"To Please a Woman Worthy of Being Pleased"

Darcymania in Jane Austen's *Pride and Prejudice*

*T*his chapter, like the following, focuses on the domestic sphere and on the role of women in creating the allure of the male leader or master. Women in both *Pride and Prejudice* and *Jane Eyre* function as important figures who can testify to the value of the leader because of their desire for equality and freedom. In these novels the female protagonists choose the hero not despite their democratic aspirations but, perversely, because of them. They help to reconcile a liberal appreciation for the individual and a hierarchical desire for submission. Ultimately, they function to naturalize hierarchy in a time in which merit challenges inherited rank as the justification for inequality.

Although, like the chapters on Byron and Hazlitt, this chapter considers the representation of male leadership during the Napoleonic wars, it examines how *Pride and Prejudice* rejects the army as a locus of British leadership. In the novel, soldiers are restless men on the make who recall the excesses of the French mob and the upstart pretensions of Napoleon. Army men offer an obstacle to unity and hierarchical order.[1] Instead, the novel represents the genesis of a different kind of leader, distanced from the army, but connected to land. Austen's representation of a hero similar to what William Wordsworth describes as the "wise and good" Governor responds to a crisis of traditional authority as well as to the threatening appeal of Napoleonic militarism.

However, the British leader Austen represents is not simply a reactionary throwback to an ideal of the British landowner who denies modernization. Austen's leader maintains traditional power by eschewing the

113

arrogance of rank and by allying himself with a liberal acceptance of commerce and the value of individual merit. Paradoxically, this acceptance of certain liberal values allows Darcy to strengthen the power and prestige of the landed elite. The crux of Darcy's change from arrogant aristocrat to effective modern leader involves a change in manners. His new manners convey respect for a certain kind of equality that makes room for meritorious individuals despite their dependence on vulgar trade. Crucially, however, Darcy maintains a profound obstinacy that suggests a virility undaunted by his new softness of manner.

This chapter examines Darcy's transformation in the context of recent historical work that describes a landed elite that maintained power despite social unrest while accommodating (to a limited degree) and managing new democratic and economic forces. It also considers similarities between Austen's Darcy and William Wordsworth's representation of the good Governor as alternatives to Napoleon. These leaders learn to rule through the mentorship of women. The Darcy/Elizabeth relationship emphasizes the importance of women in the creation of the modern leader. They teach aristocratic men to privilege merit and to adopt benevolent manners that seduce social inferiors. The chapter concludes by examining something that "sticks out," that cannot be integrated into Darcy's newly conquered domain. Wickham remains unpredictable and dangerous, a representative of those forces of disruption associated with the Revolution who, remaining unseduced by the end, troubles the reach of Darcy's charismatic power.

A Political Austen

Jane Austen's *Pride and Prejudice* (1813), famous for the repartee between a lively heroine and an arrogant hero, seems an unlikely text for a study on manly leadership. After all, Austen scholarship often eschews narrowly political questions of governance, focusing instead on the politics of the domestic sphere, marriage, and the role of women. Nonetheless, critics have long understood that the strict division between private and public is less than helpful.[2] Thinking of a condition of mutual influence rather than strict separation is more accurate. As Deidre Lynch writes, Austen's novels have been particularly important for critics and readers to tell stories about "their relations to the literary tradition or to house and home and nation and history."[3] Austen's representation of the relationship between Darcy and Elizabeth Bennet, her focus on the provincial, and the domestic speak to large concerns about the nation and national leadership. In the novel, powerful lessons about submission to manly leaders are learned in the local and the domestic. The novel models in the domestic sphere the kind of exciting intimacy that pertains to a fantasy of the leader/follower relationship in more public domains. To understand this relationship we must question not only the divide between public and private but also between liberal and conservative. Questioning whether the novels are liberal, conservative, or entirely apolitical has been a commonplace of Austen criticism.[4]

In one of the most important readings of the novel, Claudia L. Johnson argues that *Pride and Prejudice*, considered Austen's most conservative novel, speaks the language of liberalism. For Johnson, "Austen is no less than redeeming a tradition of liberal moral and political philosophy which antedates the post revolutionary controversies that called it into question. Her acceptance of happiness as a morally acceptable goal proves not that she was a closet radical but rather that she and progressives were drawing on a shared tradition."[5] The right to happiness, Johnson explains, raises questions about the legitimacy of authority because "the pursuit of happiness privileges private judgment and invites a degree of autonomy of which more conservative novelists were suspicious" (84). But this interest in certain liberal claims about the individual does not mean the novel is progressive: "*Pride and Prejudice* thus alternately verges on and recoils from radical criticism" (87). For Johnson, Austen offers only a "provisional experiment" (92) in this novel in "an effort to work through established forms—a conservative enterprise, after all—in order to transform them into the purveyors of ecstatic personal happiness" (92–93). This experiment is not repeated in later novels, which, Johnson argues, in agreement with most critics, are far less celebratory of the ruling classes. Johnson offers one of the most subtle accounts of the novel by emphasizing the persistence of liberal claims together with the novel's fascination with elite power. However, like most critics, Johnson posits an opposition between conservative and liberal elements (that in this case are experimentally, if unsatisfactorily, reconciled in a kind of fairy-tale ending).

Critics tend to see a struggle between progressive and reactionary elements in a novel that, for most, resolves its tensions in favor of a conservative worldview. Placing liberal and conservative values in opposition, however, misses the point. The novel offers a canny representation of how British elites learned to manage dangerous modern forces. In the novel, elites adopt liberal manners and the value of individual merit over rank to maintain their power. A fantasy about romantic love enables this conjunction of the seemingly opposite political values of hierarchy and individualism, revealing how marriage and courtship, apparently private concerns, cannot be separated from political questions of governance and leadership.

Aristocratic Power

Recent work on the nineteenth-century British class system helps to explain the type of political compromise Darcy enacts in the novel. Historians have revised the "traditional class-based account" of Great Britain from the 1780s to the 1840s.[6] David Cannadine writes that according

> to the traditional class-based account, it had all been very simple and straightforward: the industrial and French revolutions together transformed social structures and social relations by destroying the old, individualistic, hierarchical world of ranks, orders, and degrees and bringing about an entirely new social system based on collective and conflicting identities, a system that resulted from the making of the working and middle classes. (59)

Although historians "still recognize that the decades from the 1780s to the 1840s were disturbed and momentous" (60), and, although "these *were* years in which the British social order was wrenched and transformed by a succession of seismic shocks" (61), it "does not mean that new collective classes were being 'made' and the old individualistic hierarchies were being overthrown" (62).[7] Whereas historians now tend to believe that the lower and middle classes did not really become coherent classes in the nineteenth century, they argue that elites became more secure, more powerful, and more influential than they had been before the revolutions: "historians have become increasingly impressed by the resilience of the traditional landowning elite, by the weaknesses and divisions of the bourgeoisie, and by a working class which never fulfilled the heroic revolutionary role that Marx had prescribed."[8]

Yet, for Cannadine, what is most interesting about the power of the elite in the nineteenth century was not its venerable traditionalism but its "remarkable capacity to renew, to re-create and to re-invent itself over time...one such crucial period of renewal, re-creation, and re-invention...lasted from the 1790s to the 1820s."[9] The British elite, as Linda Colley points out, was "a working, capitalist elite, actively supportive of commerce and in love with every form of economic modernization that might enrich it."[10] According to recent historians, then, if the middle and lower classes failed to be made, the elites were caught up in a highly successful process of refashioning that allowed them to retain political, social, and economic power in Great Britain until the twentieth century.

How to Make Power Gentle: Wordsworth's Good Governor

The hero of *Pride and Prejudice*, Mr. Darcy, like the British elites, maintains traditional power against threats from the lower orders. However, Austen is not interested, as historians of the aristocracy are, in the economic and political measures elites took to safeguard their power. She is interested in how elites reinvented their manners to deflect the threats of a discontented people.[11] The novel is part of a larger trend in the literature and culture of the period to re-create elite manners to appease the threat posed by the Revolution and by Napoleonic charisma.

The period of the French Revolution faced problems of hierarchy and equality with particular urgency. If historians are right and there were no homogeneous middle and lower classes but only powerful rhetorical constructs used both to attack and to defend hierarchy, contemporaries nonetheless feared that hierarchy was really "at risk."[12] In the face of threats, many elite Britons realized that "hierarchy could no longer be left to take care of itself" (76). What was new in the early nineteenth century according to historians such as Cannadine was that "hierarchy was being aggressively defended and justified" (64) while this view of the world was "being repudiated and rejected by a succession of radical writers who inveighed on behalf of the virtuous 'people'" (67).

As Charles S. Maier writes, "it requires formidable historical effort to recall the fear of democracy that pervaded polite society after the collapse of the Napoleonic Empire. Even on the eve of the French Revolution the term had ambivalent connotations; afterwards it was associated with Jacobin dictatorship, Terror, and continuous French military aggression."[13] Maier contends that the "history of democracy in the nineteenth and twentieth centuries involves the story not so much of making the world safe for democracy... but of making democracy safe for the world" (126). Despite the fears it raised, "democracy could not simply be resisted" (126). For many observers, "society itself was evolving democratically" (126). What was at stake was not the full scale suppression of democracy but rather a powerful control of the "excesses" of democracy that might threaten property and rank.

Part of the effort to calm the "excesses" of democracy required that elites refashion themselves in response to dangerous times. Linda Colley emphasizes the change in the self-representation of elite men during and after the French Revolution. She recalls a particularly charged moment, "the first procession of the Estate General in Paris in 1789, the prelude to the French Revolution" in which "representatives of the Third Estate, dressed in sombre black, had been cheered; but the traditionally lavish costumes of the nobility and clergy had met with jeers or silent disgust."[14] Britons took particular note of this reaction: "Great Britain seems to have been one of the first European nations in which this shift from peacock male to sombre man of action became apparent. As early as the 1780s, even peers of the realm were regularly to be seen attending the House of Lords in a costume that evoked a plain, quasi-military masculinity" (187). The crucial shift was "in the direction of meritocracy" (190).

The emphasis on meritocracy raised serious problems though. Napoleon, the great enemy of Great Britain, was a spectacular example of meritocracy in action.[15] British elites needed to persuade the public that elite rule was necessary not because of divine right, or a belief in a God-given hierarchy, but because elite men were the most talented men the nation had to offer. They also needed to differentiate their merits from those of Napoleon. Colley claims that British national identity was fundamentally shaped by the extended conflict with France and that, in an attempt to validate the British political system, Britons sought to distance themselves from Napoleonic militarism: "They defined themselves against the French as they imagined them to be, superstitious, militarist, decadent, and unfree" (5).

Pride and Prejudice also attempts to conceive of a form of leadership that opposes Napoleonic militarism and tyranny and that safeguards certain liberal values while maintaining patrician power. It participates in a tradition of writing during and after the French Revolution that sought to represent a British alternative to French politics. As discussed in chapter 2, Edmund Burke offered one of the earliest and most influential accounts of modern British power in the revolutionary period. Describing chivalry, another word for British tradition, Burke writes in his *Reflections on the Revolution in France* (1790) that British monarchs maintain hierarchies by adopting a British tradition that creates a "noble equality."[16] An equality that somehow exists independently of economic and political inequalities, noble equality is sustained by the gentle manners of the Governor who knows how to temper sternness with "manners" that subdue "the fierceness of pride and power." The British leader's commitment to *noble* equality, an equality among meritorious individuals, maintains the power of the noble class.

Wordsworth's turn-of-the-century anti-Napoleonic writing echoes Burke's representation of the modern monarch and reveals typical features of the new leadership Darcy assumes. In his 1802 Sonnet "I Griev'd for Buonaparte," Wordsworth contrasts the Gallic tyranny of Napoleon with the liberal moderation of the truly British leader. The British leader establishes order and hierarchy by, paradoxically, avoiding the violence and coercion associated with war:

> I griev'd for Buonaparte, with a vain
> And an unthinking grief! the vital blood
> Of that Man's mind what can it be? What food
> Fed his first hopes? What knowledge could *He* gain?
> 'Tis not in battles that from youth we train
> The Governor who must be wise and good,
> And temper with the sternness of the brain
> Thoughts motherly, and meek as womanhood.

Wisdom doth live with children round her knees:
Books, leisure, perfect freedom, and the talk
Man holds with week-day man in the hourly walk
Of the mind's business: these are the degrees
By which true Sway doth mount; this is the stalk
True power doth grow on; and her rights are these.[17]

Wordsworth's good Governor has "true Sway" because he shares neighborly chats with ordinary men about ordinary business. This stalk on which "True power doth grow" is a kind of plant that emerges organically from the British rural world that preoccupied Wordsworth's poetic imagination. The Governor has a power that does not feel like power, which depends on benevolent interaction and understanding. In fact, the leader has learned his lesson from women who have given him "Thoughts motherly, and meek as womanhood." The model for Wordsworth's master is the mother who influences but does not compel.[18]

For J. W. Burrow the emphasis on mild manners is crucial in much eighteenth- and early-nineteenth-century thought. He traces a continuity between "eighteenth-century concepts" and "crucial elements in nineteenth-century liberalism"[19] and finds that the liberal idea of progress dates back to a Scottish Enlightenment optimism that understood the "development of civil society from rudeness to refinement," apparently revising "the historical pessimism" of republicanism's fear of commerce and luxury (27). For supporters of commercial society, modern society was fundamentally made up of "a tissue of manners and modes of social behavior, sometimes referred to by the new term 'civilization'" (28). Manners would soften the actions of governors regardless of the type of government (28). Burrow sees a line of thought extending from Hume to Constant and Macaulay, which understands the civilizing function of commerce rather than its feminizing effects: "Hume's Scottish emphasis on the progress of society and manners—so that it seemed the form of polity might be monarchical or republican with little effect on the individual, as long as manners were mild, laws observed, and private life and property respected—implied a kind of confidence in, or acceptance of, the historical process, and hence of the nature of modernity" (33–34). According to this view, what mattered in society was not politics but social manners, which controlled governments and made commercial interests run smoothly. This view of modern society was central to certain strains of Whig thought and later evident in liberal views on the anachronism of war in commercial culture; it "embraced the common language of educated society and public life as the expression of bonds of sentiment, habit, civilized manners that transcended the political, and in fact largely controlled the effects of any particular given constitution, as they also qualified and restrained the pursuit of self-interest by individuals" (38).

Burrow's description of civilized manners recalls both Burke's and Wordsworth's emphasis on the sentimental attachments that create bonds between ruler and ruled. Wordsworth's Governor communes with ordinary men learning the habits of daily life to establish bonds with those he rules. His manners, learned from women, are gentle and humane, avoiding the violence that characterizes republican and Napoleonic France. This Governor sways; he does not coerce.

Yet, the mild-mannered Governor is only one side of Wordsworth's representation because maternal feelings only temper "the sternness of the brain." The verb "to temper" has two associated meanings. "To temper" means to mix two substances together to moderate the effects of one or both. It also means to harden or make stronger a substance that has undergone a process of tempering. The verb is often associated with sword-making. Because this poem is about the untempered sternness of Napoleon, the man of war, the association of the verb "to temper" with sword-making seems inevitable. If Napoleon is untempered by womanly kindness, he is, by implication a brittle instrument of war whose power is after all limited. The speaker grieves for Napoleon as though his end were near because he lacks true sway. But if the good Governor is tempered, he is nonetheless made up of a stern substance that only gains strength when tempered by benevolence. The implication here is that however meek the leader may be, he holds in reserve a strength far more powerful than that of the man of war. The leader, whose manners are meek and who appears to elevate ordinary men to his station, holds sternness in reserve for the right occasion. The phallic associations with the sword, which the poem suggests, remain a hidden but nonetheless tantalizing quality of the leader.

The gentle power that Wordsworth describes is important but it must offer more than kindness. It is perhaps not enough to grieve for Napoleon as though one's grief could kill off his allure. As chapter 3 argues, erotically, men of war are very much alive in the public imagination and, if one is to counteract that appeal, one must create a new erotics that can rival Napoleon's seduction. Wordsworth's "true Sway" must also offer a certain erotic appeal associated with power.

In the novel, liberal claims about equality require a supplement of chivalric excitement to inspire submission to the superior man. The new liberal manners and the new paradigm of the man of merit refashion certain older notions of manly virtue. Rather than the selfish, ambitious man who only functions in the public sphere to pursue his individual interests, the bugbear of republican thought, Austen offers a leader who, while respectful of liberal equality, demonstrates an obvious superiority of merit matched by a superiority of class and wealth. Darcy, like the ideal warrior civic republican-ism celebrated, defends his community against forces of social destruction.[20] But whereas the hero of republicanism was a representative of the landown-ing class who disavowed the new commercial culture, Austen's hero learns to respect the new bourgeoisie because the man of merit may be found in any class or profession. In this effort to integrate an older ideal of a chivalric war-rior class into a liberal paradigm, Austen divorces her hero from war alto-gether.[21] However, he must figuratively do battle with the kinds of modern forces of social disruption the civic humanists saw developing in a commer-cial society. Darcy's means of battle eschew direct violence and rely instead on financial exchange. The modern hero does not kill the enemy in battle; he must "finally bribe" (212) him.

Darcymania

Austen's Mr. Darcy offers a model for how an elite in crisis adapted itself to modern conditions. If Darcy learns to function like Wordsworth's Governor, he does so by abandoning an outdated arrogance that undermines his hold over modern people. Initially, Darcy's greatest fault, a fault that produces dis-affection among those who are supposed to fall in line with his influence and power, is his pride, his relentless exhibition of caste.

If in this period of fear elites learned to appease their inferiors by no longer parading their caste superiority before the public, Darcy seems willing to incur disaster at every turn. He famously alienates an entire neighborhood, only pages into the novel. At a ball:

> Mr. Darcy soon drew the attention of the room by his fine, tall person, handsome features, noble mien; and the report which was in general circulation within five minutes after his entrance, of his having ten thousand a year. The gentlemen pronounced him to be a fine figure of a man, the ladies declared he was much handsomer than Mr. Bingley, and he was looked at with great admiration for about half the evening, until his manners gave a disgust which turned the tide of his popularity; for he was discovered to be proud, to be above his company, and above being pleased; and not all his large estate in Derbyshire could then save him.[22]

Having aroused both men and women with his fine figure and £10,000, Darcy "turned the tide of his popularity." The narrator uses the language of political elections to compare Darcy's loss of favor with a candidate's unpop-ularity with the voters. In a world in which no elite member can afford to lose popularity, in which subordinates can vote as well as rebel, there is no room for a show of pride. To power and privilege, Darcy must add the power to please. In Austen's novel, seductive leaders must pay due attention to liberal claims of equality to save themselves from confronting more radical democratic demands for popular sovereignty and the distribution of property.

The problem initially is that Darcy's manners create a prejudice that hides his merits (Elizabeth realizes that "proud and repulsive as were his manners, she had never, in the whole course of their acquaintance...seen anything that betrayed him to be unprincipled or unjust—anything that spoke of irreligious or immoral habits" [137]). Darcy says he is "ill qualified to recommend himself to strangers," (116) that "I certainly have not the talent which some people possess... of conversing easily with those I have never seen before. I cannot catch their tone of conversation, or appear interested in their concerns, as I often see done" (116). For him, manners that recommend themselves are a matter of talent; they are inborn. Lacking this talent, he is tone deaf, unable to match the tune that others play. Awkward and out of step, he never fails to offend.

But his cousin, Fitzwilliam, declares he is ill qualified because "he will not give himself the trouble" (116). The manners that recommend one to strangers require practice; they are a matter of art. Picking up Darcy's reference to music, Elizabeth explains, "My fingers...do not move over this instrument in the masterly manner which I see so many women's do....But then I have always supposed it to be my own fault—because I would not take the trouble of practicing. It is not that I do not believe *my* fingers as capable as any other women's of superior execution" (116–17). "Masterly manner[s]" require practice but, in his superior position in life, Darcy has not taken "the trouble of practicing" an art that is necessary for survival to men such as Wickham.

To Elizabeth's claims about her piano playing, Darcy responds by changing the referent of discussion: "Darcy smiled and said, 'You are perfectly right. You have employed your time much better. No one admitted to the privilege of hearing you, can think anything wanting. We neither of us perform to strangers'" (117). This is a strange and difficult response representing Darcy's first real effort to claim a connection with Elizabeth. In failing to practice the piano, Elizabeth has employed her "time much better." If it is not the piano to which she has employed her time, then it may be in the development of her manners, the other referent of this exchange. Oddly, however, Darcy concludes that she, like him, does not perform for strangers. For Darcy, strangers cannot understand or appreciate the kind of performance that he and Elizabeth offer. It is a performance for those few elect who can understand merit where strangers see nothing. Darcy attempts to suggest a certain intimacy among those few who can really hear each other. Of course, Elizabeth is, to Darcy's shock, deaf to his performance. Darcy has to learn how to seduce even those who are not strangers, even those meritorious few who can appreciate him. The novel suggests that the man of merit must rely on far more than nature to play even to Elizabeth Bennet. Austen does not allow us to forget that elite power is maintained through a subtle art of seduction.

On her visit to Pemberley, Elizabeth finds that Darcy has suddenly acquired those manners that reveal his hidden merit. In this famous scene, Darcy manifests a startling change that reveals his new allegiance to gentle power. Schooled by the humiliation of Elizabeth's rejection, Darcy learns that the power to please consists of having great power and, yet, exhibiting a condescending restraint from using it against his subordinates. This change of manners is signaled even before Darcy appears on the scene by his property, which speaks eloquently for a man who cannot speak well for himself. Instead of the ostentation Elizabeth expects from the proud Darcy family, she finds the grounds are "neither formal, nor falsely adorned" (215). The housekeeper is "much less fine, and more civil, than she had any notion of finding her" (216). Although the rooms are "lofty and handsome, and their furniture suitable to the fortune of their proprietor," his taste is "neither gaudy nor uselessly fine; with less splendor, and more real elegance, than the furniture at Rosings" (216). Darcy's home and grounds speak to "the fortune of their proprietor" but without the loud ostentation of Lady Catherine's estate. Suddenly transformed, Darcy appears to be a gentleman, so naturally suited to his position, that he has no need to show his status or humiliate his inferiors.

Elizabeth's reactions to the landscape suggest this emphasis on Darcy's natural gentlemanliness. The narrator claims that Elizabeth "had never seen a place for which nature had done more, or where natural beauty had been so little counteracted by an awkward taste" (159). Elizabeth finds a "stream of some natural importance." Like the owner of these grounds whose character is apparently laid visible in his property, the land exhibits *natural* importance that, however, is "swelled into greater, but without any artificial appearance" (159). The taste of the Darcy family, their art of picturesque landscape design is so attuned to nature that determining where nature ends and art begins is difficult.

In her work on Austen and the picturesque, Jill Heydt-Stevenson draws a distinction between two forms of the picturesque: picturesque improvement and picturesque aesthetics. The improvers called for open vistas, which often meant "the removal of villages and commons for the sake of the prospect."[23] The point of this aesthetic was to eliminate the signs of "commerce, and of laborers' homes" in favor of a "beautiful *private* park...that a few privately appreciate" (263). This kind of aesthetic, then, made power visible, made aristocratic ostentation the center of the spectacle. The second kind of aesthetic, endorsed by Uvedale Price and Richard Payne Knight, called for conservation of the natural landscape altered only by those changes that seemed to fit naturally into the existing scene. Price and Knight called for a landscape that was not controlled and arranged to magnify the power and wealth of the landowner but that was allowed to remain largely unaltered.

The picturesque Price and Knight advocated, then, naturalizes elite power by covering art and ideology with the appearance of nature. Their aesthetic complicates the nature/art distinction so important to eighteenth-century aesthetic theory. In the picturesque the "paradox of the copy and the original is unresolvable, for we cannot determine whether the landscape or the landscape sketch came first, since art and nature are engaged in a process of reflexive influence" (270).

Elizabeth's description of the landscape at Pemberley reads like a page out of Price and Knight's theories about how nature should not be "counteracted by an awkward taste." The park full of sharp turns and trees that obstruct the vista avoids the extremes of art the improvers advocated and offers a landscape in which seeing the human hand is impossible. The entire estate might stand as a model of tempering, of how to bring elements together to create something better: nature and art, vitality and moderation, power and softness. Peter Knox-Shaw writes, where "for Burke, beauty had the effect of pacifying the subject, while the sublime provoked awe and astonishment, the new category of the 'picturesque' encompassed an intermediary range of affects, so redeeming more of the natural world and everyday world for aesthetic recognition."[24] He adds that the proponents of the picturesque aesthetic called for a "rough" (76) aesthetic that would privilege "the irregular against the geometric, the abrupt against the rounded, the bold and free against the carefully finished" (76–77). For Knox-Shaw, what "sympathy had been to the cult of sensibility, priapism was to prove for [Richard Payne] Knight's version of the picturesque" (86).

As Elizabeth and the Gardiners first enter Darcy's estate, they descend into a valley and then:

> gradually ascended for half a mile, and then found themselves at the top of a considerable eminence, where the wood ceased, and the eye was instantly caught by Pemberley House, situated on the opposite side of a valley, into which the road with some abruptness wound. It was a large, handsome, stone building, standing well on rising ground, and backed by a ridge of high woody hills;— and in front, a stream of some natural importance was swelled into greater, but without any artificial appearance. (159)

From a natural phallic protuberance, the visitors are caught by the sight of an artificial one, Pemberley House. The house, however, is seamlessly integrated into the natural landscape, backed by woods and fronted by a swelling stream. The house itself resembles the man, "handsome" and "standing well on rising ground." The picturesque estate, emblem of its master's nature and art, of his phallic power associated of course with status but tied to a natural strength, represents a modern form of political and social power. It emphasizes the master's merit, his natural right to power without the extreme volatility of the sublime or the ostentatious artificiality the improvers advocated.[25] If the picturesque is that aesthetic that moderates between extremes or differing terms, if it offers a middle ground between conservatism and radicalism, it emblems the kind of political dispensation required in postrevolutionary times that allows for a liberal sense of freedom bolstered by a virile strength that protects against the extremes of revolutionary change.

The picturesque, then, offers a way to figure the very qualities that Wordsworth emphasizes in the good Governor. These qualities are most explicitly stated by Darcy's housekeeper who reminds us of the landlord's treatment of the working classes. Darcy's housekeeper offers a list of Darcy's merits: "He is the best landlord and the best master . . . that ever lived. Not like the wild young men now-a-days who think of nothing but themselves. There is not one of his tenants or servants but what will give him a good name. Some call him proud; but I am sure I never saw any thing of it. To my fancy, it is only because he does not rattle away like other young men" (161). According to the housekeeper, young men of the present day are distinguished by their selfishness. Darcy, however, only appears proud because he is not self-indulgent, addicted to his own pleasures. Like his father, he will be "affable to the poor" and always kind to servants, he has "never had a cross word" for his housekeeper (161). Underneath the appearance of pride, Darcy is a master who takes responsibility for his subordinates in the best civic republican tradition, standing in opposition to selfish and effeminate men.

Before Elizabeth discovers the new and improved Darcy himself, however, she comes across his full length portrait in the gallery of his home. The portrait offers a smile "as she remembered to have sometimes seen when he looked at her" (162). As Elizabeth examines the painting, she experiences her first moment of erotic intimacy with Darcy: she "fixed his eyes upon herself" and "thought of his regard with a deeper sentiment of gratitude than it had ever raised before; she remembered its warmth, and softened its impropriety of expression" (162). The language, here, suggests that the painting is as susceptible to Elizabeth's attractions as the original it represents. But this represented Darcy, this object hanging in the family gallery of paintings, offers a different Darcy, one softened and warmer than the original. The world of objects that belong to him magically represent a different man. But considering that Darcy attributes his pride to his poor upbringing, that he has, until Elizabeth's intervention been cold and repulsive to everyone, particularly his social inferiors, Pemberley appears as a kind of magical castle in which the beast reveals he is after all a prince. Furthermore, his house, his land, and his servant ask that we read Darcy as having always already been this man. They ask that we read him as misunderstood. We are now given the appropriate clues in this fairy-tale place for discovering the true Darcy. Darcy requires his ancestral property to speak for him and reveal his merit. In this place, things speak more eloquently for the person than the person himself. A painting's gaze solicits feelings that the original owner of the gaze fails to elicit.

As Elizabeth comically suggests when she tells Jane that she first fell in love with Darcy at the sight of his house, there is something crucial in this novel in the relation of persons to things. Darcy's things are not merely possessions, signs of his social status that can be taken from him. They are far more intimately connected to him. The land, the house, and the portrait are expressions of Darcy, emblems of his true merit, hidden by the people and places that do not belong to him and therefore cannot properly represent him. If Elizabeth falls in love first with Darcy's house this is because Darcy is his house. The house, like the portrait, seduces far better than the actual man. If Darcy does not know how to play to strangers, his things do. They seduce, they charm, they compel. The land with its valleys and phallic protuberances, its streams swelling with importance down into valleys offers an erotic landscape that "delight[s]" Elizabeth (159). If the land suggests phallic power, the nonostentatious décor, the picturesque arrangement of woods, and the testimony of the servant speak to a tempered power. The possessions are not mere objects of status and power but signs of Darcy's liberality and benevolence, his condescension and merit. The land and property are so intimately connected to Darcy that they are one and the same. A man cannot be deprived of what functions as a natural extension of the self—the man of property is his property. This is a lord who cannot be overthrown because he belongs to what he owns.

This discovery of hidden merit is matched by the sudden, magical transformation in Darcy's manners.[26] When he meets Elizabeth's aunt and uncle, he surprises Elizabeth with a request for an introduction: "This was a stroke of civility for which she was quite unprepared; and she could hardly suppress a smile, at his being now seeking an acquaintance of some of those very people, against whom his pride had revolted" (224). Darcy condescends not only to converse with Mr. Gardiner as though he were an equal but also to invite these tradespeople to his home and to treat them "with the greatest civility" (225). Darcy's relationship with Elizabeth has caused him to fall under a new political dispensation that requires elite men to please liberal sensibilities while maintaining their aristocratic power. Darcy has learned to make his power appear natural, yet imposing; to appear as a man of merit, not simply of wealth; to delight the subordinate both by the magnitude of his power and by the condescension with which he treats subordinates. Darcy must appear ordinary and extraordinary, equal and superior. This is the new prescription for social control.

But as with the Governor, Darcy's newly "softened" mind is tempered by a strength that differentiates him from all the other male characters in the novel. If softness alone were required, Bingley would become the ideal leader who can make liberal individualism and hierarchy compatible.[27] By the end of the novel, Mrs. Gardiner informs Elizabeth that "obstinacy is the real defect of [Darcy's] character after all.... Nothing was to be done that he did not do himself" (210). Tempered by good manners, Darcy is at the core powerfully obstinate.

Obsessed by manners, *Pride and Prejudice* demonstrates how "good" manners, manners that judge according to merit rather than rank, create powerful networks of interaction and affect, which suggest at first glance that the real heart of an effective community lies beyond property and caste. People may be divided by rank but people of merit enjoy an equality beyond these considerations. The love affair between subordinates and their betters must take place in the register of merit in which master and servant look beyond caste to perceive an inner equality that renders them true companions. As Burke puts it, the leader needs better manners, which "produced a noble equality... which mitigated kings into companions, and raised private men to be fellows with kings" (239). Manners make "fellows" out of superiors and inferiors so that, in Austen's novel, they may reconcile both traditional hierarchy and liberal values. A meritocracy, according to the novel, creates a powerful intimacy among special people who apparently overlook hierarchy to enjoy one another on a higher level than caste. The very act of recognizing equality of merit creates new forms of pleasurable subordination.

Darcymania is one name for the peculiar phenomenon that allows liberal minded people to genuflect with pleasure. Darcy is appealing because he is not a throwback to an aristocratic past but a modern figure, the man of merit, who learns to uphold equality of merit over actual material inequalities.

Frankness: Democratic Dispositions

Austen's Darcy resembles Wordsworth's Governor not only because he learns how to temper his power but also because he learns his lesson from a woman. Crucial to the fantasy of modern leadership, here, is a particular kind of relationship between hero and heroine. Whereas this relationship appears to answer to nearly fairy-tale-like romantic conventions, it also speaks to a fantasy about liberal inflected elite power. In the novel, Darcy becomes modern because of Elizabeth Bennet, who often functions as a representative in the novel of a liberal democratic subject.[28] As many critics have pointed out, Elizabeth is outspoken against inordinate pride of rank and is an apparent proponent of liberty and self-determination. Associated with certain liberal values, Elizabeth manifests her impatience with outdated forms of propriety in her walking and talking. For critics of Austen as well as Austen fanatics, Elizabeth is the Austen heroine most marked by her willingness to appear in the wrong place where she can say the wrong things to the delight of generations of readers. This delight receives its highest satisfaction perhaps in the much discussed scene in which Elizabeth insults the arrogant and ostentatious Lady Catherine de Bergh, the representative of a shameless and outdated pride in rank.

In the terms of the novel, Elizabeth's refusal to adapt to outdated propriety and respect for rank is described as an extraordinary "liveliness." Elizabeth defines liveliness to Darcy, "The fact is that you were sick of civility, of deference, of officious attention. You were disgusted with the women who were always speaking and looking, and thinking for *your* approbation alone. I roused, and interested you because I was so unlike *them*" (338). Her liveliness speaks to a certain democratic disposition also described in the novel as *"frankness"* (326). Both Darcy and the reader are seduced by this "liveliness" that does not stand on ceremony, that democratically judges according to merit rather than rank.

Peter Knox-Shaw argues that Isaac Bickerstaff's play, *The Sultan*, is a source that inspired Austen's early version of the novel, *First Impressions*. The sultan in the play is "weary of subservience, and secretly riveted by the spectacle of subversion" (82). He is taken with a character who resembles Elizabeth in her unwillingness to submit. This play, for Knox-Shaw, is also a model for Price's "cherished concept of the picturesque" (82). The bored sultan is matched with a bold slave who refuses to submit to his power and therefore pleases him more. If Darcy resembles the picturesque emphasis on roughness and abruptness, Elizabeth, like her precursor in *The Sultan*, "is repeatedly associated with the word 'energy.' Her physical exuberance which leads on occasion to a trail of present participles (as in 'jumping,' 'springing,' 'glowing') is one aspect of the 'wildness' by which she is regularly characterized—though the play of her (asymmetrical) features points to a deeper source, a delight in expressing herself at the risk of transgression" (83–84).

I argued earlier that Pemberley is a physical manifestation of Darcy's merit. For Heydt-Stevenson it is also symbolic of Elizabeth's liveliness. Price and Knight, arguing against the improvers, used the analogy of the female body subjected to unnatural constraints. Heydt-Stevenson sees this analogy as a sign of a feminist position that understands the tyranny of social control as a problem particularly felt and played out on women's bodies. The picturesque of Price and Knight emphasizes freedom from restraint, development toward natural inclination, and an unconcern for the strictures of propriety while avoiding the chaos of the sublime: "Thus the picturesque entered into the Burkean dichotomy of the sublime and the beautiful as a destabilizing and mediating term, taking the energy from the sublime and the languor from the beautiful and intermixing them" (469).[29] If it does not appall with its chaos and grandeur, the picturesque landscape does not offer a simply restful vista because the "playful and complex landscape invites action and response....And curiosity provokes our own energy" (269). In *Pride and Prejudice*, Heydt-Stevenson argues, Austen "highlights the vitality and energy of this kind of landscape" (271). Associated with the picturesque aesthetic, Elizabeth "challenges traditional and patriarchal assumptions about beauty, decorum, and class. Elizabeth's vitality demonstrates Austen's preference for energy over control and rigidity" (270). Although energetic and open to change, the picturesque landscape also maintains strong connections to tradition and the past by refusing to make substantial alterations. For Heydt-Stevenson, "Elizabeth's connection to Darcy and his connection to Pemberley reinforces custom and moral heritage, as did the Price and Knight picturesque" (273). The picturesque's "dual emphasis on liberty and connection" avoids the extremes of Lydia and the stultifying dullness of Catherine Bingley.

If for Jill Heydt-Stevenson Elizabeth's associations with the picturesque suggest her connection to a more open, democratic politics, these connections only allow Elizabeth to sanctify and legitimize traditional elites who have learned their manners. Elizabeth's democratic disposition, far from threatening hierarchy, makes her the indispensable companion of a new kind of leader. Elizabeth teaches the proud aristocrat how to behave in the service of a new kind of leadership that safeguards hierarchy in postrevolutionary times. Elizabeth realizes that, "by her ease and liveliness, his mind might have been softened, his manners improved" (275). At the end of the novel, Darcy confesses the success of her influence: "You taught me a lesson, hard at first but most advantageous. By you, I was properly humbled...You showed me how insufficient were all my pretensions to please a woman worthy of being pleased" (328). If Darcy represents a seductive form of aristocratic but liberal inflected leadership, Elizabeth represents that special initiate who, after the initial error to which everyone is liable, comes to see the real merit of the man. The marriage between Darcy and Elizabeth inaugurates a new political culture because it can "teach the admiring multitude what connubial felicity really was" (275). Union with Elizabeth creates the coordinates by which the multitudes may enjoy Darcy and accept economic and political inequality in good conscience. Elizabeth shows that there is a proper route for submission in these contentious times. In postrevolutionary times, elite men must learn to please, a lesson learned, as with Wordsworth's Governor, from women.

Paradoxically, then, in those moments in which the novel seems to endorse freedom and equality, it represents the most hierarchical tendencies of the nineteenth century. The affect of liberal desire needed to be incorporated into the project of maintaining elite power. For this reason, the argument often repeated that characters such as Elizabeth give up on their desire for freedom and equality by compromising themselves into marriage, cannot account for the novel's strange uses of liberalism. The novel represents a particularly devious and seductive mode of leadership that compels submission by promising liberation. By learning liberal manners, elite men most thoroughly seduce those very subjects who strive for equality and independence.

To help explain how certain liberal values could be co-opted by elite interests, I examine Chantal Mouffe's definition of liberal democracy. The type of liberal values represented in the novel speaks to what Mouffe describes as "'the paradox' of modern democracy."[30] She asks, "what is the best way to designate the new type of democracy established in the West in the course of the last two centuries?" (1). For Mouffe, the "novelty of modern democracy, what makes it properly 'modern,' is that, with the advent of the 'democratic revolution,' the old democratic principle that 'power should be exercised by the people' emerges again, but this time within a symbolic framework informed by the liberal discourse, with its strong emphasis on the value of individual liberty and on human rights" (2). These values, which are "central to the liberal tradition," are not part of "the democratic tradition whose core values, equality and popular sovereignty, are different" (2). According to Mouffe there "is no necessary relation between these two distinct traditions" other than a "contingent historical articulation" (3). Today, Mouffe contends, the "dominant tendency" is to identify democracy with "the defence of human rights, leaving aside the element of popular sovereignty" (4).

If the democratic tradition calls for "equality, identity between the governing and governed and popular sovereignty," (3) liberal democracy stands far more for liberty than for equality, for individual rights, than for social, political, and economic equality. In other words, liberal democracy as we know it today and as it was being shaped throughout the nineteenth century, privileged liberalism over democracy, forfeiting equality for individual self-development. Liberty is more consistent with a meritocracy in which everyone in theory is free to develop according to his or her talents, unhampered by traditional privilege. Meritocracy has little to do with radical democracy in that it can offer a new way to naturalize and legitimize hierarchies after the French Revolution and its assault on traditional privileges.

The novel represents how liberal manners produce an "egalitarian feeling" that allows unequal people to participate in a fantasy about personal merit that makes inferiors *feel* like equals. This fantasy entails the recognition of personal merit by a superior man. But his recognition depends on the frisson of inequality, on the thrill of the aristocratic man's condescending gaze. Most of the major characters in the novel remain fixated by this fantasy, a fantasy most effectively played out as the heterosexual romance with a superior man.

For psychoanalysis, as I argue in chapter 1, fantasy offers us the illusion that desire may be satisfied by an object so that "the subject fascinates himself—hypnotizes himself,"[31] remains caught by the object of desire. In psychoanalysis, fantasy functions like ideology, providing the subject the way to cover over political and social antagonisms. Slavoj Žižek writes:

> Ideology is not a dreamlike illusion that we build to escape insupportable reality; in its basic dimension it is a fantasy-construction which serves as a support for our "reality" itself: an "illusion" which structures our effective, real social relations and thereby masks some insupportable, real, impossible kernel (conceptualized by Ernesto Laclau and Chantal Mouffe as "antagonism": a traumatic social division which cannot be symbolized). The function of ideology is not to offer us a point of escape from our reality but to offer us the social reality itself as an escape from some traumatic, real kernel.[32]

To develop Žižek's argument in connection with *Pride and Prejudice*, we might say that in Austen's novel the problem of class inequality constitutes the antagonism that must be escaped by entering the fantasy of romantic love. Darcy, as the object of our desire, permits us to forget that kind manners do not confer political, social, and economic equality. Liberal manners only "hypnotize" us so that we may ignore what Pemberley stands for: privatized land and resources for the enrichment and empowerment of an exploitative elite. Darcymania seduces us all into loving our betters.

Wickham Unseduced

If the reactions to the BBC *Pride and Prejudice* are any guide, most readers and viewers identify with Elizabeth who learns to see the merit in a superior man who is misunderstood. The reader or viewer is, by this account, invited to become that initiate who can submit to the proper master, who finds her object of desire in the fantasy of heterosexual romance with the superior man. I argue, however, that the novel is far less simply satisfied with this solution and that Wickham and the army suggest a disturbing limit to the model of seduction the Darcy/Elizabeth relationship proposes. Wickham is the character in the novel who is most clearly unable to find or accept his object(s) of desire, who remains perpetually dissatisfied and restless.

The happy picture of a smooth resolution in which the liberal-minded Elizabeth teaches the aristocratic Darcy new manners and in which she, herself, learns to appreciate the real value of the man, suggests an untroubled evenness that the novel does not permit. If the relationship between Darcy and Elizabeth is a paradigm for how all submissive relationships should function in a hierarchical, postrevolutionary community, the novel offers serious obstacles to its success. We find a certain obduracy in Wickham that makes him blind to the appeal of the Darcy/Elizabeth model of submission. He is the embodiment of the subject who cannot be quietly hypnotized, who is driven by an unsatisfiable desire, who perpetually discards and replaces his objects of desire.

Wickham is the character most threatening to the allure of elite men.[33] His danger lies partly in the fact that as a soldier and as a man who knows how to play to strangers he provides the kind of glamour that distracts from Darcy's appeal. But he is not simply a contender for Darcy's place, the result of a meritocratic system in which aristocrats need to compete with commoners. Instead, his seductiveness is particularly dangerous because he cannot properly replace Darcy: Wickham embodies those forces of anarchic desire that critics imagined were generated by the French Revolution. Most interestingly, however, he belongs to a world in which the rules of probability are unclear; the narrator represents an army seen from a distance, in which the rules and values remain unknown. Because other characters do not know what values and standards operate in the army, they do not always know how to calculate Wickham's intentions and interests. To seduce subordinates, one must at least understand what motivates and guides them. Both Wickham's motives, which are in excess of any clear self-interested calculation, and the world he comes from, remain opaque to the civilian community.

According to Darcy, interest only motivates Wickham. But the affair with Lydia represents an excess of motives that requires pages of attempted explanation and conjecture. Wickham himself never explains his motives. If, for a calculating man, this affair seems out of character, the Bennet family learns that Wickham's conduct is not simply calculating and interested. It is excessively acquisitive; he has amassed gambling debts and debts with local merchants. Wickham consumes money, objects, and women in a manner that cannot be connected simply to a desire to improve himself. Furthermore, his choice of objects suggests a carelessness about value that baffles other characters. Wickham does not consume what others consider valuable but what is proximate, what can be got. What Elizabeth and Mr. Gardiner agree on is that the object choice is not worth the risk because it is valueless in every way. Lydia lacks not only personal merit but also the means to satisfy Wickham's worldly interests. She can only interest him as an object to consume briefly before moving on to another. In uncovering Wickham's real conduct, the characters learn that he is "imprudent and extravagant" (188); neighbors and relations report Wickham's "extravagance or irregularity" (191). Wickham's affair with Lydia produces a fantasy in Meryton of endless seduction and financial misconduct: "He was declared to be in debt to every tradesman in the place, and his intrigues, all honoured with the title of seduction, had been extended into every tradesman's family.... Elizabeth, though she did not credit above half of what was said, believed enough to make her former assurance of her sister's ruin still more certain" (191). If the village fantasy of a type of Don Giovanni who consumes goods and women for the sake of consumption without halt to his desires and without rational calculation is an exaggeration of actual conduct, it does, nonetheless, reveal the potential dangers of Wickham to every family. He is a consumer who threatens the orderly exchange of money for goods and the patriarchal exchange of women.

His excessive consumption signals an aspect of the character that functions in the service of "making trouble," of unsettling families, ruining women, and causing general mayhem. Linda Dowling writes that the French Revolution created in England a fear of the endless generativity of a mob let loose on the world. For many Britons, once the old stays of power became undone, women, the lower classes and the burgeoning capitalist economy with its speculations and transactions of wealth independent of the sure foundation of land, would overwhelm the settled agrarian world. The landed economy of Great Britain seemed under attack by an urban generativity that promised to swallow everything in its path. This fear was expressed in the language of "heterosexual promiscuity," "an idiom of that blind generativity—of bodies, of money, of value—threatening to overwhelm a middle-class world of controlled desire and legal marriage and the orderly transmission of property within society."[34] This is a world motivated by a "blind" desire for acquisition and consumption that goes beyond the careful calculations of self-interest and personal ambition. Wickham's danger lies not simply in his desire for self-advancement but in his destructive and even self-destructive capacity to seduce people and consume money.

In her analysis of *Blackwood's* reaction to the Cockney school, Linda Dowling marks a historical change in how reactionaries identified the enemy of a land based, traditionalist England. If civic republican discourse had imagined the enemy as an effeminate man, sterile, urban, disconnected from land and dependent on financial speculations, the French Revolution called on traditionalists to find a new language to describe a new threat. The

Revolution vividly demonstrated not a culture of weakness and sterility but one that was terrifyingly vibrant and generative:

> For as [*Blackwood's*] writers move from the eunuchs and effeminati of classical republican discourse to an alternative language deploring heterosexual promiscuity, they are moving as well from a symbolic vocabulary of impotence and effeminacy to an idiom of that blind generativity—of bodies, of money, of value. (21)

Wickham unleashes precisely this kind of energy as he attempts to disrupt the orderly exchanges of women and property. His desire is far more threatening than that of a calculating upstart who merely manipulates others to achieve his own secure place in the social hierarchy. Wickham functions as the embodiment of those very forces of generativity that appear so terrifying during the French Revolution.[35]

But if merit and rational calculation of self-interest cannot keep Wickham in line, then something is at play in the choices subordinates make that exceeds the appeal Darcy is able to offer them. The sensitive initiate who, despite certain errors of judgment learns to see the true merit in her social superior, is the perfect submissive subject. It is the obdurate, stupid, insensible character who cannot be easily controlled. Bingley is in some ways the comic opposite of Wickham and Lydia. The creature of Darcy's will, he makes life choices entirely according to Darcy's advice. Content with Darcy's explanations and decisions, Bingley is led blindly through life. Wickham, instead, can be neither led nor controlled and most of all he cannot be satisfied because what he wants is not clear. In some sense, Wickham and Lydia simply want to consume. We see a degree of indifference to what they actually consume that makes them particularly volatile. Lydia is indiscriminate about objects of desire from bonnets to men.[36] She and Wickham want change and sensation. They are destructive because their consuming pleasure cannot be satisfied by a particular object. They will always require more but this "more" is not simply what a commodity culture promises. In that system there would presumably be a hierarchy of goods and desires. Instead, Wickham may be as taken with Lydia Bennet as with Elizabeth. He and Lydia have no clear or stable hierarchy of objects that might partially fixate their wandering desires to limit and control their behavior. If, as the narrator states, Wickham will not long enjoy his wife, surely the same (pace Elizabeth and the narrator) may be imagined of Lydia who, without the restraint of shame, will consume again and again perpetuating the very problem Darcy stepped in to redress. As the Gardiners and Darcy work to establish a controlled, respectable, and meritorious vision of a hierarchical society, Wickham and Lydia suggest that commodity culture unleashes a far less controllable desire. Neither the desire of the proper consumer nor the desire of the parvenu who can be bribed, Wickham's desire threatens to break the boundaries established even by a reformed Darcy. If

Darcy's first attempt to control Wickham (perhaps with the threat of a duel) unleashes Wickham on the world, his second attempt through bribery promises only a temporary solution. Neither aristocratic violence nor economic persuasion can quite contain Wickham.

Even more disturbing to any effort to establish stable hierarchy, however, is the presence of the army in the novel. The "voices of reason" in the novel, such as Elizabeth and the narrator, attempt to imagine a world in which one may calculate motives and in which values are stable. However, the army represents a limit point beyond which reasonable calculation no longer holds. Mr. Gardiner and Elizabeth attempt to determine the probable actions of a character who has committed the improbable. Not only can they not determine what is probable for Wickham himself, but they are also unsure of what is probable in his sphere of life. To Mr. Gardiner's claim that Wickham will not threaten his position in the army by ruining Lydia, Elizabeth responds, "As to what restraint the apprehension of disgrace in the corps might throw on a dishonourable elopement with her, I am not able to judge; for I know nothing of the effects that such a step might produce" (183). What constitutes disgrace in the world of Meryton is perfectly clear but the army is both a part of and disconnected from polite society. The army is a place in which probabilities cannot be calculated and in which its members may commit seemingly improbable actions that cannot be predicted and avoided.

In the most interesting recent work on Jane Austen, William Galperin argues that several of Austen's contemporaries called for a "realist" novel that would represent only the natural and therefore probable. These claims in literary theory were similar to those put forth by the proponents of the picturesque such as Price, Knight, and Gilpin. Galperin argues, "the privileged term" in picturesque theory is nature "which slides imperceptibly...into other totalizing terms such as 'truth' or 'reality.'"[37] In other words, "nature becomes under the aegis of the picturesque not simply the only nature we know on earth; it becomes...the only nature—the only 'all'—we apparently need to know" (20). The novel, like the landscape, must be made to conform to these laws of nature. For Galperin:

> Theorists of the picturesque recommend representations of human and social life in narrative fiction that, like the representations of nature they endorse in art and in gardening, are not only both probable *and* partial, or "natural" *by virtue* of their partiality; they urge representations whose conflation of truth and subject matter ultimately serves specific social and ideological interests. (20)

Galperin finds, however, that Austen's practice is to undermine expectations of probability, to disrupt this naturalizing effort so dear to picturesque and literary theorists.

Wickham, Lydia, and the army itself put pressure on any notion of the probable because what rules of probability rule with such characters and in such organizations is not clear.[38] Is it probable that a middle-class girl should be completely unaware and unconcerned about her reputation? Is it probable that a soldier should insult his colonel's hospitality or that he should ruin himself? Or, as Elizabeth suggests, is it even probable that he would be ruined in the army for his elopement? In the world of the picturesque theorist, every object, action, and word has its place in an already scripted narrative. Nothing is out of place even though everything seems to occupy its place as if by nature's design. But Wickham erupts into this seemingly ordered picture with an action probably improbable. Or not. Elizabeth finds herself without the coordinates to judge. Wickham's actions are even more troubling than the example Galperin offers of the gypsies in *Emma* who appear out of place in the landscape. Galperin argues that at "base in Gilpin's discrimination is a hierarchy of orders (and desires) in which the probable is the only legitimate representation of life, whose privilege is therefore tied to a containment or suppression of the extraordinary and the improbable" (21). It is, then, "completely unacceptable—given the limits placed by picturesque on the improbable—for gypsies to materialize in the flesh out of nowhere" (21). If the gypsies seem to be a disruption in an otherwise orderly universe, Wickham's disruption makes it unclear what universe it takes place in. By what and by whose standards should such an act be judged? In what world are these actions probable? For whom are they improbable? Wickham's elopement suggests competing visions of probability, which is even more disturbing than the irruption of the improbable in an orderly universe. Elizabeth's confusion about what may be probable in the army suggests a far more difficult problem about order. How can one organize and seduce those whose motives cannot be understood by shared rules of probability?

If *Pride and Prejudice*, then, offers the most seductive of Austen's heroes in what appears to be her most reactionary novel, the intransigence of Wickham suggests the presence of desires that cannot be calculated or controlled in the world Darcy inhabits. A novel that represents how liberal and hierarchical ends work together, also reveals how the fears of a commercial culture that plagued eighteenth-century republicans still reverberates in the nineteenth century. If elites in the novel learn to control their inferiors for a time, Wickham suggests, however subtly by the end of the novel, that such efforts are not certain of permanent success.

Chapter 7

Dependent Masters and Independent Servants

The Gothic Pleasures of British Homes in Charlotte Brontë's *Jane Eyre*

*L*ike Austen's *Pride and Prejudice*, Charlotte Brontë's *Jane Eyre* (1847) has rarely if ever been examined as a novel about British leadership. Viewed as a domestic novel, *Jane Eyre* is most often studied as a representation of the patriarchal constraints of the home and of the racist ideologies that validate domestic British womanhood. Whereas earlier feminist critics celebrated Jane's struggle for self-determination against oppressive patriarchal forces in what they took to be an at least partially satisfying conclusion, more recent work qualifies Jane's victories against patriarchal oppression, claiming that she is trapped within stereotypes of ideal bourgeois femininity and racist views that seriously qualify her rebellion.[1] Much recent work sees Jane as either betraying her earlier commitment to feminist and racial equality or as remaining, throughout the novel, crucially conflicted about her political allegiances.[2] There is, however, a different way of understanding the relationship between the novel's democratic and hierarchical politics. The novel never betrays a commitment to feminist autonomy and racial equality because Jane's desires are never simply about radical equality. Jane's goal in the novel is a very qualified kind of freedom; not the directly political freedom that requires equality, that undermines hierarchies of class, as well as gender and race. Instead, freedom for Jane Eyre consists of the right to experience exciting adventure, particularly Gothic adventure in which maintaining hierarchical difference gives the narrative its true erotic edge.[3] The novel adopts the language of liberalism by touting the values of merit and individual liberty to connect an apparent quest for freedom and self-determination with the desire for mastery.

137

The domestic space in the novel turns out to be not a place separate from the public sphere but the most cathected space in which British men and women learn to reconcile liberal and hierarchical politics. The home is that privileged site where two seemingly irreconcilable political dispositions come together to safeguard a covert but deeply cathected love of submission. The domestic sphere for Brontë offers a particularly effective space for naturalizing a perverse kind of modern power that thrives on the appearance of equality. This apparent equality, however, only serves to cover the underlying presence of the master. This novel represents a certain kind of liberal democratic commitment as the ultimate means by which the relationship with the master not only survives but also thrives as the only modern adventure worth having.

Pervaded throughout by language of mastery and equality, the novel asks to be read as a representation of how English democracy should work. Modern democratic subjects, by the end of the novel, appear free, equal, and empowered even on the economic level, but this independence only licenses a hidden commitment to one's idol or master to whom one can more freely genuflect. The plot of the novel works to exile most forms of overt hierarchical power from the British home. It establishes another space, typically in India, the Caribbean, or even in continental Europe, where overt masters can lead inferiors without the constraints pertaining to the British context. But, in England, once the inequalities that torment the protagonist seem at least superficially removed from her relationship with the master, the novel reveals how the last bastion of true inequality is found at the level of erotic gender fantasy. The lower classes and women remain wedded to their aristocratic masters because their masters make modern life exciting by lending a Gothic intensity to an otherwise mundane existence.

The novel's plotting of the aristocratic master's survival in Great Britain speaks to a reality about class in the nineteenth century that historians have recently come to terms with. As the previous chapter argued, recent historical work has shown that aristocratic classes were remarkably resilient and able to reinvent themselves to thrive in a modern world. Like Austen's Darcy, Rochester recreates himself to appease democratic demands. Elite men must learn to minimize the differences of race, class, and gender to suggest a more important equality of merit. Yet, both novels also show how, at a deeper level, a superior virility distinguishes the master from inferior men and legitimizes his continued social, political, and economic superiority. The exciting equality Darcy and Rochester hold out to Elizabeth and Jane is only truly appealing because it is always enacted against the backdrop of the master's superiority and, in the case of *Jane Eyre*, his eventual reassertion of violent power.

Bullies for Empire

Jane Eyre examines characters who, by ascribing to hierarchical politics and by ignoring liberal claims, produce rebellion in inferiors. The novel offers these characters as examples of failed mastery, marking the oppressive characters as fundamentally inadequate for Great Britain. The novel works to displace overtly hierarchical politics to the periphery, the colonies, and the continent.

Two characters crucially represent this failure to engage with British values. Their expulsion from the narrative and from England allows the novel to define a specifically British power in difference from the colonies. The explicitly hierarchical forms of power that define the positions of Bertha Mason and St. John Rivers relegate them irrevocably to colonial spaces.

In the novel, as Nancy Armstrong argues, the aristocratic women, unlike middle-class women, perpetuate a rigid sense of hierarchy.[4] Additionally, by standing in for outdated hierarchy, aristocratic women in the novel forfeit their Englishness and become figuratively, if not literally in all cases, not-English. They are all connected by non-Western physical characteristics. Bertha is a Creole, an English woman presumably, but whose appearance suggests she is at least figuratively not white.[5] Blanche Ingram, a stand-in for Bertha whose French name ironically highlights her whiteness, has an "oriental eye" (183) and skin as "dark as a Spaniard" (196).[6]

If non-Western features indicate that elites and aristocrats do not embody true Englishness, Bertha, more than any other elite woman, suggests an added dimension to the elite woman's connection to oppressive power because Bertha Mason is the effect of the most overt kind of imperial oppression.[7] Jenny Sharpe sees Bertha's equivocal race and nationality not only as very much in line with the critique of the upper-class woman but also as a critique of a certain kind of imperialism. She writes, in England, Creole "was a derogatory name for the West Indian sugar plantocracy. *Jane Eyre* is a novel of the 1840s, a time when slavery was so unpopular that only those who directly benefited from it continued to defend it."[8] For Sharpe, Bertha represents a common stereotype in English representations of slave owners whose moral degeneracy leads to insanity (46). My claim here is that Bertha represents an unacceptable form of power that the liberal values of the novel work to eliminate. As such and as a serious impediment to Rochester's rebirth into a new modality of power, she must be eliminated from the novel.

St. John Rivers is also relegated to the colonies and to an early death. His relation to power is likewise hierarchical but, nonetheless, different from Bertha's connection to slavery. Sharpe differentiates between the representation of slave-owning colonies such as Jamaica and of colonies such as India where labor was presumably paid. The abolitionist movement successfully represented slavery as "not only an inferior labor system but as an immoral one as well" (27). By constructing the British right to expand its empire as a matter of "moral superiority," the discourses of empire and slavery became incompatible. By turning to India, however, conceiving of the morality of British expansion without the taint of slavery was possible. In India "the British saw themselves as freeing natives from the bondage of ignorance and cruel religious practices" (28). British intervention in India was authorized by a fixed sense of racial, national, and religious superiority.

If Bertha represents the first and more illegitimate form of colonial power, St. John Rivers represents the second, associated with India rather than the slave-owning colonies. A devoted missionary, St. John Rivers practices a religion that licenses a strict hierarchical view of the world and legitimizes his arrogant assumption of power.[9] Power remains static and fixed for him in a rigid hierarchy that makes him, as Jane describes him, a cold despot.[10] In the course of the novel, this hierarchical understanding of religion becomes good only for death and the colonies.

But the novel does not get rid of St. John Rivers as thoroughly as it eliminates Bertha. On the last page, the narrator describes St. John River's heroic achievements:

> As to St. John Rivers, he left England: he went to India. He entered on the path he had marked for himself; he pursues it still. A more resolute, indefatigable pioneer never wrought amidst rocks and dangers. Firm, faithful, and devoted; full of energy, and zeal, and truth, he labours for his race: he clears their painful way to improvement; he hews down like a giant the prejudices of creed and caste that encumber it. He may be stern; he may be exacting; he may be ambitious yet; but his is the sternness of the warrior Greatheart, who guards his pilgrim-convoy from the onslaught of Apollyon. (501)

With St. John Rivers finally gone from England, the reader can breathe a sigh of relief. But the passage refuses to let him go with a mere mention. Instead it inflates his importance in a novel that is purportedly about other characters.

The question of why the novel ends with St. John Rivers has remained unresolved for critics.[11] But one way that St. John and his sacrifice signify by the end is that they define a modality of power that, although relegated to the colonies where it can only be justified by the "backwardness" of the colonized people, is nonetheless a necessary support for a more truly "English" power that defines itself in the course of the novel by opposing the colonial other represented by Bertha. The static hierarchies that characterize St. John's missionary work, although partly endorsed at the end of the novel by religion and imperialist ideology, do not belong in England. Sequestered in the colonies, this kind of power functions as a marker of how far democratic England has come but it reassures that, when necessary, the patriarchal and despotic power of a Greatheart can still defend the empire and perpetuate its interests. This novel shows how a seemingly democratic commitment not only coexists with imperial power but also requires it to exist. The cold despot is necessary to the empire, but he is not acceptable for domestic consumption.[12]

Jane Eyre never allows the reader to forget how domestic and national power depend on the colonies. Crucial for the resolution of the novel is Jane's inheritance of her uncle's colonial wealth, a fortune earned in England's slave-owning colonies. This inheritance suggests perhaps the darkest hint of complicity between the democratic ethos in England and the oppressive condition of the colonies because, as Spivak argues, the English woman's freedom and equality depend on the unacknowledged oppression of the colonized. This wealth, furthermore, finances St. John River's own mission to India suggesting greater connections between Bertha and St. John's colonial world than the novel explicitly acknowledges.

British Homes, Gothic Thrills

If overly oppressive politics belong in the colonies and are necessary for empire and for the maintenance of British comfort and power, a rather different politics is suitable in Great Britain itself. Britons enjoy a seemingly more liberal political climate that, nonetheless, maintains an exciting commitment to violent masters. Jane learns to desire the master's power in her childhood because the attachment to masters is taught in British homes where little girls dream of Gothic adventure.

In the first page of the novel, Jane escapes the attention of her hostile relations by hiding in a secluded window seat and leafing through the pages of Thomas Bewick's *History of British Birds*. She gazes on pictures of "bleak shores," "death white realms," a "cold and ghastly moon" above "a wreck just sinking" (14–15). As Jane W. Stedman claims, Jane is most fascinated by Bewick's supernatural images in which fiends in bird shape stand over gibbets and tombstones. This book, which purports to be about the natural world but which offers Gothic images instead, is particularly interested, according to Stedman, in British homes: "many pictures in *British Birds* suggest Thornfield Hall as Jane imagines it in her dream and as she finds it after the fire."[13] This book suggests what Jane will later learn—that exciting masters live in Gothic homes and that young girls find their life adventure in the home. Jane learns her fascination for the master from Gothic books.[14]

Yet, in her childhood, the home appears to shut out Gothic adventure even as it produces the desire for it.[15] This desire for excitement and Jane's frustration at being trapped in the home appears most famously in the passage on the leads at Thornfield. Looking out over the landscape below, Jane sees her continued interdiction from adventure as the effect of her domestic servitude. Her condition of servitude, which Rochester refers to as her "governessing slavery" (303), limits her experience of life, forcing her to occupy liminal spaces that promise escape but only continue to trap her. She seeks out the roof of this house as she sought out the retired window seat of the Reed home to see "bright visions." Imagining a greater world, she "let my heart be heaved by the exultant movement which while it swelled it in trouble, expanded it with life" (125). This imaginary life is filled with "trouble" but also offers "a tale my imagination created, and narrated continuously; quickened with all of incident, life, fire, feeling, that I desired and had not in my actual existence" (125). Daydreams of adventure cannot be actualized, for Jane, because she belongs to the oppressed classes:

> It is in vain to say human beings ought to be satisfied with tranquillity: they must have action; and they will make it if they cannot find it. Millions are condemned to a stiller doom than mine, and millions are in silent revolt against their lot. Nobody knows how many rebellions besides political rebellions ferment in the masses of life which people earth. (125)

Like millions of others, Jane is condemned not so much to starvation or disenfranchisement, as she is to "tranquillity."

The passage becomes more specific:

> women feel just as men feel; they need exercise for their faculties, and field for their efforts as much as their brothers do; they suffer from too rigid a restraint, too absolute a stagnation, precisely as men would suffer.... It is thoughtless to condemn them, or laugh at them, if they seek to do more or learn more than custom has pronounced necessary for their sex.
>
> When thus alone, I not unfrequently heard Grace Poole's laugh: the same peal, the same low, slow ha! Ha! Which when first heard had thrilled me. (125–26)

This passage has been read as Jane's most explicitly feminist statement. Cora Kaplan finds that even though "Bertha must be killed off" in favor of a "Protestant femininity, licensed sexuality," "the text cannot close off or recuperate that moment of radical association between political rebellion and gender rebellion, cannot shut down the possibility of a positive alliance between reason, passion and feminism."[16] This passage, for Kaplan, offers a radical moment in which Jane imagines her alliance with the oppressed, an alliance that also validates the anger and passion that are anathema to proper femininity.

For many critics, this passage and the scenes of Jane's childhood represent the most radical phase of the novel. Yet the passage on the leads is not simply about a desire for feminist and class equality. It speaks to Jane's early childhood interest in adventure or Gothic narrative. For Jane, the oppression of women and the lower classes consists first and foremost in a refusal to offer them the pleasures of adventure. Condemned to boredom because of their gender and poverty, women and the working class can experience none of the excitements available to men of property. This recognition, however, is not explicitly a call for suffrage and economic equality. It is first and foremost a call for the right to experience excitement, for access to Gothic pleasures. At this point, the home is a place devoid of the master's presence. Here, women can only confine "themselves to making puddings and knitting stockings, to playing on the piano and embroidering bags" (125). The thrill of danger available to men is missing. Rochester brings the pleasures of the master home to Jane so that she can put aside the boredom of domestic life and create a new kind of home.

Associated with revolutionary anger at the restrictions on women, Bertha's famous laugh also hails the beginning of a new narrative—the Gothic tale that Jane has wanted to inhabit throughout her life. Jane's sense of the dullness of domesticity is answered by two of the novel's most Gothic effects—the mad woman's laugh and Rochester's appearance as a demon. Rochester brings adventure into the home by replacing the relations of stable equality between Jane and the housekeeper, Mrs. Fairfax, with the exciting power struggle between master and servant. The conjunction of this passage, the eerie laugh, and Rochester's arrival suggest that the servant and the woman's boredom end when the master returns home.[17]

Gothic Homes: The True Pleasures of British Life

Jane finds all the adventure she will ever need with Rochester in his home. If Jane has throughout desired an escape from the domestic so that she may experience the Gothic, she discovers that the Gothic is properly found at home. Jane's life story, organized around a series of rejections in which several characters fail to seduce her, culminates in a successful seduction by her master. Rochester succeeds where others have failed because he and Jane develop a compelling Gothic eros that is both intimate and political.

Most accounts of the Gothic as a literary genre understand it as crucially about a social or psychic disruption that suspends "normality."[18] For Cyndy

Hendershot, the "Gothic disrupts. It takes societal norms and invades them with an unassimilable force."[19] According to David Punter, the Gothic is about "a fracture, an imbalance, a 'gap' in the social which would not go away" (Punter 1987: 26)."[20] Responding to Punter's reference to fractures and gaps, Robert Miles turns to Foucault for a historical understanding of the Gothic that eschews the notion of the fragmentation of some previous cohesion and focuses instead on the Gothic as "a moment [that] arises from the clash of incommensurate 'archives,' where the one has lost its hold and the other only begins to assert its grip. This clash problematizes the discourses that traverse it so that, in the repeat of the old, we find the destabilizations of the new" (28). The Gothic, according to much recent work, reveals incompatible forms of power usually narrating a confrontation between older power structures (aristocratic, religious, and so forth) and newer more bourgeois and democratic structures. However, most Gothic texts stage a confrontation in which either each side is destroyed or in which the older power is eliminated. In other words, the Gothic manifests a problem that leads to a destructive antagonism.

I claim, instead, that by the end of *Jane Eyre*, the Gothic manifests a perverse suspension of an antagonism. My reading of Gothic effects in *Jane Eyre* emphasizes how the Gothic is necessary for the "normal" state of things to continue. The Gothic in this novel does not offer a nightmare vision that reveals the terrors of everyday life. The dangers of the master expose no hidden reality in this novel because the normal state of English democracy is Gothic. Incapable of unmasking the pretensions of ideology, the Gothic is merely the effect of an ideology that eerily sustains incompatible desires at the same time. The Gothic in this novel, then, is neither the effect of a disruption in the normal fabric of social existence, nor of the clash of antagonistic forms of power. Rather the Gothic, here, is ideology at its most effective insofar as it reconciles impossible antagonisms. As Slavoj Žižek claims, reality is formed from fantasies pervaded with contradictory desires and identifications.[21] As chapter 1 argued, Žižek understands fantasy as a means of covering a social antagonism that would otherwise reveal "the inconsistency of our own ideological system" (48). What the Gothic allows the novel to hold together is the belief in equality and in superior men who possess the natural right to rule. These contradictory beliefs are reconciled in the novel's representation of companionate marriage, which allows for contradictions to become naturalized. Fantasy, here, is indistinguishable from ideology but it preserves the sense that, although ideology organizes symbolic material or "reality" for everyone in a culture, it can be experienced as a manifestation of a personal, intimate, and entirely unique desire. In the novel, ideology becomes reality when symbolic processes become domesticated, drawn into the sphere of personal and intimate life. By defining political relations as the expression of a unique and personal disposition, the novel turns these Gothic desires into the norm, a norm in which every exceptional and unique reader finds herself in an exciting Gothic adventure.

The fulfillment of Jane's Gothic desire begins with Rochester's arrival at Thornfield and the development of their courtship as a complex power struggle. Initially, Rochester appears to have all the power in this relationship and like an oriental tyrant, he will enslave Jane. However, even though Jane feels that Rochester's "smile was such as a sultan might, in a blissful and fond moment, bestow on a slave his gold and gems had enriched" (291), she also knows that she has "a sense of power over him" (298).

Although the problem of Rochester's excessive power is not resolved until the end of the novel, Brontë shows how, throughout the relationship, Rochester and Jane are not erotically compelled by a simple master and slave dynamic. Their interactions are more complex because, despite Rochester's actual social superiority, he does not clearly know himself who has real power in their relationship. He describes how power circulates between them:

> I never met your likeness, Jane: you please me, and you master me— you seem to submit, and I like the sense of pliancy you impart; and while I am twining the soft, silken skein round my finger, it sends a thrill up my arm to my heart. I am influenced—conquered; and the influence is sweeter than I can express; and the conquest I undergo has a witchery beyond any triumph *I* can win. (293)

On the one hand, Rochester claims that Jane masters him but she does so by seeming to submit. Because of this "sense of pliancy" in her, Rochester feels assured of his own strength in binding her to himself. But "while I am twining the soft, silken skein around my finger," his control over her is reversed and he finds that "I am influenced—conquered." His strength is weak compared to her influence, which, although submissive, is more triumphant. Jane's influence here seems to echo Nancy Armstrong's important claim that women are empowered to reform violent men through their gentling influence. Armstrong describes a cultural shift in which an apparently egalitarian ethos replaces a concern with "the intricate status system that had long dominated British thinking" (4). Women become the agents of this modernizing cultural change because the home over which they preside offers a safe haven from the male public world of political and economic struggle. In opposition to the aristocratic lady, the bourgeois woman oversees a domestic space where "the most basic qualities of human identity" (3) developed. Women, in nineteenth-century novels, then, function as mediating figures whose influence transforms an older aristocratic culture into a modern bourgeois culture. In the home, under her purview, differences of power ideally disappear and merit, not status, accounts for differences among people.[22] For Armstrong, the home safeguards the values of merit and minimizes the inequalities that repress the egalitarian energies of a nascent bourgeois culture. Yet, *Jane Eyre* offers a rather different representation of the woman's influence, which perversely works both to institute liberal equality and to preserve the master's power.

The complex and apparently contradictory nature of Jane's influence becomes clear in the moment when Rochester's power threatens to become most overwhelming. When Jane announces that she must leave him, Rochester responds, "By God! I long to exert a fraction of Samson's strength, and break the entanglement like tow!"—threatening to actualize the violence hinted at in his earlier description of the silken skein (340). To bend her to his will, Rochester warns:

> "Jane! Will you hear reason?" (he stooped and approached his lips to my ear) "because if you won't, I'll try violence." His voice was hoarse; his look that of a man who is about to burst an insufferable bond and plunge headlong into wild licence [*sic*]. I saw that in another moment, and with one impetus of frenzy more, I should be able to do nothing with him. The present—was the passing second of time—was all I had in which to control and restrain him; a movement of repulsion, flight, fear, would have sealed my doom,—and his. (340–41)

Ready to burst his bonds of self-control, the thwarted master is on the verge of revealing the enormous power he wields, but, Jane saves them both.

Their doom would be to reduce their relationship simply to one of brute oppression and to establish an explicit hierarchy. But Jane's reaction is unusual. Rather than express the anxiety she often feels during their courtship, she claims:

> I was not afraid: not in the least. I felt an inward power; a sense of influence, which supported me. The crisis was perilous; but not without its charm: such as the Indian, perhaps, feels when he slips over the rapid in his canoe. I took hold of his clenched hand; loosened the contorted fingers; and said to him, soothingly,—"Sit down; I'll talk to you as long as you like." (341)

Jane's influence does not constitute her as the angel in the home, here, the figure of domestic benevolence and civility. Rather, her capacity for influence resembles a savage Indian negotiating a rapid. Influence does not so much tame the wild force about to burst its bounds as avert its dangers. The crisis is perilous but charming because Rochester's threatened violence is the occasion for Jane's adventure. His power is the "field" for her exertions as she discovers that her strength is stimulated by his mastery. Here, influence means the capacity to engage with a greater power while enjoying one's capacity to keep it in check. However, the crucial point here is that keeping it in check is a means of keeping it. The Indian riding the rapids tests his strength against a far greater power, not to destroy or eliminate the danger, but to participate in and share that power while exerting force over the rapids by controlling their effects.

If, for Armstrong, the domestic sphere is invested with the "basic qualities of human identity," in *Jane Eyre* the nature of those qualities is not simply egalitarian. *Jane Eyre* naturalizes the desire for mastery as one of these "basic qualities" at the same time that it also naturalizes a desire for equality and freedom. In the home and under Jane's purview, the erotic pleasures of mastery and the desire for democratic freedom coexist as the most intimate truths of "human identity."

In a subsequent scene, Rochester acknowledges that he too understands the dangers of explicit mastery:

> I could bend her with my finger and thumb: and what good would it do me if I bent, if I uptore, if I crushed her? Consider that eye: consider the resolute, wild, free thing looking out of it, defying me, with more than courage—with a stern triumph....Of your own you could come with soft flight and nestle against my heart, if you would: seized against your will you will elude the grasp like an essence. (357)

As with the image of the wild Indian, Jane here is not on the side of civilization but on the side of nature. A "wild, free thing," a "savage, beautiful creature," she is not the domestic woman who teaches restraint to the violent aristocrat.[23] Rather, her natural freedom, her wildness restrains him from attacking the "brittle frame." If images of savages recur with very negative connotations in descriptions of Bertha and of colonized subjects, here the novel evokes a discourse of the noble savage whose connection to nature ensures not ignorance and bestiality, but an avoidance of false social conventions in favor of essential qualities. The Indian figures a certain kind of subjectivity free of oppressive social determinants.

Jane here is not only a woman and a servant, but also more generally a natural "democratic" subject, one who cannot be mastered but who must choose her own master. In the moments in which Jane no longer experiences anxiety about the dangers of Rochester's power but instead finds excitement in contending with him, in exerting her own power to control his, Jane ceases to be specifically gendered or classed and functions as an exemplar of the follower who freely chooses his or her master. This follower finds life's purpose and pleasure in engaging the master.

Many critics claim that Gothic manifestations, such as despotic patriarchs and supernatural occurrences, figure the horrors of the patriarchal home for women.[24] But Jane's evident pleasure in her struggle with the master suggests a more perverse attachment, reminiscent of Brontë's own youthful interest in Byronic heroes.[25] Gothic plots and characters do not come into being simply as manifestations of patriarchal injustice, but rather to provide Jane with a "field" of adventure. Part of the adventure involves learning how to negotiate dangers so they can be enjoyed without allowing the master to become either an oppressor or an overly benevolent figure.

To establish a permanent field of Gothic pleasures, the novel must come to terms with the obstacles of class and gender. If the great social difference between Rochester and Jane represents a barrier to her enjoyment of Rochester's power, the novel concludes by engaging in a fantasy about how to escape these obstacles of culture and return to "nature." In place of a politics that recognizes specific social identities and forms of oppression, the conclusion proposes a fantasy in which subjects, naturally free, lose their social determinants to become their most "natural" selves. To effect this change, Rochester's socially superior strength must become less overt. The point of the narrative is to eliminate inequality that is not freely chosen.

The rest of the novel, after Jane leaves Rochester, sets in place the conditions by which Jane can eliminate her excessive weakness to maintain the pleasure of submission that Godwin, Byron, Hazlitt, Carlyle, and Austen's followers experience. The inequalities of caste and gender can be minimized in favor of a new inequality that allows Jane to submit with pleasure.

English Democracy and Blind Samson

The end of the novel works to minimize overt inequalities between Jane and Rochester only to produce a crucial but "natural" superiority that no longer depends on social and economic advantages but on some inner virility that justifies Jane's submission. If Jane returns to Thornfield an "independent" woman, who no longer fears Rochester's economic and social power or his physical superiority now that he has been reduced to dependency after the fire, the novel suggests that Rochester's strength has actually only increased. This strength comes both from physical weakness that only subordinates his followers more thoroughly and from a sublime inner strength the novel figures by comparing Rochester to Samson.

On the one hand, Rochester's power to subjugate Jane results from his new weakened condition. Jane returns to Thornfield to find, instead of a "stately house," only "a blackened ruin" (472). The ruin is "very fragile looking, perforated with paneless windows, no roofs, no battlements, no chimneys—all had crashed in" (472). This description seems to suggest that the master of Thornfield has suffered a similar fate and is now Armstrong's obsolete aristocrat, who has fallen with his ancestral home. Rochester's near equal, Jane can now become his servant freely and willingly: "I will be your companion—to read to you, to walk with you, to sit with you, to wait on you, to be eyes, and hands to you. Cease to look so melancholy, my dear master; you shall not be left desolate, so long as I live" (483). She makes her decision to serve him without compulsion because as she tells him, "I am an independent woman now" (483). Rochester, however, is now dependent: "The water stood in my eye to hear this avowal of his dependence: just as if a royal eagle, chained to a perch, should be forced to entreat a sparrow to become its purveyor" (488). But the sparrow who "will have to wait on" the eagle commits no sacrifice of its liberty because Jane tells him, "I love you better now, when I can really be useful to you, than I did in your state of proud independence, when you disdained every part but that of the giver and protector" (495). As with the repentant Falkland, the chastened Darcy, Wordsworth's wise Governor, and Carlyle's stuttering, incoherent heroes, softened, weakened men only gain a greater hold over their inferiors when they lose or abandon overt claims to superior power. Inferiors are only more thoroughly seduced by a castrated master.

But Jane's first sight of Rochester also suggests another dimension to his ability to seduce her. Jane recognizes, "it was my *master*, Edward Fairfax Rochester, and no other" (479, my emphasis). She describes his appearance:

His form was of the same strong and stalwart contour as ever: his port was still erect, his hair was still raven-black; nor were his features altered or sunk: not in one year's space, by any sorrow, could his athletic strength be quelled, or his vigorous prime blighted. But in his countenance I saw a change: that looked desperate and brooding—that reminded me of some wronged and fettered wild beast or bird, dangerous to approach in his sullen woe. The caged eagle, whose gold-ringed eyes cruelty has extinguished, might look as looked that sightless Samson. (479)[26]

Rochester's infirmities call forth his strengths. Jane's description of Rochester carefully maintains a balance between weakness and strength, vulnerability and power. The wild beast is fettered. The eagle eyes are blind. But fettered beasts, especially wild ones, may break the binds that hold them and blind Samson regains his lost strength as Rochester eventually regains his eyesight. The master's "blind ferocity" promises a future return of vision and strength (479).

This image of a blind Samson allows Brontë to create an effective scene of seduction in which the hero reveals a power that "passes shew," as Hazlitt and Hamlet would describe it. This power no longer depends on advantages of caste. Furthermore, his masculinity seems to have undergone a transformation in that the body, once the source of his threatening physical strength, has become dependent on the strength of others. But, oddly, this visible weakness only highlights an invisible strength. The wounded body has become like a cage that traps the "eagle." The power is now within, invisible, sublime, promising to burst forth. Whatever his physical sufferings, Rochester has a power that survives all adversity. Slavoj Žižek describes this sublime self as that "other 'indestructible and immutable' body which persists beyond the corruption of the body physical—this other body...is like the corpse of the Sadeian victim which endures all torments and survives with its beauty immaculate. This immaterial corporeality of the 'body within the body' gives us a precise definition of the sublime object."[27] When Jane sees the sublime body through the mutilated physical body, she recognizes her "master." If earlier in the novel Rochester wished to "exert a fraction of Samson's strength, and break the entanglement like tow," he actually has more strength now that he has lost Samson's strength. Like Burke's weak sovereign, Rochester's physical weakness can exert far more power to keep Jane entangled. As Rochester acknowledges earlier about the wild bird, "Of your own you could come with soft flight and nestle against my heart, if you would: seized against your will you will elude the grasp like an essence" (357). At the moment that Rochester's masculinity seems most imperiled, it ceases to become a matter of the physical body and becomes, instead, a sublime object that seduces Jane. This strength, not of the body, offers a new virility seemingly unrelated to social power. Whereas, throughout the novel, Rochester's male power is indistinguishable from a position of social privilege (Jane compares Rochester to kings, sultans, and pirates whose violent masculinity is as much a function of their status as of their physical prowess), it now stands alone free of both social conventions and of the body. On the one hand, then, Jane's and Rochester's equality seems visibly confirmed in the ruin of Thornfield, in the ruin of Rochester's amputated arm, and in his blindness. On the other, this leveling of their positions engenders a sublime power in Rochester that seems to mark him as the indisputable master, as a man whose power has become entirely "natural." Like an eagle, Rochester's strength is his natural inheritance. His mastery now exceeds the limitations of his body or his socioeconomic status. This is a mastery that emerges, as it were, out of the ashes of a purifying fire that burns off the social superfluities of caste and gender leaving the essential nature. His virility now passes for a sign of nature rather than culture.

The eagle and the sparrow, recalling Bewick's book on birds, figure the "natural" power difference between Jane and Rochester. The free play of power between the two must depend on this natural hierarchy, which subsists despite every flaunting of convention, every claim of equality and every avowal of Jane's mastery. But the images of birds that figure the natural differences between master and servant are, of course, textual images, impressed on Jane at a young age. In Bewick's book, the drawings of birds do not represent scientifically accurate images of the natural world. Instead Bewick's images represent the natural sublime. A sublime imagery that teaches Jane as a child to love a certain kind of power reappears at the end of the novel as a naturalized inequality. True British birds, Jane and Rochester discover their inequality in a text about British nature that is really a text about British power. Figured as a savage Indian or wild bird, the democratic subject can never be compelled into servitude but can freely choose to nestle on the master's bosom. Inequality, then, is freely established based not on social and economic differences but on a fantasy of sublime power. The fantasy persists despite every material determination. Material inequality must be minimized so that Jane and Rochester can indulge in the much more tenacious inequality constituted by this fantasy. By locating the development of this new master in the home, the novel naturalizes mastery as responsive to the most intimate human desires.

The "Preface" to Jane Eyre, Conventionality, and Literature

To conclude, I return to the beginning. In the "Preface" to *Jane Eyre*, Brontë comments on the function of this novel as a socially redemptive kind of literary production in contrast to merely conventional writing. At the heart of Brontë's claim about the value of her novel is its representation of how to recognize and be recognized by a master.

The novel argues that, like the followers Wordsworth, Godwin, Byron, Hazlitt, Carlyle, and Austen described, Jane has the rare capacity to see beyond the vulgar crowd and gain insight into the master's true value. This insight is pitted against the merely conventional assessments of others. Although convention should keep Jane and Rochester apart, for Jane this view is merely "a slavish notion of inferiority" (185). Convention should also make Rochester an unlikely object of admiration: "I compared him with his guests. What was the gallant grace of the Lynns, the languid elegance of Lord Ingram,— even the military distinction of Colonel Dent, contrasted with his look of native pith and genuine power?"(198). Summoning a conventional gaze, Jane avers, "I could imagine that most observers would call them attractive, handsome, imposing; while they would pronounce Mr. Rochester at once harsh-featured and melancholy looking" (198). The common observer merely sees the conventions of class, missing the real power in Rochester. According to Jane as she observes the guests, "the light of the candles had as much soul in it as their smile; the tinkle of a bell as much significance as their laugh" (198). But Rochester, instead, has a "penetrating" look. The mere conventions of class that place him among these guests are little compared to the fact that "he is not of their kind. I believe he is of mine...though rank and wealth sever us widely, I have something in my brain and heart, in my blood and nerves, that assimilates me mentally to him" (199).

This unique insightfulness is echoed in Brontë's "Preface" as a literary capacity to recognize the truly original and insightful text rather than merely "conventional" writing. Brontë's "Preface" addresses the "timorous or carping few who doubt the tendency of such books as *Jane Eyre*" (5). One of those few was Elizabeth Rigby who claimed disparagingly in the *Quarterly Reviewer*, "every page burns with moral Jacobinism."[28] To these critics, Brontë answers, "Conventionality is not morality" (5). She writes, "appearance should not be mistaken for truth; narrow human doctrines, that only tend to elate and magnify a few, should not be substituted for the world-redeeming creed of Christ" (6). Firmly differentiating between worldly values that empower the few and true values, Brontë claims, the "world may not like to see these ideas dissevered, for it has been accustomed to blend them; finding it convenient to make external show pass for sterling worth—to let white-washed walls vouch for clean shrines" (6). The person "who dares scrutinize and expose—to raze the gilding, and show base metal under it—to penetrate the sepulcher, and reveal charnel relics" can never become popular and society "may hate him: but hate as it will, it is indebted to him" (6).

Brontë follows this defense of her work as the antithesis of the conventional by offering an example of a fellow writer whose value she alone recognizes: "There is a man in our own days whose words are not framed to tickle delicate ears: who, to my thinking, comes before the great ones of society, much as the son of Imlah came before the throned kings of Judah and Israel: and who speaks truth as deep, with a power as prophet-like and as vital" (6). Brontë celebrates Thackeray "because I think I see in him an intellect profounder and more unique than his contemporaries have yet recognized; because I regard him as the first social regenerator of the day—as the very master of that working corps who would restore to rectitude the warped system of things" (6–7). Thackeray as a master of "that working corps" is also her master, for Brontë sees herself as working to "restore rectitude." Brontë can recognize this master because she alone among her contemporaries has the correct insight, an insight into Thackeray's value as a reformer of society. This capacity to see correctly, to recognize the master, is of crucial benefit to the world for the master and his corps are the "social regenerator[s] of the day." If *Jane Eyre* is commonly read as a novel about a hero and heroine who abandon the world to indulge in their own private relationship, the "Preface" offers a perspective that considers the capacity to perceive one's master as fundamental not simply to one's own personal pleasure but to the very regeneration of society. Jane and Rochester's love affair, from this perspective, figures how literary masters influence their protégés in the creation of works that "restore to rectitude the warped system of things."

In the spirit of the perversity of this novel, one might want to put pressure on this last phrase and wonder whether the novel's function is ultimately to rectify the system of things or rather to restore this warped system to prominence. Does the novel critique a warped system or revive and create it? On the one hand, as many have argued, Jane's attainment of a relationship relatively free of the limitations of class and gender is a form of wish fulfillment, a fantasy that highlights the actual constraints of the society the novel represents. On the other hand, however, the novel claims that fantasy is far more powerful than material reality. Rochester is more a real master once the only support for his power is a fantasy about his "natural" superiority and Jane is more truly subjected when she is most materially empowered. These contradictions mark out a "warped system of things" as confounding and contradictory for critics today as for Brontë's contemporaries.

Notes

Chapter 1. Introduction: Fantasies of National Virility and William Wordsworth's Poet Leader

1. Marie F. Busco, "The 'Achilles' in Hyde Park," *Burlington Magazine* 130 (1988): 920.

2. Linda Colley, *Britons: Forging the Nation, 1707–1837* (New Haven, CT: Yale University Press, 1992), 258.

3. Busco, 924.

4. Busco points out how pranksters disfigured the statue by placing a broomstick in the fist (923).

5. Michele Cohen argues that silence became a manly characteristic in Great Britain by the end of the eighteenth century: "the monosyllabic English tongue and the taciturnity of its native speakers were fused into a common national trait, manliness. English, a 'plain, rational, and monosyllabic tongue' was suited to its 'manly and laconic' speakers. By contrast, French was a language suited only for 'graceful trifling.'" *Fashioning Masculinity: National Identity and Language in the Eighteenth Century* (London: Routledge, 1996), 107.

6. Edmund Burke, *Reflections on the Revolution in France*, ed. J. C. D. Clark (Stanford, CA: Stanford University Press, 2001), 238.

7. Stefan Dudink and Karen Hagemann, "Masculinity in Politics and War in the Age of Democratic Revolutions, 1750–1850," in *Masculinities in Politics and War: Gendering Modern History*, ed. Stefan Dudink, Karen Hagemann, and John Tosh (Manchester, England: Manchester University Press), 6.

8. Catherine Hall, Keith McClelland, and Jane Rendall, *Defining the Victorian Nation: Class, Race, Gender and the British Reform Act of 1867* (Cambridge, England: Cambridge University Press, 2000), 34.

9. Leonore Davidoff and Catherine Hall, *Family Fortunes: Men, and Women of the English Middle Class, 1780–1850* (Chicago: University of Chicago Press, 1987), 13.

10. Hannah Barker and Elaine Chalus, *Gender in Eighteenth-Century England: Roles, Representations and Responsibilities* (London: Longman, 1997), 19.

11. See, for example, Sonya O. Rose, *Limited Livelihoods: Gender and Class in Nineteenth-Century England* (Berkeley: University of California Press, 1992).

12. See Catherine Hall, "Competing Masculinities: Thomas Carlyle, John Stuart Mill and the Case of Governor Eyre," in, *White Male and Middle Class: Explorations in Feminism and History,* ed. C. Hall (Cambridge, England: Cambridge Polity Press, 1992), 255–95; Mrinalini Sinha, *Colonial Masculinity: The "Manly Englishman" and the Effeminate Bengali in the Late Nineteenth Century* (Manchester, England: Manchester University Press, 1995).

13. See Amanda Vickery, "Historiographical Review: Golden Age to Separate Spheres? A Review of the Categories and Chronology of English Women's History," *Historical Journal* 36 (1993): 383–414; Joyce Thomas, "Women and Capitalism: Oppression or Emancipation? A Review Article," *Comparative Studies in Society and History* 30 (1988): 534–49.

14. See, for example, Colley who argues that the virulent call for women to remain in the domestic sphere did not reflect the reality of women's lives but was rather an attempt to persuade them away from their involvement in political activity. *Britons*, 281.

15. See Jeff Weintraub, "The Theory and Politics of the Public/Private Distinction," in *Public and Private in Theory and Practice,* ed. Jeff Weintraub and Krishan Kumar (Chicago: University of Chicago Press, 1997), 1–42. Joan Wallach Scott, "Gender: A Useful Category of Historical Analysis," in *Gender and the Politics of History*, ed. Joan Scott (New York: Columbia University Press, 1988).

16. Hall, McClelland, and Rendall, 34.

17. For historical work see, for example, John Tosh, "What should historians do with masculinity? Reflections on nineteenth-century Britain," *History Workshop Journal* 38 (1994): 179–202, *Manful Assertions: Masculinities in Britain since 1800,* ed. Michael Roper and John Tosh. (London: Routledge, 1991).

18. See Philip Carter, "Men about Town: Representation of Foppery and Masculinity in Early Eighteenth-Century Urban Society," *Gender in Eighteenth-Century England: Roles, Representations, and Responsibilities,* ed. H. Barker and E. Chalus (London: Longman, 1997).

19. See James Eli Adams, *Dandies and Desert Saint: Styles of Victorian Manhood* (Ithaca, NY: Cornell University Press, 1995).

20. John Tosh, "The Old Adam and the New Man: Emerging Themes in the History of English Masculinities, 1750–1850," in *English Masculinities, 1660–1800,* ed. Tim Hitchcock and Michele Cohen (London: Longman, 1999), 222.

21. See Lawrence Stone, *The Family, Sex and Marriage in England, 1500-1800* (New York: Harper & Row, 1977); G. J. Barker-Benfield, *The Culture of Sensibility: Sex and Society in Eighteenth-Century Britain* (Chicago: University of Chicago Press, 1992).

22. Tosh, "The Old Adam and the New Man," 223.

23. Bryce Traister, "Academic Viagra: The Rise of American Masculinity Studies," *American Quarterly* 52.2 (2000): 292–93.

24. Traister points to the influential work of James Eli Adams, Herbert Sussman, and Richard Dellamora. For other examples of this approach in Romantic studies see Tim Fulford, *Romanticism and Masculinity: Gender, Politics and Poetics in the Writings of Burke, Coleridge, Cobbett, Wordsworth, De Quincey, and Hazlitt* (Hampshire, England: St. Martin's, 1999), and Ellen Brinks, *Gothic Masculinity: Effeminacy and the Supernatural in English and German Romanticism* (Lewisburg, PA: Bucknell University Press, 2003). Brinks refers to a "distressed masculinity" (11) or "Dispossessed masculinity" (12) and asks, "if a male subject can be inhabited, displaced, or self-alienated, even temporarily, by uncanny forces that unleash, precipitate or coincide with effeminizing effects, in what sense does he possess a masculine identity?" (12).

25. Hazlitt's lack of popular success cannot be simply attributed to his championing of an enemy of England. Napoleon, among many radicals, was a popular figure even during the war and certainly after his defeat in the years in which Hazlitt wrote his biography. "Sympathy for Napoleon, though an unbroken strand in British radical thought during the years of his rule, took on new overtones in the wake of Waterloo. He became a tragic figure, a melancholy hero, a child as much of misfortune as of fortune.... British sympathizers... ascribed to Napoleon a dignity in adversity that attested to his strength of character as no act of state could." Stuart Semmel, *Napoleon and the British* (New Haven, CT: Yale University Press, 2004), 222.

26. Mark Francis and John Morrow, *A History of English Political Thought in the Nineteenth Century* (New York: St. Martin's, 1994), 11.

27. James Vernon, *Politics and the People: A Study in English Political Culture, c. 1815–1867* (Cambridge, England: Cambridge University Press, 1993), 6.

28. Jonathan Perry, *The Rise and Fall of Liberal Government in Victorian Britain* (New Haven, CT: Yale University Press, 1993), 12.

29. Hall, McClelland, and Rendall, 10.

30. Boyd Hilton, *A Mad, Bad, and Dangerous People? England 1783–1846* (Oxford, England: Oxford University Press, 2006), 31.

31. Don Herzog, *Poisoning the Minds of the Lower Orders* (Princeton, NJ: Princeton University Press, 1998), 53.

32. See also J. G. A. Pocock, *The Machiavellian Moment: Florentine Political Thought and the Atlantic Republican Tradition* (Princeton, NJ: Princeton University Press, 1975), 231, 492.

33. Crane Brinton, *English Political Thought in the Nineteenth Century* (New York: Harper & Brothers, 1962), 87.

34. Linda Dowling, *Hellenism and Homosexuality in Victorian Oxford* (Ithaca, NY: Cornell University Press, 1994), 14. See also Walter E. Houghton, *The Victorian Frame of Mind 1830–1870* (New Haven, CT: Yale University Press, 1985), 54–58.

35. Hilton, 629.

36. See, for example, *Nervous Reactions: Victorian Recollections of Romanticism*, ed. Joel Faflak and Julia M. Wright (Albany, NY: State University of New York Press, 2004); Andrew Elfenbein, *Byron and the Victorians* (Cambridge, England: Cambridge University Press, 1995); Richard Cronin, *Romantic Victorians: English Literature, 1824–1840* (New York: Palgrave, 2002).

37. C. A. Bayly, *The Birth of the Modern World 1780-1914: Global Connections and Comparisons* (Malden, MA: Routledge, 2004), 86.

38. Yoon Sun Lee, *Nationalism and Irony: Burke, Scott and Carlyle* (New York: Oxford University Press, 2004), 4.

39. William Anthony Hays, *The Whig Revival, 1808–1830* (New York: Palgrave, 2005), 14.

40. Francis and Morrow, 106.

41. Peter Mandler, *Aristocratic Government in the Age of Reform: Whigs and Liberals, 1830–1852* (Oxford, England: Oxford University Press, 1990), 25.

42. Samuel Taylor Coleridge, *A Lay Sermon* (1817), in *The Major Works*, ed. H. J. Jackson (Oxford, England: Oxford University Press, 1985), 662.

43. Francis and Morrow, 124.

44. Hilton, 30.

45. Herzog, 503.

46. Mandler, 25

47. Hays, 5.

48. Hays, 177–178.

49. Burrows writes that the tendency has been to understand liberalism in the nineteenth century as concerned with "autonomous individuals, rationally seeking the satisfaction of given wants.... Liberalism so defined is readily presented as the philosophical counterpart to *laissez-faire* Political Economy. It makes the central political issue of liberal thought, and hence, by extension of nineteenth-century England, that of state intervention in economic life" (3). But due to the "work of historians of political thought over the past couple of decades, this model no longer offers convincing guidance to any large-scale interpretation of political theory in the seventeenth and eighteenth centuries," although it does still often shape our sense of "nineteenth-century political thought" (3). For Burrows, this narrative of laissez-faire liberalism tends

to obscure the much richer connections between whiggism and liberalism in the nine-teenth century, which reveal that concerns about the excesses of commerce and democracy were pervasive.

50. Francis and Morrow, 6.

51. See, for example, Stefan Collini, *Public Moralists: Political Thought and Intellectual Life in Britain 1850–1930* (Oxford, England: Oxford University Press, 1991). Collini sees liberals as concerned with the problem of "altruism and egoism" (72). Even John Stuart Mill was not "the voice of the textbook stereotype of liberal individualism" when he deplored "the self-interested attitudes fostered by much com-mercial competition" (71).

52. Lauren M. E. Goodlad, *Victorian Literature and the Victorian State: Character and Governance in a Liberal Society* (Baltimore, MD: Johns Hopkins University Press, 2003), viii.

53. Richard Bellamy, "Introduction," in *Victorian Liberalism: Nineteenth-Century Political Thought and Practice*, ed. Richard Bellamy (London: Routledge, 1990), 2.

54. H. S. Jones, *Victorian Political Thought* (New York: St. Martin's, 2000), 1–2.

55. John Robertson, "The Legacy of Adam Smith: Government and Economic Development in the *Wealth of Nations*," in Bellamy, 21.

56. Jones, 8.

57. For work on the limits of liberalism's egalitarian and democratic politics see Celeste Langan, *Romantic Vagrancy: Wordsworth and the Simulation of Freedom* (Cambridge, England: Cambridge University Press, 1995). For Langan, the vagrant figures the condition liberalism created, which offers an illusion of freedom but in fact produces dispossessed subjects. The injunction to walk that motivates Wordsworth's peripatetic poet suggests the kind of freedom and mobility associated with liberalism. However, the poet finds the landscape peopled by homeless vagrants whose condition speaks to the limitations on freedom enclosures and private property imposed. Another instance of a critique of British liberalism in the period is *Liberalism and Empire* in which Uday Singh Mehta argues that conservatives did not provide the strongest justifications for the British rule in India but, rather, British lib-erals. The paradox of liberalism is that "the period of liberal history is unmistakably marked by the systematic and sustained political exclusion of various groups and 'types' of people." *Liberalism and Empire: A Study in Nineteenth-Century British Liberal Thought* (Chicago: University of Chicago Press, 1999), 46. Christopher Newfield turns to nineteenth-century America to show how liberalism allows for exciting forms of submission among white, middle-class American males. In *The Emerson Effect*, Newfield argues, "in fable and song the United State is the land of the free and the home of the brave." *The Emerson Effect: Individualism and Submission in America* (Chicago: University of Chicago Press, 1996), 1. Yet the American liberal

tradition, which seems so committed to the claims of the individual over those of community, actually resolves itself into "a habit of submission to authority that weakens autonomy and democracy alike" (1). For important work on the limits of liberalism for women and women's rights see Joan B. Landes, *Women and the Public Sphere in the Age of the French Revolution* (Ithaca, NY: Cornell University Press, 1988); Jean Bethke Elshtain, *Public Man, Private Woman: Women in Social and Political Thought* (Princeton, NJ: Princeton University Press, 1981); Carole Pateman, *The Disorder of Women: Democracy, Feminism, and Political Theory* (Cambridge, England: Cambridge University Press, 1989).

58. Stuart Semmel points to widespread British anxieties about effeminacy particularly during the wars with France. Semmel writes, "though the passing century had seen Britain's commerce grow, the *Courier* feared that Great Britain had 'in proportion' with this success, 'departed from the old principles of liberty; a general apathy has seized all ranks; we no longer speak in the firm and manly tone of our ancestors'" (39). In 1801 the *Courier* echoes the language of republicanism about the effeminacy of a commercial nation. See also, Semmel 67, 69–70. Philip Shaw points to how the Battle of Waterloo was often "invoked as a means of validating a claim to authority: as guarantor of national unanimity; as symbol of triumph of the 'martial spirit' over the vitiating effects of commercialism; as a key stage in the rise of middle class individuation." *Waterloo and the Romantic Imagination* (New York: Palgrave, 2002), 4.

59. See C. B. Macpherson, *The Political Theory of Possessive Individualism* (Oxford, England: Oxford University Press, 1962).

60. For work on the relationship between liberalism and republicanism, see John P. Diggins, *The Lost Soul of American Politics: Virtue, Self-Interest, and the Foundations of Liberalism* (New York: Basic Books, 1984); Joyce Appleby, "The Social Origins of American Revolutionary Ideology," *Journal of American History* 64 (Mar. 1978): 935–58; Appleby, *Capitalism and the New Social Order: The Republican Vision of the 1790's* (New York: New York University Press, 1984); Michael P. Zuckert, *Natural Rights and the New Republicanism* (Princeton, NJ: Princeton University Press, 1994).

61. Vickie B. Sullivan, *Machiavelli, Hobbes, and the Formation of Liberal Republicanism in England* (Cambridge, England: Cambridge University Press, 2004), 1.

62. Philip Carter reminds us of Hume's defense of commercial society in which he attempted to argue that "modern manners would lead to new forms of manliness, combining traditional virtues such as moderation, industry and courage (themselves improved by refinement) with more innovative qualities." *Men and the Emergence of Polite Society, Britain 1660–1800* (Harlow, England: Longman, 2001), 132. In his 1752 essay, "Of Refinement in the Arts and Sciences," Hume reconciles "military life not only with men's involvement in female society but also with the broader phenomenon of an emerging commercial economy" (76).

63. J. W. Burrow, for example, argues that we can find civic republican ideas in John Stuart Mill's work where the "republican and Country echoes are loud and clear." *Whigs and Liberals: Continuity and Change in English Political Thought* (Oxford, England: Oxford University Press, 1988), 81.

64. J. G. A. Pocock, *The Machiavellian Moment*, 201.

65. "Indeed, before republicanism could become truly liberal, it had to shed its romance with military adventures" (Sullivan, 16); "Ultimately, when it come[s] to the means by which glory is to be gained, however, Cato distances himself from Macchiavelli and reveals himself to be a true liberal. He renounces the battlefield as the venue where glory is to be won in order to embrace trade as the vehicle by which England can compete and best other nations" (229).

66. Benjamin Constant, *Political Writings*, trans. and ed. Biancamaria Fontana (Cambridge, England: Cambridge University Press, 1988).

67. Richard Teichgraeber reminds us of support for commerce as an alternative to war in the British press. He quotes the *Analytical Review* (Sept.–Dec. 1790):

> The genius of commerce is gone forth amongst the nations of the earth, everywhere carrying peace and plenty and freedom in her train. The old wars were for dominion, now they are for trade, and therefore will be fewer of them; because all war is destructive to trade. The first kings of the earth were tyrants and despots... now they are merchants and traders. The kingdoms of Europe may be said to have become warehouses; the courts, counting-houses; the prime-ministers, bookkeepers; and the secretaries of states, clerks and porters. (94, fn. 16)

"Adam Smith and Tradition: *The Wealth of Nations* before Malthus," in *Economy, Polity and Society: British Intellectual History, 1750–1950*, ed. Stefan Collini, Richard Whatmore, and Brian Young (New York: Oxford University Press, 2000).

68. H. S. Jones argues that the "central point about Victorian liberalism is that its assumptions were absorbed into the mainstream and were embraced by Conservatives as much as by party Liberals" (20).

69. See Jerome McGann, *The Romantic Ideology: A Critical Investigation* (Chicago: University of Chicago Press, 1983).

70. G. J. Barker-Benfield, *The Culture of Sensibility.*

71. For some examples of important work in Romantic studies that emphasizes the political significance of the literature of the period see James K. Chandler, *England in 1819: The Politics of Literary Culture and the Case of Romantic Historicism* (Chicago: University of Chicago Press, 1999); Saree Makdisi, *Romantic Imperialism: Universal Empire and the Culture of Modernity* (Cambridge, England: Cambridge University Press, 1998); Katie Trumpener, *Bardic Nationalism: The Romantic Novel and the British Empire* (Princeton, NJ: Princeton University Press, 1997). For work on Victorian literature that sees it as crucially concerned with public issues such as

political economy and democracy see, for example, Andrew H. Miller, *Novels behind Glass: Commodity Culture and Victorian Narrative* (Cambridge, England: Cambridge University Press, 1995); Lauren Goodlad, *Victorian Literature and the Victorian State*; Jeff Nunokawa, *The Afterlife of Property: Domestic Security and the Victorian Novel* (Princeton, NJ: Princeton University Press, 1994).

72. As the following chapters argue, although Carlyle is not a narrative writer in the sense of a novelist, his writing does "tell stories"; he offers historical examples so devoid of scholarly apparatus, so mystified, as to function as parables and archetypal narratives. Their effect is always heightened by Carlyle's famous hyperbolic style that inspires precisely that attachment to the leader that his stories seek to encourage. Hazlitt's biography, although not fiction, offers the kind of fantasy to be distinguished from daydream, which is particularly powerful in that it is a story that purports to describe a real story of self-development. Napoleon's biography, one could argue, represents the ultimate example of nineteenth-century fantasy—the self-made man who achieves everything through merit.

73. Slavoj Žižek, *The Plague of Fantasies* (London: Verso, 1997), 11.

74. Todd McGowan, "*Lost on Mulholland Drive:* Navigating David Lynch's Panegyric to Hollywood," *Cinema Journal* 43.2 (2004): 69.

75. Žižek, 7.

76. See Langan, 15, 225–26.

77. The eighteenth century sees the rise of the novel, the bourgeois genre par excellence, and the bildungsroman becomes a popular subgenre of the novel in the nineteenth century. One important example of a bildungsroman about finding one's proper place and about answering the "che vuoi?" would be Dickens's great best seller *Great Expectations*. Likewise, Romantic poetry is famous for its innovative interest in the inner workings of the mind, the development of the self. Wordsworth's *The Prelude* about the growth of the poet's mind is a particularly pointed example of the modern interest in the individual subject.

78. See M. H. Abrams, *Natural Supernaturalism: Tradition and Revolution in Romantic Literature* (London: Oxford University Press, 1971); Antony Easthope, *Wordsworth Now and Then: Romanticism and Contemporary Culture* (Buckingham, England: Open University Press, 1993); Richard Bourke, *Romantic Discourse and Political Modernity: Wordsworth, the Intellectual and Cultural Critique* (New York: St. Martin's Press, 1993); Ian Reid, *Wordsworth and the Formation of English Studies* (Burlington, VT: Ashgate, 2004).

79. Many critics argue that Wordsworth's efforts to carve out a manly role for the poet responded to multiple provocations. He reacted to the popularity of women poets and to a culture of sensibility that seemed to undermine the manliness of poetry. Simon Bainbridge claims that the "closing decades of the eighteenth century had witnessed the increasing feminization of poetry as it became characterized as a pursuit most suitable for women, heightening one popular construction of the male

poet as effeminate." *British Poetry and the Revolutionary and Napoleonic Wars* (Oxford, England: Oxford University Press, 2003), 105. See also Marlon B. Ross, *The Contours of Masculine Desire: Romanticism and the Rise of Women's Poetry* (New York: Oxford University Press, 1989), and Judith W. Page, *Wordsworth and the Cultivation of Women* (Berkeley: University of California Press, 1994). On the manliness of the "Preface" itself see *Eighteenth-Century Women Poets: An Oxford Anthology*, ed. Roger Lonsdale (Oxford, England: Oxford University Press, 1990), xl–xli. For Bainbridge, Wordsworth's sense that his poetic identity was in crisis was only heightened by the war years in which poets felt called on to masculinize the nation (117).

80. William Wordsworth, "Essay Supplementary to the Preface of 1815," in *The Prose Works of William Wordsworth*, ed. W. J. B. Owen and J. W. Smyser, vol. III (Oxford, England: Oxford University Press, 1974), 82.

81. Ian Reid argues that Wordsworth was a "political inspiration" for leaders such as President Woodrow Wilson and Australian Prime Minister Alfred Deakin (ix).

82. William Wordsworth, "Preface to *Lyrical Ballads,*" in *The Prose Works of William Wordsworth*, ed. W. J. B. Owen and J. W. Smyser, vol. I (Oxford, England: Oxford University Press, 1974), 128.

83. On Wordsworth's critique of a commodity culture in the "Preface" see Robert Anderson, "'Enjoyments of a [...] more exquisite nature': Wordsworth and Commodity Culture," *Romanticism on the Net: An Electronic Journal Devoted to Romantic Studies* 26 (Mar 2002): 66.

84. Bainbridge argues that Wordsworth's interest in Milton signals a commitment to manly writing, to the masculinization of poetry (103, 117–18).

85. Elizabeth Fay, "The 'Honourable Characteristics of Poetry': Two Hundred Years of Lyrical Ballads: Wordsworth's Balladry: Real Men Wanted," in *Romantic Circles* http://www.rc.umd.edu/praxis/lyrical/fay/balladry.html

86. Simon Bainbridge argues, "Wordsworth was a poet with a strong sense of martial identity" (91).

87. William Wordsworth, *The Convention of Cintra*, in *The Prose Works of William Wordsworth*, ed. W. J. B. Owen and J. M. Smyser, vol. I (Oxford, England: Oxford University Press, 1974), 289.

88. Brian Folker, "Wordsworth's Visionary Imagination: Democracy and War," *English Literary History* 69.1 (2002): 186.

89. Wordsworth, *The Convention of Cintra*, quoted in Folker, 191.

90. Wordsworth, *The Convention of Cintra*, 338.

91. William Wordsworth, "Lines: Composed a Few Miles above Tintern Abbey," in *English Romantic Writers*, ed. David Perkins (Fort Worth, TX: Harcourt Brace Jovanovich, 1967), 209.

92. William Wordsworth, *The Prelude* (1805), ed. Jonathan Wordsworth, M. H. Abrams, and Stephen Gill (New York: Norton, 1979).

Chapter 2. "A Left-Handed Way": Modern Masters in William Godwin's Caleb Williams

1. William Godwin, *Caleb Williams*, ed. David McCracken (New York: Norton, 1977), 112.

2. See Linda Colley, *Britons: Forging the Nation, 1707–1837* (New Haven, CT: Yale University Press, 1992), 147–93.

3. Slavoj Žižek, *The Metastases of Enjoyment: Six Essays on Woman and Enjoyment* (London: Verso, 1994), 54.

4. Slavoj Žižek, *The Ticklish Subject: The Absent Center of Political Ontology* (London: Verso, 1999), 362.

5. For another Lacanian reading of the novel see David Collings, "The Romance of the Impossible: William Godwin in the Empty Place of Reason," *English Literary History* 70.3 (2003): 847–74. Collings's reading of the novel differs from mine in particular because he sees the final scene in court as a moment of ethical insight in which both Falkland and Caleb move beyond the fantasy that they can control or fully know their world. They discover that they are "participants in a story whose ultimate import is unknown" (861). I see the court scene as the realization of Caleb's most cherished fantasy, that of union with his master, rather than a breaking out of illusion.

6. James Thompson, "Surveillance in William Godwin's *Caleb Williams*," in *Gothic Fictions: Prohibition/Transgression*, ed. Kenneth W. Graham (New York: AMS Press, 1989), 179.

7. Monika Fludernik, "William Godwin's *Caleb Williams*: The Tarnishing of the Sublime," *English Literary History* 68.4 (2001) 879.

8. See James T. Boulton, *The Language of Politics in the Age of Wilkes and Burke* (London: Routledge & Keegan Paul, 1963), 226–32; Fludernik, 858–59. Pamela Clemit quotes Godwin on Burke as "a memorable example, of the power of a corrupt system of government, to undermine and divert from their genuine purposes, the noblest faculties." *The Godwinian Novel: The Rational Fictions of Godwin, Brockden Brown, and Mary Shelley* (Oxford, England: Oxford University Press, 1993), 40. Nancy E. Johnson writes, "Falkland often echoes Burke's *Reflections*, and he falls victim to emotion in the same way that Burke does in the essay." Falkland "voices Burke's backward-looking vision in the revolution debates." *The English Jacobin Novel on Rights, Property and the Law: Critiquing the Contract* (New York: Palgrave, 2004), 124.

9. Edmund Burke, *Reflections on the Revolution in France*, ed. J. C. D. Clark (Stanford, CA: Stanford University Press, 2001), 239.

10. Mark Girouard, *The Return to Camelot: Chivalry and the English Gentleman* (New Haven, CT: Yale University Press, 1981), 17.

11. Burke's claims about a British elite who adapted their manners to calm the discontent of their inferiors echoes recent work on the eighteenth- and nineteenth-century aristocracy. As many historians have pointed out, late-eighteenth-century aristocrats altered their appearance from that of a leisured and pampered class to that of a class of men with work to do. As David Cannadine writes, the new elite "saw themselves as men of affairs, disinterestedly and heroically doing their best for their country." *Aspects of Aristocracy: Grandeur and Decline in Modern Britain* (New Haven, CT: Yale University Press, 1994), 21.

12. See Colley, 195–236.

13. John Barrell, "Sad Stories : Louis XVI, George III, and the Language of Sentiment," in *Refiguring Revolutions: Aesthetics and Politics from the English Revolution to the Romantic Revolution*, ed. Kevin Sharpe and Steven N. Zwicker (Berkeley: University of California Press, 1998), 94.

14. Marilyn Morris, *The British Monarchy and the French Revolution* (New Haven, CT: Yale University Press, 1998), 178.

15. Morris, 177.

16. Falkland has a "voice that seemed supernaturally tremendous" (7); "his visage gradually assumed an expression of supernatural barbarity" (113); "Did his power reach through all space, and his eye penetrate every concealment?" (240).

17. Caleb describes his investigations in erotic terms. Falkland's angry efforts to prevent his curiosity only arouse him:

> That there was danger in the employment [of spying] only served to give an alluring pungency to the choice. I remembered the stern reprimand I had received, and his terrible looks; and the recollection gave a kind of tingling sensation, not altogether unallied to enjoyment. The farther I advanced, the more the sensation was irresistible. I seemed to myself perpetually on the brink of being countermined, and perpetually roused to guard my designs. The more impenetrable Mr. Falkland was determined to be, the more uncontrol[l]able was my curiosity. (107–108)

Caleb is aroused by Falkland's determination to be "impenetrable." The "irresistible" sensation, Falkland's anger aroused, also compels Caleb to prevent Falkland from penetrating him in turn. Always on the brink of being found out, Caleb is "perpetually roused to guard my designs." Each pursues the other in an erotic game of cat and mouse in which the danger and promise of penetration is itself the stimulus. This game will be played out when each is penetrated by the other in the final court scene of the novel.

18. Eve Kosofsky Sedgwick, *Between Men: English Literature and Male Homosocial Desire* (New York: Columbia University Press, 1985), 116.

19. Gary Handwerk, "Of Caleb's Guilt and Godwin's Truth: Ideology and Ethics in *Caleb Williams*," *English Literary History*, 60. (Winter 1993) 949–50.

20. Doubting the veracity of Caleb's claims about his own feelings has become a critical commonplace. For work on Caleb as an unreliable narrator see Mitzi Myers, "Godwin's Changing Conception of *Caleb Williams*," *Studies in English Literature 1500–1900* 12 (1972): 591–628; Eric Rothstein, "Caleb Williams," *Systems of Order and Inquiry in Later Eighteenth-Century Fiction* (Berkeley: University of California Press, 1975).

21. Slavoj Žižek, *Enjoy Your Symptom: Jacques Lacan in Hollywood and Out* (New York: Routledge, 1992), 158.

22. Examples of Caleb's desire to experience Falkland's power abound. Even when he knows that one of his disguises has been connected with his true identity he refuses to change it, "Indeed it was a piece of infatuation in me for which I am now unable to account, that, after the various indications which had occurred in that affair proving to them that I was a man in very critical and peculiar circumstances, I should have persisted in wearing the same disguise without the smallest alteration" (252–53). His desire to connect with the master is disappointed when Caleb is brought before a magistrate and faced with criminal prosecution. Caleb finds, to his consternation, that the charges are dropped:

> The effect which this incredible reverse produced upon my mind it is impossible to express. I, who had come to that bar with the sentence of death already in idea ringing in my ears, to be told that I was free to transport myself whithersoever I pleased! Was it for this that I had broken through so many locks and bolts, and the adamantine walls of my prison; that I had passed so many anxious days, and sleepless spectre-haunted nights; that I had racked my invention for expedients of evasion and concealment; that my mind had been roused to an energy of which I could scarcely have believed capable.... (279)

Caleb's stated elation at being released from prison ("my heart was too full of... exultation" [279]) is tinged with a disappointment that Falkland has given him up, that the game seems played out.

To be the object of persecution is to remain engaged with the master. Throughout the novel Caleb becomes sick and listless in those moments when he seems to have escaped the most immediate persecution—in London he experiences "an extacy of despair" (259) and "fits of despondence" (268). It is only when he is caught again and thrown into prison that "I recovered my health" (278). Caleb falls into depression when he is not the direct object of Falkland's persecuting gaze. When he feels that persecution most directly, Caleb becomes healthy and strong.

23. Similarly, Pamela Clemit argues that the revised ending validates a "sympathetic community" created by Caleb's "eloquence" at the trial in which he shows pity for Falkland (68). Godwin emphasizes "the need for human warmth and responsive-

ness" (68). This chapter argues differently that sympathy is fatal, that coldness and distance would better serve the interests of justice, and that sentimentality is the last, most powerful tool of a threatened ruling class.

24. For a critique of sympathy in the novel see John Bender, "Impersonal Violence: The Penetrating Gaze and the Field of Narration in *Caleb Williams,*" in *Vision & Textuality*, ed. Stephen Melville and Bill Readings (Durham, NC: Duke University Press, 1995), 265–68, 271.

25. See, Alex Gold Jr., "It's Only Love: The Politics of Passion in Godwin's *Caleb Williams,*" *Texas Studies in Literature and Language* 19 (1977), 142–43; Mona Scheuermann, "From Mind to Society: *Caleb Williams* as a Psychological Novel," *Dutch Quarterly Review* 7 (1977), 117; Donald R. Wehrs, "Rhetoric, History, Rebellion: *Caleb Williams* and the Subversion of Eighteenth-Century Fiction," *Studies in English Literature* 28 (1988), 497–511.

26. Several critics have pointed to Godwin's suspicion of the possibilities of enlightened knowledge particularly when infected by sentimentality. Andrew Mccann argues that Godwin feared the seductive effect of sentimental discourse that could overwhelm reason and produce the wrong kind of public opinion:

> The novel's eponymous protagonist discovers, in his relationship with his aristocratic patron Falkland, that public opinion mediated through the dissemination of textual objects and the formation of a national reading public synonymous with the boundaries of the emerging nation-state, far from facilitating the bright dawn of political justice, is in fact emptied of all capacity for independent thought and thoroughly integrated into a regime of administered consciousness.

Cultural Politics in the 1790's: Literature, Radicalism and the Public Sphere (New York: St. Martin's, 1999), 71.

Chapter 3. Political Seductions: The Show of War in Lord Byron's Sardanapalus

1. Sonia Hofkosh, "The Writer's Ravishment: Women and the Romantic Author—The Example of Byron," in *Romanticism and Feminism*, ed. Anne K. Mellor (Bloomington: Indiana University Press, 1988), 94; see also Nicola J. Watson, "Trans-figuring Byronic Identity," in *At the Limits of Romanticism: Essays in Cultural, Feminist, and Materialist Criticism*, ed. Mary A. Favret and Nicola J. Watson (Bloomington: Indiana University Press, 1994), 185–206.

2. See, for one example among many, Anne K Mellor, *Romanticism and Gender* (New York: Routledge, 1993).

3. See Louis Crompton, *Byron and Greek Love: Homophobia in Nineteenth-Century England* (Berkley: University of California Press, 1985) for a study of the homosexual eros of Byron's work and a biographical account of his erotic seductions

of men. See also, more recently, Ellen Brinks, *Gothic Masculinity: Effeminacy and the Supernatural in English and German Romanticism* (Lewisburg, PA: Bucknell University Press, 2003), 68–90.

4. Charles Donelan, *Romanticism and Male Fantasy in Byron's Don Juan: A Marketable Vice* (London: Macmillan, 2000), 15.

5. William Hazlitt, *The Spirit of the Age* (1824, 1825), in *English Romantic Writers*, ed. David Perkins (Fort Worth, TX: Harcourt Brace Jovanovich, 1967), 698.

6. See Robert F. Gleckner, *Byron and the Ruins of Paradise* (Baltimore, MD: Johns Hopkins University Press, 1967), 299; Phillip W. Martin, *Byron: A Poet before His Public* (Cambridge, England: Cambridge University Press, 1982), 147.

7. Richard Lansdown, *Byron's Historical Dramas* (Oxford, England: Oxford University Press, 1992); Malcolm Kelsall, "The Slave-Woman in the Harem," *Studies in Romanticism*, 31 (Fall 1992), 315–31; Jerome J. McGann, "Hero with a Thousand Faces: The Rhetoric of Byronism," *Studies in Romanticism* 31 (Fall 1992): 295–313; Daniel P. Watkins, *A Materialist Critique of English Romantic Drama* (Gainesville, FL: University Press of Florida, 1993); Jerome Christensen, *Lord Byron's Strength: Romantic Writing in Commercial Society* (Baltimore, MD: Johns Hopkins University Press, 1993); Julie Carlson, *In the Theatre of Romanticism: Coleridge, Nationalism, and Women* (Cambridge, England: Cambridge University Press, 1994); Michael Simpson, *Closet Performances: Political Exhibition and Prohibition in the Dramas of Byron and Shelley* (Stanford: Stanford University Press, 1998).

8. In *The Corsair*, Conrad indulges in moments of explosive violence. In battle he becomes "A glutted tiger mangling in his lair!" (II.iv.190). Lord Byron, *The Corsair, in Lord Byron: Selected Poems* eds. Susan J. Wolfson and Peter J. Manning (London: Penguin, 2006).

9. Lord Byron, *Sardanapalus, Byron: The Complete Poetical Works*, vol. VI, ed. Jerome J. McGann and Barry Weller (Oxford, England: Oxford University Press, 1991).

10. Christensen, *Lord Byron's Strength*, 276.

11. Constant, "The Spirit of Conquest," quoted in Christensen, 277.

12. J. W. Burrow, *Whigs and Liberals: Continuity and Change in English Political Thought* (Oxford, England: Oxford University Press, 1988), 27.

13. Linda Colley, *Britons: Forging the Nation, 1707–1837* (New Haven, CT: Yale University Press, 1992), 223.

14. Often this attempt to define the benevolence of British power in opposition to that of France focused on Napoleon as the oppressor of all benevolent feeling, as the enemy of women, and as a brutal negation of civilized society. In his sonnet, "On the Extinction of the Venetian Republic," Wordsworth figures Napoleon's conquest of Venice as "a maiden City" "violate[d]." *English Romantic Writers*, ed. David Perkins (New York: Harcourt Brace Jovanovich, 1967) 286–87. Likewise Coleridge writes

about Napoleon's war in Spain: "But had Bonaparte anything to fear from Spain?....Was she not in his arms, and did he not, while she was clasped around him, stab her to the heart?" (209). Coleridge claims that Napoleon's reign will be short lived in a world that has progressed beyond martial violence. He warns, "The finger of enlightened Europe points at [French] fetters" (331), forcing the French to see the barbarism of their leader. Emphasizing the French ruler's cruelty and violence, Coleridge claims that enlightened Europe will end Napoleon's rule, which is nothing more than a strange anachronism in a modern world. Samuel Taylor Coleridge, *Essays on His Times, The Collected Works of Samuel Taylor Coleridge*, vol. 3, ed. D. V. Erdman (Princeton, NJ: Princeton University Press, 1969), 325–28.

15. Colley, 225.

16. "Even before his death, a significant Nelson cult had developed. He was mobbed wherever he went, his progresses through the country in 1802 establishing a quasi-regal status that rivalled the popularity of George III." Gillian Russell, *The Theaters of War: Performance, Politics, and Society, 1793–1815* (Oxford, England: Oxford University Press, 1995), 8.

17. Scott Hughes Myerly, *British Military Spectacle: From the Napoleonic Wars through the Crimea* (Cambridge, MA: Harvard University Press, 1996), 140.

18. Gillian Russell overtly connects the figure of the soldier to that of the actor in this period of British history. Not only did soldiers perform in military spectacles, not only did actors play soldiers in some of the most successful theatrical presentations, but the profession of soldiering itself also transformed the individual enlisted man into an actor. Soldiers assumed a role when they wore their uniforms. Military costumes metamorphosed them into new men for "becoming a soldier was...at a fundamental level, a theatrical experience. It meant the realization of the capacity to take on another identity, to perform the military or naval role. In late Georgian culture going for a soldier also implied that one was lost to civilian society in the same sense as joining the stage implied estrangement from the respectable norm"(182). Men who would never otherwise have left small villages became travelers to foreign countries and moved far outside the world and the identity they could have imagined for themselves had they not entered the army.

19. Marilyn Butler, "John Bull's Other Kingdom: Byron's Intellectual Comedy," *Studies in Romanticism* 31 (1992): 292. Susan Wolfson notes the parallel between Sardanapalus's separation from his wife and George IV's marital difficulties. He, like the Asian monarch, is a "scandalously derelict husband." "'A Problem Few Dare Imitate': Sardanapalus and 'Effeminate Character,'" *English Literary History* 58 (1991): 882. Also, like George IV, Sardanapalus seems addicted to private pleasures at the expense of the public welfare. The Assyrian king's pleasure palace is as scandalous to his people as George's extravagant Brighton Pavilion. According to Jerome McGann, George IV's extravagantly expensive "pleasure dome," which "summed up the world of the Regency is recalled to our attention in the sybaritic scenery of Byron's play." Jerome McGann, "Hero with a Thousand Faces: The Rhetoric of Byronism," *Studies in Romanticism* 31 (1992): 309.

20. George IV "ordered enormous quantities of clothing and accessories throughout his lifetime, including every variety of uniform, and could remember every article of dress he had ever obtained in the past fifty years" (Myerly, 33).

21. Colley, 215.

22. Much of Byron's late writing offers an explicit indictment of British claims to moral superiority. In *Don Juan*, Byron ridicules his hero for believing that "here [in Britain] is Freedom's chosen station. / Here peals the people's voice, nor can entomb it / Racks, prisons, inquisitions." *Don Juan*, ed. T. G. Steffan, E. Steffan, and W. W. Pratt (London: Penguin, 1973), XI.9. In the preface to *Sardanapalus*, Byron claims that he has "attempted to preserve... the 'unities.'" He has done so, fully "aware of the unpopularity of this notion in present English Literature." If the unities are no longer popular in England, they are "still so in the more civilized parts" of the world. This notion of a barbaric England constitutes a deliberate provocation in the face of frequent contemporary claims about British moral superiority. For other readings of the Preface see Susan Wolfson, "A Problem Few Dare Imitate," 889, and Jerome Christensen, *Lord Byron's Strength*, 278.

23. Linda Dowling, *Hellenism and Homosexuality in Victorian Oxford* (Ithaca, NY: Cornell University Press, 1994), 6.

24. Others suggest the possibility of Sardanapalus's immanent power, too. After Sardanapalus spares his life, the rebel soldier Arbaces declares, "Methought he look'd like Nimrod as he spoke, / Even as the proud imperial statue stands / Looking the monarch of the kings around it, / And sways, while they but ornament, the temple" (II.i.352–55).

25. Byron's representation of Assyria might be understood as an exercise in imagining archaic cultures ruled by barbaric violence. But as many critics have argued, Byron's Assyria is more interestingly understood as a representation of Great Britain and its imperial culture. Marilyn Butler sees Assyria as an imperial power, aggressively bent on conquest. Butler reads Semiramis, Sardanapalus's bloodthirsty female ancestor, as an embodiment of "the motherland.... In the play's scheme of political symbolism, Semiramis is Britannia sated with battles and conquests and turned monstrous." Assyria's capital, Nineveh, is for Butler, "like London," the capital of an empire-building nation. An imperial culture requires Semiramis to maintain the empire. To refuse violence is to refuse to sustain the very foundation of British power. Marilyn Butler, "John Bull's Other Kingdom," 292–93.

26. Russell, in her work on the relationship between war and theater in early nineteenth-century England, argues that seeing the military leader and sharing his power, his experience of the battle, was a very popular spectacle. English theater underwent a significant change during the war in which the emphasis shifted from overtly artificial theatrical representation to simulations that attempted to represent actual battles realistically. The emphasis on realism led to the development of a form of entertainment that claimed to offer the viewer a panoptic, bird's eye view of simulated battles. Russell writes, "The desire to see or 'take' the battlefield was instrumen-

tal in the development of another kind of spectacularization of war...— the panorama." This new development "represented another attempt to realize the field of battle to the sight. The advantage which it had over the theater was its capacity to suggest the actual dimensions of the battlefield." What the panorama offered the spectator was a more intense experience of "war" because it allowed the audience to occupy a position that "was in effect analogous to that of the military leader" who could "command the view of the battlefield" (75–77). The panorama's power, then, came from its ability to create an identification with the most important actor in the war, the leader himself. The English public, separated from the visual pleasure of the actual battle, was offered the pleasure of reliving a spectacle it had missed.

27. G. Wilson Knight goes as far as to claim that the king "is conceived as, in essence, a saint" (188) and as "Christ." "'Simple and Bright': Sardanapalus" (1939), in *The Plays of Lord Byron*, ed. Robert Gleckner and Bernard Beatty (Liverpool, England: Liverpool University Press, 1997), 189. See also Jerome J. McGann's *Fiery Dust: Byron's Poetic Development* (Chicago: University of Chicago Press, 1968), 237–38. Critics such as Wolfson, Christensen, and Daniel Watkins place the blame for the problems of Assyria both on the culture of violence the king opposes and on his own program. Watkins writes, "The initial actions of the play dramatize the struggle between equally unsatisfactory social philosophies." *A Materialist Critique of English Romantic Drama* (Gainesville: University Press of Florida, 1993), 164.

28. Vincent Carretta, *George III and the Satirists from Hogarth to Byron* (Athens: University of Georgia Press, 1990), 7.

29. "Sad Stories: Louis XVI, George III, and the Language of Sentiment," in *Refiguring Revolutions: Aesthetics and Politics from the English Revolution to the Romantic Revolution*, ed. Kevin Sharpe and Steven N. Zwicker (Berkeley: California University Press, 1998), 96.

30. Michael Simpson claims that the king's most apparently egalitarian and benevolent moments mask a commitment to absolutist power. If Sardanapalus avows a desire to give everyone what they desire, this apparent largesse only speaks to "the King's ultimate fantasy of absolute power. Since almost everyone always agrees with Sardanapalus, because he is the King, the only possible development of this scenario is one in which they already agree and identify with him before he enunciates his desire." Michael Simpson, *Closet Performances: Political Exhibition and Prohibition in the Dramas of Byron and Shelley* (Stanford, CA: Stanford University Press, 1998), 148. This benevolence cannot countenance disagreement or disaffection. His relationship with his slave, Myrrha, seems to model an ideal relationship to his people. Simpson points to the sentimental discourse between Myrrha and the king in which he "dare not breathe [his] own desire, / Lest it should clash with thine"(I.ii.22–23) as an example of the king's fantasy of a condition of mutually satisfiable desire. Simpson writes, "None of this transaction is, of course, overtly political. It is exactly this absence of an avowed politics that allows the sentimental discourse of this relationship to be projected as the civic paradigm that is supposed to replace political relations in Assyria" (145). The failure of this project, as Simpson points out, is clear not

only because the people do not share the king's pleasures or his desires, but also because this benevolence fails even in his treatment of the slave whom he can order out of the room at will (IV.i.438–48). By speaking for the people's desire, the king remains a tyrant. The leader, whose will cannot be distinguished from the people's desire, merely replaces the defunct fiction of divine right with a new fiction about monarchical power. Imagining himself as a man like any other licenses the despotic presumption that he wants what others want. Susan Wolfson reminds us of "the relation of Sardanapalus's pacifism to a social structure sustained by slavery, hereditary privilege, and royal prerogative—one in which the king may deal with people as property and treat wife and children as political factors." "A Problem Few Dare Imitate," (881).

31. Barrell, 96.

32. Wolfson, 874.

33. Margaret J. Howell, "A Panorama of Assyria," *Byron Tonight: A Poet's Plays on the Nineteenth-Century Stage* (Surrey, England: Springwood, 1982) 55–95.

34. George Henry Lewes's reaction to Kean's 1853 production of the play. Quoted in Howell, *Byron Tonight,* 78–79.

35. Much has been written about the tendency of Romantic writers to eschew the stage in favor of what they called "mental theater." Closet drama was meant to replace the vulgarity of contemporary stage productions with the superior refinement of individual imagination. For one of the earliest discussions of closet dramas see, Samuel C. Chew, *The Drama of Lord Byron: A Critical Study,* 1915. Reprint (New York: Russell and Russell, 1964). For a more recent study see Alan Richardson, *A Mental Theater: Poetic Drama and Consciousness in the Romantic Age* (University Park: Pennsylvania State University Press, 1988). But as Michael Simpson argues,

> Casting themselves as closet dramas, and so denying themselves a theatrical materialization, these dramatic texts seem nonetheless to be projecting a realization of themselves. They page the stage, in both senses: even as they insist that they are merely texts, these plays' dramatic signatures refigure them as scripts for action. The very denial of theatrical production seems to invest the texts themselves with a paradoxical insistence that they be performed, and the political plots of many of the dramas can be read to recommend a directly political materialization of their texts' imperatives. (2)

Whether intended for the stage or as closet drama, *Sardanapalus,* points not only to its own existence as a staged event, but also to the audience and its involvement with and reaction to spectacle.

36. "That the central syllable of the name *Semira*mis chimes with *Myrrha* predicts on the subrational level of phonics the nightmare's figurative logic." Wolfson, "A Problem Few Dare Imitate," 887.

37. Wolfson comments, "Sexuality and violence, two energies Sardanapalus had thought to keep opposed, are here wound together, even as they were when he

entered battle 'as though it were a bed of love' (3.1.224). Neither the feminine nor the erotic offers an escape from violence" (888).

38. Julie A. Carlson claims that female characters in romantic drama typically lack "introspection" and are figures of "action" rather than thought. The capacity to achieve critical self-awareness or distance is a feature of "superior men." *In the Theatre of Romanticism*, 180.

39. Judith Butler has importantly addressed the effect of posturing on the construction of gender. For her, "it is only *within* the practices of repetitive signifying that a subversion of identity becomes possible." *Gender Trouble: Feminism and the Subversion of Identity* (New York: Routledge, 1990), 145. Butler calls for parody that repeats these signifying practices by offering a "denaturalized performance that reveals the performative status of the natural itself" (146). This effect of parody appears to be what stage productions of *Sardanapalus* sought to edit out of view. To complicate matters, however, Sardanapalus himself claims, at times, that parody is actually a masculine ability to refuse a feminine overinvestment in a mere social role. He thus reclaims the radical potential of Butler's understanding of parody in the service of shoring up a virility that exceeds performance. But this apparent misogyny can be read as the ultimate act of identifying not with essential identities but with the nothing that he claims to be. He destroys anything that can reify the king.

Chapter 4. Sublime Democracy and the Theater of Violence: Authoritarianism in William Hazlitt's The Life of Napoleon Buonaparte

1. William Hazlitt, *Complete Works of William Hazlitt*, ed. P. P. Howe (London: Dent, 1931), 20:97. All references from Hazlitt's writing are from this edition and will be included in the text.

2. In numerous published essays such as, "The Tendency of Sects," 1815 (*The Round Table*, 4:47); "On Envy (A Dialogue)" (*The Plain Speaker*, 12:97); "On Egotism" (12:157); "On Jealousy and Spleen of Party" (12:365); "Party Spirit" (*Miscellaneous Essays*, 20:321); "The Spirit of Controversy,"(20:306); "Envy,"(20:311); and "Prejudice"(20:316), Hazlitt examines what he takes to be the prevailing spirit of self-promotion. The world seems made up of men on the make who are willing to sacrifice truth, justice, and honor for the sake of their personal ambition or the ambitions of their "sects" (a term that Hazlitt uses to refer to vehicles for self-advancement). Whereas, at one time, people truly had faith in what they fought for and were willing to stake their lives on it, in the present, men are "enlightened" out of their "prejudices" and use belief only as a means to defeat a rival for power. Now that divine right rule is known to be merely a superstition, "envy is the ruling passion of mankind." Everyone "looks upon himself in the light of a dethroned monarch, and the rest of the world as his rebellious subjects and runaway slaves, who withhold the homage that is his natural due, and burst the chains of opinion he would impose

upon them: the madman in Hogarth (sooth to say), with his crown of straw and wooden sceptre, is but a type and *common-place* emblem of every-day life" ("Trifles Light as Air," 1829, 20:280).

3. In the present, Hazlitt seems unable to extend this capacity for commitment to women. If Lambrun was a credible fanatic in the past, women in the present appear as the most unredeemable subjects of a culture of fashion and publicity. When most modern men are incapable of committing themselves to a cause, women become the more extreme example of the problem that afflicts modernity. In his essay, "On the Spirit of Monarchy" (1823), Hazlitt claims that everyone in the present knows that a king is "a mere cypher" (19:257) who offers up an image in which every man can see himself reflected. Subjects see themselves "all over in the glass of royalty" (19:255). Hereditary kingship inspires self-love because "we see the symbols of majesty, we enjoy the pomp, we crouch before the power, we walk in the procession, and make part of the pageant, and we say in our secret hearts, there is nothing but accident that prevents us from being at the head of it" (19:256). Women are the subjects most willing to sell themselves to false idols for "what female heart can indeed withstand the attractions of a throne" (19:262). The spirit of monarchy, Hazlitt goes on to assert in a footnote, "implies in it the *virtual* surrender of the whole sex at discretion" (19:263). Only "a manly strength of character" is "proof against the seductions of a throne" (17:287). Women in Hazlitt's work often figure the weakness of the public. Consequently, for Hazlitt, Napoleon wisely removes women from the economy of seduction altogether. In 1815 Hazlitt asserts, "the women of France, it is said, were never favourable to Bonaparte, because under the old *regime* every thing was done through them, and under the new dynasty nothing" (19:129).

4. Gary Kelly argues that "by 1789, circulation libraries were a central institution in the rapidly expanding leisure industry and a controversial element in the world of fashionable consumption where class attitudes, values, and cultures met, came into conflict, and were worked out." *English Fiction of the Romantic Period: 1789–1830* (London: Longman, 1989), 4.

5. Edmund Burke, *Reflections on the Revolution in France*, ed. J. C. D. Clark (Stanford, CA: Stanford University Press, 2001), 239.

6. Ralph M. Wardle, *Hazlitt* (Lincoln: University of Nebraska Press, 1971), 426. Despite the fact that Hazlitt saw *The Life of Napoleon* as his most important work, critics have largely ignored it. Herschel Baker dedicates a few pages to it in his biography describing it as a "monumental failure." *William Hazlitt* (Cambridge, MA: Harvard University Press, 1962), 461. Wardle claims that Hazlitt saw Napoleon as an "apostle of freedom" (446) but Wardle sees the biography as a historical failure and as the work of a "broken man." (449). John Kinnaird writes that the biography "need not detain us long" (325). For him, Hazlitt believed that "the future of the modern world...lies with democracy, and that Napoleon's mastery lay precisely in his command of the modern ethos of equality—the principle of 'equality of pretension' being 'the chief maxim of his reign'(13:8)" (330). Kinnaird claims that Hazlitt "is unwilling to recognize" what "Napoleon himself understood with brutal clarity...whether the

democratic ethos is capable of developing, without autocratic rule" (331). Before dismissing the work altogether, Kinnaird writes, "Perhaps it is wrong to expect much clear thinking in the *Life.*" *William Hazlitt: Critic of Power* (New York: Columbia University Press, 1978), 331. If Hazlitt has anything interesting to say about democracy, he writes it "elsewhere in these same years". P. P. Howe, *The Life of William Hazlitt* (Westport, CT: Greenwood , 1972), 331.

7. Quoted in Stanley Jones, *Hazlitt: A Life From Winterslow to Frith Street* (Oxford, England: Oxford University Press, 1989), 172.

8. Kinnaird, *Critic of Power*, 83.

9. David Browmich, *Hazlitt: The Mind of a Critic* (New Haven, CT: Yale University Press, 1999), 313.

10. Simon Bainbridge, *Napoleon and English Romanticism* (Cambridge, England: Cambridge University Press, 1995), 207.

11. See Jones, 183–84.

12. The similarities between Hazlitt and Habermas's conceptions of the enlightened public sphere are many. For Habermas, the bourgeois public sphere "was intended to change domination as such." *The Structural Transformation of the Public Sphere: An Inquiry into a Category of Bourgeois Society,* trans. Thomas Burger (Cambridge, MA: MIT Press, 1991), 28. The public sphere comprised "private people" coming together to debate the common good (26). Within the public sphere, "laws of the market were suspended as were laws of the state" (36). Each private individual left behind his personal interests and became part of a public engaged in rational debate to reach a consensus about the public good.

This public sphere, which understood itself as constituted by free and equal individuals, "challenged the established authority of the monarch" (52). Publicity, the mass dissemination of reasoned discourse in textual form, was integral to this process of opposition because "just as secrecy was supposed to serve the maintenance of sovereignty,...so publicity was supposed to serve the promotion of legislation based on *ratio*" (53). The bourgeois public sphere, for Habermas, was, then, a "democratic association" informed by public debate and publicity that in principle opposed itself to political inequalities. Nancy Fraser, "Rethinking the Public Sphere: A Contribution to the Critique of Actually Existing Democracy," in *Habermas and the Public Sphere*, ed. Craig Calhoun (Cambridge, MA: MIT Press, 1997), 109–42. Its goal was to create an enlightened "public opinion" from the process of rational debate (Habermas, 89).

Implicit in Habermas's view of the public sphere, as it is in Hazlitt's account, is the need to conceive of the public as dependent on unity of thought and belief. Nancy Fraser claims that for Habermas, "the proliferation of a multiplicity of competing publics is necessarily a step away from, rather than toward, greater democracy, and that a single, comprehensive public sphere is always preferable to a nexus of multiple publics" (117). In this unified bourgeois public sphere debate occurs within certain shared assumptions about public discourse and is conducted by a homogeneous group of citizens. This homogeneity speaks to a desire for a singular will that guides the multitude rather than an acknowledgment of the problem of democratic plurality. Habermas and Hazlitt share a belief in the necessary homogeneity of public discourse that makes multiple and varied discourses threatening to political action. If Habermas sees the eighteenth-century public sphere as a force for democratic power, he does so only because he imagines the public sphere as in some sense not democratic at all.

13. Immanuel Kant, *The Metaphysics of Morals* (Cambridge, England: Cambridge University Press, 1993), 132.

14. Alenka Zupancic, *Ethics of the Real: Kant, Lacan* (London: Verso, 2000), 85.

15. If this vision of disunity in the biography is most often directed against the French public, much of Hazlitt's other writing sees this state as a sign of enlightened times. Annette Wheeler Cafarelli claims, "Hazlitt saw the spirit of his own age as possessing the worst forms of cultural anarchy, far before Arnold saw the dangers of doing as one likes. The character of the age is uniform in its predation and confusion, a time of 'wild beast[s]' and 'hunting animals,' each rushing its own way under 'lawless, unrestrained impulses.'" The spirit of this age is "a spirit of disunity and animosity." *Prose in the Age of Poets: Romanticism and Biographical Narrative from Johnson to De Quincey* (Philadelphia: University of Pennsylvania Press, 1990), 131.

16. Claude Lefort, "The Image of the Body and Totalitarianism," in *The Political Forms of Modern Society: Bureaucracy, Democracy, Totalitarianism*, ed. John B. Thompson (Cambridge, MA: MIT Press, 1986), 305.

17. W. J. T. Mitchell, *Iconology: Image, Text, Ideology* (Chicago: University of Chicago Press, 1986), 110.

18. Uttara Natarajan, *Hazlitt and the Reach of Sense: Criticism, Morals, and the Metaphysics of Power* (Oxford, England: Oxford University Press, 1998), 24–25.

19. Edmund Burke, *A Philosophical Enquiry into the Origin of Our Ideas of the Sublime and the Beautiful*, ed. James T. Boulton (Notre Dame, IN: University of Notre Dame Press, 1958), 59.

20. Burke, 113.

21. Bainbridge, 199.

22. In his *Political Essays* Hazlitt evokes similar views about the French. In 1814 Hazlitt writes, a "want of *keeping* is the distinguishing quality of the French character. . . . They are blown about like a weather-cock" (7:85). To the French, only the

> spirit of liberty, at the Revolution, gave them an impulse common to humanity; the genius of Bonaparte, gave them the spirit of military ambition. Both of these gave an energy and consistency to their character, by concentrating their natural volatility on one great object. But when both of these causes failed, the Allies found that France consisted of nothing but ladies' toilettes. The army are the muscular part of the state. (7:85)

23. Hazlitt emphasizes Napoleon's anachronistic proximity to savage violence. Napoleon has "an agust fibre, a heat of blood evidently borrowed from the East. He was a Tamerlane or Genghis Khan" with an "extremity of purpose" (14:105). His is "a soul of fire without water or clay, that nothing could tame, could soften or deter" (14:120).

24. That barbaric ambition actually makes Napoleon strong is further suggested in the last volume of the biography. This strength of purpose associated at first with Napoleon becomes by the end a feature of Napoleon's enemies. The Russian troops "came from the eastward of Moscow; and among them were seen tribes of wandering Baskirs and Tartars, figures unknown to European war, wearing sheep-skins, and armed with bows and arrows; men brought from the very wall of China, to show the narrow range of despotic sway, and stop the overwhelming tide of modern civilization" (15:141). The Russians reveal an extremity of purpose that baffles the west when they burn Moscow. What Napoleon does not calculate in his attack on Russia is the "resistance barbarism could make" (15:18) so that "for once he found himself surpassed by barbarous daring and resolution" (15:66). The burning of Moscow "implied the greatest strength of purpose. It was heroic, disinterested, the *ideal* of a barbaric virtue" (15:70). By the end of the biography, Napoleon has lost his barbarism and fallen prey to modern softness so that he cannot defeat the Russians. Hazlitt claims that Napoleon can no longer force a fickle public to support him because he has, himself, become corrupted by the theatricality of France. Ultimately, exposure to modern France destroys him because "notwithstanding the grasp and manly strength of his mind, the air of Paris had perhaps made him lay rather too much stress on artificial advantages" (15:18). By the end of his reign, Napoleon acts like a modern ruler; a man of show rather than merit, he is incapable of fighting the war with the single-minded purpose of his earlier days. Having come to rely on "artificial advantages," Napoleon loses his strength: "There is no doubt that an accumulation of adventitious honours and distinctions, like a weight of golden armour, clogs the mind and presses on the nerve of action; and they are therefore fittest for those who have nothing to do either to gain or keep them" (15:36).

25. Carl Schmitt, *The Concept of the Political*, trans. George Schwab (Chicago : University of Chicago Press, 1996), 26.

26. Carl Schmitt, *The Crisis of Parliamentary Democracy*, trans. Ellen Kennedy (Cambridge, MA: MIT Press, 1992), 70.

27. Napoleon described his battles as dramatic productions:

> A battle is a dramatic action which has its beginning, its middle, and its end. The battle order of the opposing armies and their preliminary maneuvers until they come to grips form the exposition. The counterma-neuvers of the army which has been attacked constitute the dramatic complication. They lead in turn to new measures and bring about the crisis, and from this results the outcome or denouement.

The Mind of Napoleon: A Selection from His Written and Spoken Words, ed. and trans. J. Christopher Herold (New York: Columbia University Press, 1955), 203.

28. Theresa M. Kelley points out that British representations of Napoleon, both pictorial and literary, tend to show Napoleon in either gigantic or miniature form. He rarely appears in human scale. For Kelley, "by the late eighteenth century, the 'extremes of creation' made available by the inventions of the telescope and microscope were understood as two sides of the same scientific and philosophical inquiry" (364). Napoleon's absurd extremes of size make him the object of an intense and hostile "scientific" scrutiny designed to expose the emperor's weakness or overweening ambition. Looking through the wrong lens is both a French and an English error, as Hazlitt's insistent attacks on the conservative English press suggest. Fitting the object to telescopic or microscopic vision particularly in England is an attempt to domesticate Napoleon. But, as Kelley argues, it may also indicate an unconquered fear because "make him big, make him small, these images seem to say, Napoleon is still the bogey-man...the extensive use of miniature images of Napoleon in English children's toys between 1803 and 1805 may register a childlike fear behind the adult English response to Napoleonic imperialism and threats of invasion" (364). "J. M. W. Turner, Napoleonic Caricature, and Romantic Allegory," *English Literary History* 58 (1991): 351–82.

29. Despite the magical effect of Napoleon's image on the people during his reign, his first defeat instantly breaks the spell. Because they are characterized by "dastardliness and effeminacy," the French cannot "[persist] in a losing cause" and prefer "to go over to the enemy" (15:205). But when Napoleon returns triumphant from Elba, he "seemed from his first landing to bestride the country like a Colossus" (15:230). The people fall under his "spell" again because he inspires "fear and personal awe." He is again "sublime." But this sublime effect requires the actual, physical presence of the leader: "Even if the French had forgot themselves and him, would not their former sentiments be revived in all their force by his present appearance among them, so full of the bold and marvelous?" (230), On his return, Napoleon becomes a literary character, both the "Child Roland of the Revolution" and "Ulysses" who "slew the suitors." As "the hero of some lofty poem or high-wrought romance," he satisfies the literary and theatrical tastes of the French who need the immediacy and excitement of his presence to compel their support (230). Of course, after the Battle of Waterloo, the French abandon Napoleon again because his magical hold falters. Without the presence of the leader, without his embodied reality, all the images that represent him fail because the French are incapable of using their imagination.

30. Mitchell, 143.

31. *The Rights of Man,* quoted in Mitchell, 146.

32. For commentary on Hazlitt's prose style see Bromwich, *Hazlitt: The Mind of a Critic,* 345–61; Graham Goode, *The Observing Self: Rediscovering the Essay* (London: Routledge, 1988), 71–89; Thomas McFarland, *Romantic Cruxes: The English Essayists and the Spirit of the Age* (Oxford, England: Oxford University Press, 1987), 53–89; Tom Paulin, *The Day Star of liberty: William Hazlitt's Radical Style* (London: Faber and Faber, 1998). Some of his contemporaries emphasized Hazlitt's complexity: Leigh Hunt "called Hazlitt 'a connoisseur in the spirit of contradiction,'"

and Allan Cunningham described Hazlitt as "...a lover of paradox...who could only utter odd and remarkable things." Annette Wheeler Cafarelli, *Prose in the Age of Poets,* 131–32.

33. Wardle, 448.

34. Hazlitt borrows from eyewitnesses to Napoleon's reign such as Constant, Las Cases, O'Meara, and Antommarchi.

35. Hazlitt describes Napoleon's efforts to create visual correlatives of inner merit by instituting a system of honors and by publicizing emblems of Napoleonic glory. Hazlitt writes, "titles and external marks of distinction should be confined to represent external advantages only" (14:114) because "there can be no outward and visible sign of an inward and invisible grace; for the question of real desert is one which is always left reserved in the human breast, and a bit of red ribbon in the button-hole does not alter our opinion in this respect" (14:114). Napoleon loses this "invisible grace" by attempting to represent and parcel out his merit. Visible rewards are "inadequate symbols," which suggest a reversion to barbarism, "to the old-fashioned tinsel and Gothic forms" (14:116). To see outward signs as adequate expressions of inner merit is "to tread back our steps instead of advancing with the spirit of the age" (14:116).

36. Hazlitt describes an African man who once saw Napoleon on the battlefield and who is stunned to learn about Napoleon's defeat. The visual impact of Napoleon on the African spectator appears to create the response that Hazlitt approves—a lifelong commitment of absolute devotion and faith to the leader. The African spectator is a subject of what, for Hazlitt, is an inescapably archaic world. This spectator is so far removed from the culture of publicity that the news of Napoleon's fall does not reach him with any certainty ("It is impossible that Napoleon has been conquered, that he is at St. Helena!"([14:54[).

37. Paul de Man, "Sign and Symbol in Hegel's *Aesthetic,*" in *Aesthetic Ideology,* ed. Andrzej Warminski (Minneapolis: University of Minnesota Press, 1996), 101.

38. See Orrin Wang, "Disfiguring Monuments: History in Paul de Man's 'Shelley Disfigured' and Percy Bysshe Shelley's 'The Triumph of Life,'" *English Literary History* 58 (1991) on the need for historical specificity in de Man's deconstructionist readings of Romanticism.

Chapter 5. Communities in Mourning: Making Capital Out of Loss in Thomas Carlyle's Past and Present and Heroes

1. Carlyle's representations of leadership and the necessity of heroes have long been a focus of critical commentary on his work: B. H. Lehman, *Carlyle's Theory of the Hero: Its Sources, Development, History and Influence on Carlyle's Work* (Durham, NC: Duke University Press, 1928); Herbert Grierson, *Carlyle and Hitler* (Manchester, England: University of Manchester Press, 1930); Robert A. Donovan,

"Carlyle and the Climate of Hero Worship," *University of Toronto Quarterly* 42 (1973): 122–41; Philip Rosenberg, *The Seventh Hero: Carlyle and the Theory of Radical Activism* (Cambridge, MA: Harvard University Press, 1975); Jules P. Seigel, "Carlyle and Peel: The Prophet's Search for a Heroic Politician and an Unpublished Fragment," *Victorian Studies* 26 (1983): 181–95; Chris R. Vanden Bossche, *Carlyle and the Search for Authority* (Columbus: Ohio State University Press, 1991)

2. Thomas Carlyle, *Past and Present*, ed. Richard D. Altick (New York: New York University Press, 1965), 211.

3. Carlyle's Irish widow left to die in the street because her neighbors will not take her in is his most famous example of laissez-faire in *Past and Present*. The irony of that case is, of course, that the widow proves her sisterhood with the world by infecting her neighbors: "Never before did I hear of an Irish Widow reduced to 'prove her sisterhood by dying of typhus-fever and infecting seventeen persons,'—saying in such an undeniable way, 'You *see*, I was your sister!'" (210).

4. J. W. Burrow, *Whigs and Liberals: Continuity and Change in English Political Thought* (Oxford, England: Oxford University Press, 1988), 32.

5. The Sphinx is both a feminine and an eastern image. By implication, the call for a virile penetration of the Sphinx's mystery is also a call for imperial conquest of those inchoate places of the world that require English enlightenment. Carlyle writes in *Past and Present* that part of bringing new vigor to England depends on the expansion of the English empire: "Our little isle is grown too narrow for us; but the world is wide enough yet for another Six Thousand Years. England's sure markets will be among new Colonies of Englishmen in all quarters of the Globe" (264).

6. The only important image of women being that of the dead body of the Irish widow. Dead or acted upon, women and the feminine have no agency in the making of the nation.

7. Herbert Sussman, *Victorian Masculinities: Manhood and Masculine Poetics in Early Victorian Literature and Art* (Cambridge, England: Cambridge University Press, 1995), 5.

8. The male hero, not the all-male community, must be safely distanced in history. This distance is necessary precisely to make that community possible in modernity.

9. Alan Sinfield, *The Wilde Century: Effeminacy, Oscar Wilde and the Queer Moment* (New York: Columbia University Press, 1994), 27.

10. Thomas Carlyle, *On Heroes, Hero Worship, and the Heroic in History* (New York: Chelsea House, 1983), 251.

11. Many critics have commented on Carlyle's style and on his mixed genre of writing. His work attempts to revitalize an enervated culture by offering startling phrases and by combining seemingly disparate genres: "at a time when the study of history...was becoming increasingly scientific and aiming above all at academic

objectivity, Carlyle...believed in a philosophy of history that was inspirational rather than rational, subjective rather than objective, impressionistic rather than precise." *Thomas Carlyle: Selected Writings*, ed. Alan Shelston (London: Penguin, 1986), 23. History writing and biography are means, for Carlyle, of creating myth and prophecy: Sussman argues that "Carlyle's works quite self-consciously seek to establish a foundation myth of manliness for an industrial society" (16). In the attempt to author a powerful myth, Carlyle, after *Sartor*, changed genres: Bossche claims that Carlyle "once described *Sartor* as a 'Didactic Novel'" but then "his concept of the literary text" shifts "from the transcendental novel toward epic history" (55). On Carlyle's view of history as prophecy and revelation see Rosenberg, 49–51. For a discussion of Carlyle's language and its effects see Mary Desaulniers's *Carlyle and the Economics of Terror: A Study of Revisionary Gothicism in The French Revolution* (Montreal: McGill-Queen's University Press, 1995). Desaulniers argues that Carlyle's language seeks to redeem a fallen language in which signifiers have become arbitrary. In agreement with Coleridge, Carlyle sees the sign as "not merely a figure of speech or an abstracted name, but a material signifier that is 'part' and 'representative' of a 'unity'" (120–21).

12. James Eli Adams, *Dandies and Desert Saint: Styles of Victorian Manhood* (Ithaca, NY: Cornell University Press, 1995), 36.

13. This separation was profoundly influential. "Mid-Victorian writers commonly employed this strategy," and "some successful Victorian businessmen...tried to adapt their lives" to the model of a manufacturer who resembled "the virile, all-conquering warrior chieftains of old." G. R. Searle, *Morality and the Market in Victorian Britain* (Oxford, England: Oxford University Press, 1998) 104.

14. Andrew Parker points to a similar anxiety in Marx about "non-productive" labor. Parker sees Marx caught up in "the nineteenth century's obsessive fantasy of an authentic self immune from the dangers of theatricality." "Unthinking Sex: Marx, Engels, and the Scene of Writing," in *Fear of a Queer Planet: Queer Politics and Social Theory*, ed. Michael Warner (Minneapolis: University of Minnesota Press, 1993), 30. For Parker, this threat to authenticity represented by a theatrical or false self stems largely from "male homosexual panic" (30). To assert the value of productive labor, Marx links it to heterosexual reproduction. Carlyle labors under a similar anxiety that, however, as I have argued, focuses less on homosexual panic and more on the fear of effeminacy, a fear less clearly linked to sexuality in the nineteenth century than in the present.

15. Walter Benjamin, "Art in the Age of Mechanical Reproduction," in *The Critical Tradition: Classic Texts and Contemporary Trends*, ed. David H. Richter (New York: St. Martin's, 1989), 573.

16. Much like the French in Hazlitt's biography.

17. For a deconstructive reading of monuments and their defacement see Paul de Man, "Shelley Disfigured," in *The Rhetoric of Romanticism* (New York: Columbia University Press, 1984), 93–124.

18. Herbert Sussman, however, argues that Carlyle feels "revulsion at the male body" (21). For Sussman, "Repelled by the male body, by male sexuality, by what he sees as the miasmic swamp of the male psyche, Carlyle imagines the interior of the male as polluted, unclean" (24). In *Past and Present*, the male body that has not undergone the discipline of work is not masculine at all, but effeminate. Sussman points out how manhood emerges from a process of self-discipline that harnesses male energy for the work of industrial production (25). But he does not distinguish between the body of the worker that must be saved from the miasmic swamp of effeminacy from the body of the leader that represents the central authority of masculine power.

19. *The French Revolution* (1837), the book that made Carlyle famous, stands as a warning that similar events may occur in England. Carlyle's book "is no history, but a warning to England that what happened in France 'can happen here.'" Albert J. Lavalley, *Carlyle and the Idea of the Modern: Studies in Carlyle's Prophetic Literature and its Relation to Blake, Nietzsche, Marx, and Others* (New Haven, CT: Yale University Press, 1968), 184.

20. Jean-Joseph Goux, *Symbolic Economies: After Marx and Freud*, trans. Jennifer Curtiss Gage (Ithaca, NY: Cornell University Press, 1990), 130.

21. Edmund Burke, *Reflections on the Revolution in France*, ed. J. C. D. Clark (Stanford, CA: Stanford University Press, 2001), 401.

22. Goux, 124.

23. Carlyle's vision of the dynamics of power recalls Freud. See Freud's *Totem and Taboo: Some Points of Agreement between the Mental Lives of Savages and Neurotics*, trans. and ed. James Strachey (New York: Norton, 1989) in which Freud argues that the leader and father becomes all the more powerful after death. His death organizes the emergence of a new civilization.

24. Karl Marx, *The Marx-Engels Reader*, 2nd ed., ed. Robert C. Tucker (New York: Norton, 1978), 313.

25. Marx, 324.

26. Yoon Sun Lee also describes Carlyle's work in terms of fetishism. Interestingly, he focuses on reading as a process of fetishistic disavowal. Carlyle's writing offers an alternative to the failure of authority in modern times. In *Past and Present*, fetishism's "features are invoked . . . through a reading of the nation's history." *Nationalism and Irony: Burke, Scott, Carlyle* (Oxford, England: Oxford University Press, 2004), 135. Reading history involves the process of forgetting, for Carlyle, forgetting that one has made the thing one now believes in: "By means of this veiling, history can be regarded as a 'thing' to be read, either metaphorically or literally. In this way, history can instill in the nation a regard for permanence, productivity, and earnest disavowal of one's own labor: in short, for masculinity" (142). The process of reading, then, ideally creates a reader who "produces an object, disavows or forgets his

own act, and stands lost in rapt contemplation before what he has made, hoping to receive his own identity from it" (145).

27. Slavoj Žižek, *The Sublime Object of Ideology* (London: Verso, 1989), 18.

Chapter 6. *"To Please a Woman Worthy of Being Pleased"*: *Darcymania in Jane Austen's* Pride and Prejudice

1. If Austen represents the army as inimical to domestic order in *Pride and Prejudice*, she offers a very different representation of the navy in her last novel, *Persuasion*, in which navy captains are the source of national security and domestic happiness. For work on Austen's interest in the navy, see B. C. Southam, *Jane Austen and the Navy* (New York: Hambledon and London, 2000). Of course, Austen was not alone in viewing the army askance: Great Britain had a tradition of viewing the army as dangerous to the stability of any neighborhood that came in contact with soldiers. The navy, instead, more frequently represented Great Britain's martial glory.

2. See Joan B. Landes, "Further Thoughts on the Public/Private Distinction," *Journal of Women's History* 15.2 (2003): 28–39. "There is a broad consensus on the limitations of overly universalizing or excessively rigid representations of the public/private division" (34).

3. Deidre Lynch, ed., "Introduction: Sharing with Our Neighbors," in *Janeites: Austen's Disciples and Devotees* (Princeton, NJ: Princeton University Press, 2000), 20.

4. Devoney Looser writes, "as those familiar with the last several decades of criticism on Austen must know, a good deal of debate has centered around whether we should call Austen's novels—or Austen herself—'feminist.'" *Jane Austen and the Discourses of Feminism*, ed. Devoney Looser (New York: St. Martin's, 1995), 2. Looser adds, the "version of Austen that was handed down from one critical generation to another—from the late Victorian period up until the work of Marilyn Butler in the mid-1970's—is that of an apolitical author" (3). For the conservative Austen, see most importantly, Alistair M. Duckworth, *The Improvement of the Estate* (Baltimore, MD: Johns Hopkins University Press, 1971); Marilyn Butler, *Jane Austen and the War of Ideas* (Oxford, England: Oxford University Press, 1975); and, more recently, *Jane Austen's Business: Her World and Her Profession*, ed. Juliet McMaster and Bruce Stovel (New York: St. Martin's, 1996). For a more subversive Austen, see Margaret Kirkham, *Jane Austen, Feminism and Fiction* (New York: Methuen, 1986); Alison G. Sulloway, *Jane Austen and the Province of Womanhood* (Philadelphia: University of Pennsylvania Press, 1989); and, more recently, Gabriela Castellanos, *Laughter, War and Feminism: Elements of Carnival in Three of Jane Austen's Novels* (New York: Lang, 1994). Claudia L. Johnson sees Austen as somewhere in between, torn between the claims of pleasure and authority, *Jane Austen: Women, Politics, and the Novel* (Chicago: University of Chicago Press, 1988).

5. Johnson, 78.

6. David Cannadine, *The Rise and Fall of Class in Britain* (New York: Columbia University Press, 1999), 59.

7. The historians who revised the class-based account claim that the language of class was indeed pervasive with three models particularly important: a hierarchical model, a three-class model, and a two-class model (rich and poor). But, according to Dror Wahrman's important account, the models of a two- or three-classed society had rhetorical force but not accurate descriptive power. The uses of the term "middle class" were multiple and were not so much a reflection of an actually existing middle class empowered by a new industrial economy, as "a pointed rhetorical weapon serving a political agenda." Dror Wahrman, *Imagining the Middle Class: The Political Representation of Class in Britain, c. 1780–1840* (Cambridge, England: Cambridge University Press, 1995), 16. For Wahrman the reality of class power and the discourses of class did not necessarily reflect one another: he argues for a "*degree of freedom which in fact exists in the space between social reality and its representations*" (6).

8. David Cannadine, *Aspects of Aristocracy: Grandeur and Decline in Modern Britain* (New Haven, CT: Yale University Press, 1994), 9.

9. Cannadine, *Aspects of Aristocracy*, 10.

10. Linda Colley, *Britons: Forging the Nation, 1707–1837* (New Haven, CT: Yale University Press, 1992), 154.

11. For a different focus on manners in Austen see Jenny Davidson, *Hypocrisy and the Politics of Politeness: Manners and Morals from Locke to Austen* (Cambridge, England: Cambridge University Press, 2004). Davidson argues that, for Austen, hypocrisy has its value particularly for dependents and women: "Tact has become a form of power that people are willing to acknowledge, giving it a new legitimacy" (168). Concealment of one's desires and motives is, then, not altogether without virtue. In *Mansfield Park,* Austen explores how patronage may be "compatible with virtue but that virtue must often be a matter of negotiating dependence" (169). Davidson almost completely ignores *Pride and Prejudice* in her discussion of Austen, a novel in the which the dependent heroine is famous for flaunting convention and politeness when they seem in opposition to virtue or her own desire.

12. Cannadine, *The Rise and Fall of Class,* 71.

13. Charles S. Maier, "Democracy since the French Revolution," in *Democracy: The Unfinished Journey, 508 BC to AD 1993,* ed. John Dunn (Oxford, England: Oxford University Press, 1992), 125.

14. Colley, 187.

15. Colley points out that most "of the officers in Napoleon's *grande armee*, like the bulk of his imperial nobility, possessed no claim to land or ancient lineage, but had risen to prominence since the Revolution through their own exertions. In this

sense, Napoleonic France could still be seen—and was seen by its British opponents—as a meritocracy" (150).

16. Edmund Burke, *Reflections on the Revolution in France,* ed. J. C. D. Clark (Stanford, CA: Stanford University Press, 2001), 239.

17. William Wordsworth, "1801 (*I grieved for Buonaparte, with a vain),*" in *English Romantic Writers,* ed. David Perkins (Fort Worth, TX: Harcourt, 1967), 286.

18. For influential work on Wordsworth's appropriation of mothers and the feminine, see Alan Richardson, "Romanticism and the Colonization of the Feminine," in *Romanticism and Feminism,* ed. Anne K. Mellor (Bloomington: Indiana University Press, 1988), 16–17.

19. J. W. Burrow, *Whigs and Liberals: Continuity and Change in English Political Thought* (Oxford, England: Oxford University Press, 1988), 20.

20. Burrow sees important echoes in the nineteenth century of republican ideas of civic virtues, often adapted to more modern concerns (77–100).

21. Some hint of the aristocrat's warrior roots might appear in the possibility of the duel. Mrs. Bennet fears her husband will call Wickham out when he seduces Lydia. But this entirely unlikely possibility in the case of the absentee father might be much more likely imagined of Darcy when Wickham attempts to elope with Georgiana. Kenneth Hodges has noted to me that Darcy writes to Wickham after discovering the attempted elopement and that Wickham's subsequent escape from him might suggest a threat of a duel in the letter.

22. Jane Austen, *Pride and Prejudice,* ed. Donald Gray (New York: Norton, 2001), 8.

23. Jill Heydt-Stevenson, "Liberty, Connection, and Tyranny: The Novels of Jane Austen and the Aesthetic Movement of the Picturesque," in *Lessons of Romanticism,* ed. Thomas Pfau and Robert F. Gleckner (Durham, NC: Duke University Press, 1998), 263.

24. Peter Knox-Shaw, *Jane Austen and the Enlightenment* (Cambridge, England: Cambridge University Press, 2004), 76.

25. Knox-Shaw argues that Pemberley is to be understood in opposition to Lady Catherine's estate, Rosings, which "owes its layout to the genius of Capability Brown" (93) who, Heydt-Stevenson points out, calls for an aesthetic that aggrandizes the power of the owner with grand vistas cleared of peasant homes.

26. Knox-Shaw claims that critics who see the novel as "anti-Jacobin" emphasize the change in Elizabeth rather than in Darcy. But Darcy "undergoes a radical transformation in the course of the novel, powered by the spell of Elizabeth and by all that disposes him to her, and no other character alters as much" (95). This chapter argues that Darcy's change, although more important and meaningful than any in Elizabeth, is not radical in the political sense of the term: it is rather an accommodation to a modern world that, nonetheless, maintains social hierarchy largely in place.

27. Elizabeth considers Bingley's faults: "much as she had been disposed to like him, she could not think without anger, hardly without contempt, on that easiness of temper, that want of proper resolution which now made him the slave of his designing friends" (90).

28. Some critics argue that Elizabeth Bennet speaks a feminist, enlightened humanism. In her examination of contemporary feminist writing, Allison G. Sulloway claims, "Elizabeth speaks with the voices of the feminists." *Jane Austen and the Province of Womanhood* (Philadelphia: University of Pennsylvania Press, 1989), 174. Like Claudia Johnson, Sulloway sees Austen as reacting to the attacks on Wollstonecraft and elaborating a more muted and less overt feminism. See also Margaret Kirkham, *Jane Austen: Feminism and Fiction* (Totowa, NJ: Barnes & Noble, 1983). Deborah Kaplan finds evidence for Austen's feminism less in her strong female characters and more in her participation in a "woman's culture." *Jane Austen among Women* (Baltimore, MD: Johns Hopkins University Press, 1992).

29. Knox-Shaw also argues that by "the time Jane Austen started on 'First Impressions' the school of the picturesque had taken on the character of a reformist rather than a radical movement" (98).

30. Chantal Mouffe, *The Democratic Paradox* (London: Verso, 2000), 1.

31. Mikkel Borch-Jacobsen, *Lacan: The Absolute Master*, trans. by Douglas Brick (Stanford, CA: Stanford University Press, 1991), 238.

32. Slavoj Žižek, *The Sublime Object of Ideology* (London: Verso, 1989), 45.

33. Some minor examples would be Mrs. Bennet and Lydia Bennet. Mrs. Bennet who, on the one hand, appears to be a vulgar matchmaker for her daughters, who strikes out for the richest men in the neighborhood, demonstrates an excess of desire unconnected with financial interest. After all, as she declares to her daughters, she, too, was once the lover of a red coat. Regiments of second sons and dispossessed young men provide a sexual excitement wholly disconnected from the prudential concerns of caste and wealth. If Charlotte disturbs Elizabeth by exposing the wholly materialistic calculations involved in marriage for a well-bred woman, Mrs. Bennet and Lydia are disturbing because they reveal a form of desire that does not depend on reasoned calculation and cannot be controlled by morality and the dynamics of shame.

34. Linda Dowling, *Hellenism and Homosexuality in Victorian Oxford* (Ithaca, NY: Cornell University Press, 1994), 21.

35. The danger of Wickham is compounded by the fact that he is himself generated by fathers who fail to control. As critics have long noted, the novel is marked by ineffectual fathers. Darcy's father produces a son whose pride is unchecked and a foster son who, likewise, knows no limits to his desire for acquisition. Mr. Bennet, the novel's most glaring example of a failed father, consumes his family's wealth without thought to his daughters' future and allows Lydia to become prey to Wickham's seductions. He, like Mr. Darcy the elder, never checks the rampant desires of his

children allowing Lydia to pursue her desires with the reckless abandon of Wickham. This novel has no return of the father, no figure of traditional authority who can take over and compel the prodigal back to the paternal law. Instead, once the father has died, the struggle between brothers preoccupies the novel.

36. Elizabeth claims about Lydia that Wickham "never distinguished *her* by any particular attention, and, consequently, after a moderate period of extravagant and wild admiration, her fancy for him gave way, and others of the regiment, who treated her with more distinction, again became her favorites" (185). Elizabeth believes, "Lydia had wanted only encouragement to attach herself to any body. Sometimes one officer, sometimes another had been her favorite, as their attentions raised them in her opinion. Her affections had been continually fluctuating but never without an object" (181). When Lydia elopes, she writes Mrs. Forster a letter: "I am going to Gretna Green, and if you cannot guess with who, I shall think you a simpleton, for there is but one man in the world I love, and he is an angel" (189). After declaring her devotion, her mind wanders: "Pray, make my excuses to Pratt, for not keeping my engagement, and dancing with him to night" (189).

37. William Galperin, "The Picturesque, the Real, and the Consumption of Jane Austen," *Wordsworth Circle* 28. 1 (Winter 1997), 20.

38. Many critics agree with Galperin when he writes, *Pride and Prejudice* "is arguably Austen's most successfully conservative work." *The Historical Austen* (Philadelphia: University of Pennsylvania Press, 2003), 64. The limits of Darcy's control and appeal suggest to me, however, that the novel offers an important check on the fantasy of elite power.

Chapter 7. Dependent Masters and Independent Servants: The Gothic Pleasures of British Homes in Charlotte Brontë's Jane Eyre

1. See Elaine Showalter, "Charlotte Brontë: Feminine Heroine," in *New Casebooks: Jane Eyre*, ed. Heather Glen (New York: St. Martin's, 1997), 68–77; Adrienne Rich, "Jane Eyre: The Temptations of a Motherless Woman," *On Lies, Secrets and Silence: Selected Prose 1966–1978* (New York: Norton, 1979) for more celebratory accounts of Jane's feminism. For more qualified views, Sandra M. Gilbert and Susan Gubar, *The Madwoman in the Attic: The Woman Writer and the Nineteenth-Century Literary Imagination* (New Haven, CT: Yale University Press, 1979); Cora Kaplan, "Pandora's Box: Subjectivity, Class and Sexuality in Socialist Feminist Criticism" in *Feminisms: An Anthology of Literary Theory and Criticism*, ed. Robyn R. Warhol and Diane Price Herndl (New Brunswick, NJ: Rutgers University Press, 1993) 857–77. Several critics point out how Jane's feminist and democratic commitments fail to extend to nonwhite and non–middle–class women or how her identification with others is in conflict with her desire for Rochester: Gayatri C. Spivak, "Three Women's Texts and Critique of Imperialism" *Feminisims*, 798–814;

Terry Eagleton, *Myths of Power: A Marxist Study of the Brontës* (London: Macmillan, 1975), 15–32; Jenny Sharpe, *Allegories of Empire: The Figure of Woman in the Colonial Text* (Minneapolis: University of Minnesota Press, 1993).

2. Jina Politi in "*Jane Eyre* Class-ified" argues that the revolutionary thrust of the first part of the novel disappears in the second. The novel "is marked by a contradiction in form. The first ten chapters ... organise the writing on the conventions of realism, but once Jane is out of the Charity Institution and into the world the writing incarcerates her in an a-temporal fantasy mode.... After the tenth chapter what the writing is striving to do is silence, efface, inscribe *over* its narrative past." *New Casebooks: Jane Eyre*, 88. Other critics, however, have offered a more nuanced reading in which democratic and reactionary concerns can be traced throughout the novel. Susan Meyer writes, "Brontë's major fiction reveals a conflict between sympathy for the oppressed and a hostile sense of racial superiority" ("Colonialism and the Figurative Strategy of *Jane Eyre*," *New Casebooks: Jane Eyre*, 95). Countering Spivak's more one-sided reading of race and empire in the novel, Meyer claims that "*Jane Eyre* is characterized not by Spivak's 'unquestioned ideology' of imperialism, but by an ideology of imperialism that is questioned—and then reaffirmed—in interesting and illuminating ways" (97). Although Politi is less convinced by the novel's more democratic claims and sees them as absent in the second part, Meyer assumes a continuity of democratic concerns that are, throughout, in conflict with the novel's support for empire.

3. Jane's interest in the Gothic as a means of connecting with the master resembles Caleb Williams's interest in romance.

4. Nancy Armstrong, *Desire and Domestic Fiction: A Political History of the Novel* (New York : Oxford University Press, 1987), 4.

5. It "was a savage face ... the roll of the red eyes and the fearful blackened inflation of the lineaments." Charlotte Brontë, *Jane Eyre*, ed. Michael Mason (London: Penguin Books, 1996), 317.

6. Many of the other upper-class women in the novel have similar descriptions: Blanche's mother has:

> an expression of almost insupportable haughtiness.... She had Roman features and a double chin, disappearing into a throat like a pillar: these features appeared to me not only inflated and darkened, but even furrowed with pride.... She had, likewise, a fierce and hard eye: it reminded me of Mrs. Reed's; she mouthed her words in speaking; her voice very deep, its inflections very pompous, very dogmatical,—very intolerable, in short. A crimson velvet robe, and a shawl and turban of some gold-wrought Indian fabric, invested her (I suppose she thought) with a truly imperial dignity. (195)

Wearing the power of her status overtly in her expression and in her attire, Dowager Lady Ingram appears in the narrator's description as a character of ostentation and wealth. Her "truly imperial dignity" is clownish and her efforts to mark her superiority only repulse those who are meant to feel inferior. Like Mrs. Reed, she is a hard tyrant but one who only inspires slave revolts. Here, darkness of skin becomes the result of an excessive pride of caste that marks the upper-class woman so deeply as to furrow her face. Much like Bertha Mason's face, as it appears later in the novel, swollen and black, Lady Ingram's face has become monstrous from pride and, as her attire suggests, this pride of caste orientalizes her into an Eastern tyrant.

7. For Gilbert and Gubar, Bertha represents Jane's repressed rage and sexual desire; for Spivak, Bertha functions as the white English woman's defining opposite, a monstrous other who allows the white woman to achieve individuality at the expense of her ambiguously raced colonial counterpart; for Susan Meyer, Bertha is not simply racially suspect but actually black. She is part of a larger tendency in Brontë's work to appropriate "non-white races for figurative ends," an appropriation that stresses the "shared oppression" of blacks and women but does not also "preclude racism" (97). Turning away from the imperial context, Armstrong sees Bertha as representative of Rochester's aristocratic class. Bertha, like him, must be purged from the novel in her outmoded form. Unlike Rochester who can be redeemed into a bourgeois subject, the aristocratic lady is replaced by the bourgeois Jane.

8. Sharpe, *Allegories of Empire*, 45.

9. See Marianne Thormahlen, *The Brontës and Religion* (Cambridge, England: Cambridge University Press, 1999), 211.

10. For a discussion of St. John's despotism see Q. D. Leavis, *Collected Essays*, vol. 1, ed. G. Singh (Cambridge, England: Cambridge University Press, 1983), 178, 188.

11. For an influential reading of the novel's conclusion that focuses on Jane's appropriation of the Bible, see Carolyn Williams, "Closing the Book: The Intertextual End of *Jane Eyre*" in *The Brontë Sisters: Critical Assessments*, vol. III, ed. Eleanor McNees (East Sussex, England: Routledge, 1997), 352–74.

12. "It is revealing that while Jane and her creator castigate patriarchalism at home—as embodied in the world of the great house and its sundry patriarchs—they most heartily applaud patriarchalism abroad, in the shape of religious and political empire-building." Parama Roy, "Unaccommodated Woman and the Poetics of Property in *Jane Eyre*" in *The Bronte Sisters*, 384.

13. Jane W. Stedman, "Charlotte Brontë and Bewick's *British Birds,*" *The Brontë Sisters,* 184.

14. This escape into adventure narrative occurs throughout the novel. As a child, Jane believes that *Gulliver's Travels* is "a narrative of facts" (28) and she "doubted not that I might one day, by taking a long voyage, see with my own eyes the little fields, houses, and trees, the diminutive people, the tiny cows, sheep and birds of the one realm; and the corn-fields forest-high, the mighty mastiffs, the monster cats the tower-like men and women, of the other" (29). Adventure in Jane's narrative also has a landscape. At Lowood, when the weather is bad, the "obscure chaos" of a storm

makes Jane "reckless and feverish," and she wishes "the wind to howl more wildly, the gloom to deepen to darkness, and the confusion to rise to clamour" (65). A similar interest in stormy landscapes and adventure narratives is evident in Jane's adult drawings (142–43). And the weather at Thornfield itself always responds to Jane's personal dramas by breaking out in terrific storms in times of crisis.

15. However, the famous haunting in the red room in which Jane imagines that an irate paterfamilias avenges her wrongs, hints early on that Gothic horrors and pleasures belong in the home.

16. Cora Kaplan, "Pandora's Box: Subjectivity, Class and Sexuality in Socialist Feminist Criticism," _Feminisims,_ 874.

17. In previous homes, the master is either absent or inadequate. Mr. Reed is dead and the Reverend Brocklehurst is an absurd figure of religious hypocrisy and cruelty.

18. Critical discussion about the Gothic in _Jane Eyre_ is long-standing, but in one of the most influential early essays, Robert B. Heilman focused on the Gothic only to undermine its significance in what he saw as an essentially realist novel. Heilman argues that Charlotte Brontë "modifies" the "relatively simple thrill or momentary intensity of feeling sought by primitive gothic" by moving toward "new levels of human reality, and hence from stock responses toward a new kind of passionate engagement." "Charlotte Brontë's 'New Gothic'" in _Victorian Literature: Modern Essays in Criticism,_ ed. Austin Write (London: Oxford University Press, 1961), 74. For Heilman, Brontë's novel imbeds Gothic effects within a realist novel to intensify feelings while downplaying Gothic claptrap. This reading seeks to reduce the Gothic to a convenient tool for amplifying an underlying realist narrative. The Gothic becomes an expression of a disturbed mind, an inner psychological state manifested outwardly. In contrast to this inner state lies an outer human reality against which to test and correct mental confusion. See also Eugenia C. DeLamotte's _Perils of the Night: A Feminist Study of Nineteenth-Century Gothic_ (New York: Oxford University Press, 1990), 193–228, which reads the novel's Gothic effects as an exteriorization of women's domestic entrapment and rage. Margaret Homans argues that the Gothic's literalization of internal, subjective states lends itself to exploring "the cultural identification of 'woman' with the literal" (308). For her, Charlotte Brontë "uses the Gothic with ambivalence and uses her ambivalence to protest the objectification of the feminine that the Gothic enacts." "Dreaming of Children: Liberalization in _Jane Eyre_" in _The Brontë Sisters,_ 309.

19. Cyndy Hendershot, _The Animal Within: Masculinity and the Gothic_ (Ann Arbor: University of Michigan Press, 1998), 1.

20. David Punter's review of Elizabeth Napier's _The Failure of the Gothic,_ quoted in Robert Miles, _Gothic Writing 1750–1820: A Genealogy_ (London: Routledge, 1993), 1.

21. Slavoj Žižek, _The Sublime Object of Ideology_ (London: Verso, 1989), 45.

22. This stress on the moral superiority of women became particularly important during the wars with France. According to Linda Colley, the period during and after the Revolution saw an increased emphasis on the moral power of women and their crucial importance in the production of cultural values and beliefs. English women became "Great Britain's moral arbiters," whereas French women became the embodiment of everything that seemed wrong to many Britons about the French Revolution. Linda Colley, *Britons: Forging the Nation, 1707–1837* (New Haven, CT: Yale University Press, 1992), 276. Licentious, immoral, intemperate, French women signified the degeneracy of the French State. In the same way, the moralizing influence of women in England produced a superior nation tempered by the "moral superiority" of women who functioned as "the nation's conscience" (280–81).

According to Nancy Armstrong, this desire to cast women and their moral influence as a means of civilizing the public sphere, of making violence if not obsolete at least invisible was also crucial beyond the years of Revolution and war. She argues that in the nineteenth century, writers attempted to soften the coerciveness of power by replacing violence with persuasion, the sword with the pen, the king's law with public opinion, the influence of men with the influence of women. Adopting more subtle methods of social control in the early nineteenth-century meant that literature, education, and the home became privileged sites of influence replacing overt political power (79).

23. Mary Poovey argues that her very position as governess raises questions about whether Jane Eyre can even function as the proper domestic figure who reforms the aristocrat. "Because the governess was like the middle-class mother in the work she performed, but like both a working-class woman and man in the wages she received, the very figure who theoretically should have defended the naturalness of separate spheres threatened to collapse the difference between them." The governess was a threat to the "domestic ideal" (170), whereas the proper woman, ideally, "was living proof that the commodification of labour, the alienation of human relations, the frustrations and disappointments inflicted by economic vicissitudes stopped at the door of the home" (186). The governess provides an exception to domestic ideology by highlighting how potentially cruel masters exist in the home as well as in the public sphere. If Byron, Hazlitt, and Carlyle stress how public power relations are erotic, Brontë, like Austen and Godwin, shows how private erotic relations are about power. Mary Poovey, "The Anathematized Race: The Governess and *Jane Eyre*," in *New Casebooks*, 170.

24. See, for example, Diane Hoeveler, *Gothic Feminism: The Professionalization of Gender from Charlotte Smith to the Brontës* (University Park, PA: University of Pennsylvania Press, 1998).

25. Hendershot writes that for Jane, "Rochester is a fantasy lover whose textual predecessors are Montoni, Schedoni, Melmoth, and Byron's heroes" (166).

26. Toward the end of the novel, Brontë repeatedly compares Rochester to Samson. Samson as God's champion struggling against a treacherous seductress might be an analogy for Rochester's struggle against Bertha. But Jane herself also

inevitably figures as Delilah, as an innkeeper who informs Jane of Rochester's fate suggests: "when gentlemen of his age fall in love with girls, they are often like as if they were bewitched" (474). Jane, as Delilah, has hurt Rochester who "had a courage and a will of his own, if ever man had. I knew him from a boy, you see: and for my part I have often wished that Miss Eyre had been sunk in the sea before she came to Thornfield" (475). For discussions of the association of Jane and Rochester with Samson and Delilah, see R. B. Martin, *The Accents of Persuasion: Charlotte Brontë's Novels* (New York: Norton, 1966), 100, and Philip C. Rule, "The Function of Allusion in *Jane Eyre*" (1985), in *The Brontë Sisters*, 298–305.

27. Slavoj Žižek, *The Sublime Object of Ideology*, 18.

28. Miram Allot, ed., *The Brontës: The Critical Heritage* (London: Routledge, 1974), 90.

Bibliography

Abrams, M. H. *Natural Supernaturalism: Tradition and Revolution in Romantic Literature*. London: Oxford University Press, 1971.

Adams, James Eli. *Dandies and Desert Saint: Styles of Victorian Manhood*. Ithaca, NY: Cornell University Press, 1995.

Allot, Miriam, ed. *The Brontës: The Critical Heritage*. London: Routledge, 1974.

Anderson, Robert. "'Enjoyments of a [...] more exquisite nature': Wordsworth and Commodity Culture." *Romanticism on the Net: An Electronic Journal Devoted to Romantic Studies* 26 (May 2002): 66.

Appleby, Joyce. *Capitalism and the New Social Order: The Republican Vision of the 1790's*. New York: New York University Press, 1984.

———. "The Social Origins of American Revolutionary Ideology." *Journal of American History* 64 (Mar. 1978): 935–58

Armstrong, Nancy. *Desire and Domestic Fiction: A Political History of the Novel*. New York: Oxford University Press, 1987.

Austen, Jane. *Pride and Prejudice*. Ed. Donald Gray. New York: Norton, 2001.

Bainbridge, Simon. *British Poetry and the Revolutionary and Napoleonic Wars*. Oxford, England: Oxford University Press, 2003.

———. *Napoleon and English Romanticism*. Cambridge, England: Cambridge University Press, 1995.

Baker, Herschel. *William Hazlitt*. Cambridge, MA: Harvard University Press, 1962.

Barker-Benfield, G. J. *The Culture of Sensibility: Sex and Society in Eighteenth-Century Britain*. Chicago: University of Chicago Press, 1992.

Barker, Hannah, and Elaine Chalus. *Gender in Eighteenth-Century England: Roles, Representations and Responsibilities*. London: Longman, 1997.

Barrell, John. "Sad Stories : Louis XVI, George III, and the Language of Sentiment." In *Refiguring Revolutions: Aesthetics and Politics from the English Revolution to the Romantic Revolution*. Ed. Kevin Sharpe and Steven N. Zwicker. Berkeley: University of California Press, 1998.

Bayly, C. A. *The Birth of the Modern World 1780–1914: Global Connections and Comparisons*. Malden, MA: Routledge, 2004.

Bellamy, Richard, ed. *Victorian Liberalism: Nineteenth-Century Political Thought and Practice*. Ed. Richard Bellamy. London: Routledge, 1990.

Bender, John. "Impersonal Violence: The Penetrating Gaze and the Field of Narration in *Caleb Williams.*" In *Vision and Textuality*. Ed. Stephen Melville and Bill Readings. Durham, NC: Duke University Press, 1995.

Benjamin, Walter. "Art in the Age of Mechanical Reproduction." In *The Critical Tradition: Classic Texts and Contemporary Trends*. Ed. David H. Richter. New York: St. Martin's, 1989.

Borch-Jacobsen, Mikkel. *Lacan: The Absolute Master*. Trans. Douglas Brick. Stanford, CA: Stanford University Press, 1991.

Bossche, Chris R. Vanden. *Carlyle and the Search for Authority*. Columbus: Ohio State University Press, 1991.

Boulton, James T. *The Language of Politics in the Age of Wilkes and Burke*. London: Routledge & Keegan Paul, 1963.

Bourke, Richard. *Romantic Discourse and Political Modernity: Wordsworth, the Intellectual and Cultural Critique*. New York: St. Martin's, 1993.

Brinks, Ellen. *Gothic Masculinity: Effeminacy and the Supernatural in English and German Romanticism*. Lewisburg, PA: Bucknell University Press, 2003.

Brinton, Crane. *English Political Thought in the Nineteenth Century*. New York: Harper & Brothers, 1962.

Brontë, Charlotte. *Jane Eyre*. Ed. Michael Mason. London: Penguin, 1996.

Browmich, David. *Hazlitt: The Mind of a Critic*. New Haven, CT: Yale University Press, 1999.

Burke, Edmund. *A Philosophical Enquiry into the Origin of Our Ideas of the Sublime and the Beautiful*. Ed. James T. Boulton. Notre Dame, IN: University of Notre Dame Press, 1958.

————. *Reflections on the Revolution in France.* Ed. J. C. D. Clark. Stanford, CA: Stanford University Press, 2001.

Burrow, J. W. *Whigs and Liberals: Continuity and Change in English Political Thought.* Oxford, England: Oxford University Press, 1988.

Busco, Marie F. "The 'Achilles' in Hyde Park." *Burlington Magazine* 130 (1988): 920–24.

Butler, Judith. *Gender Trouble: Feminism and the Subversion of Identity.* New York: Routledge, 1990.

Butler, Marilyn. "John Bull's Other Kingdom: Byron's Intellectual Comedy." *Studies in Romanticism* 31 (1992): 281–94.

Butler, Marilyn. *Jane Austen and the War of Ideas.* Oxford, England: Oxford University Press, 1975.

Byron, George Gordon. *The Corsair.* In *Lord Byron: Selected Poems.* London: Penguin, 2006.

————. *Don Juan.* Ed. T. G. Steffan, E. Steffan, and W. W. Pratt. London: Penguin, 1973.

————. *Sardanapalus. Byron: The Complete Works.* Vol. vi. Ed. Jerome J. McGann and Barry Weller. Oxford, England: Oxford University Press, 1991.

Cafarelli, Annette Wheeler. *Prose in the Age of Poets: Romanticism and Biographical Narrative from Johnson to De Quincey.* Philadelphia: University of Pennsylvania Press, 1990.

Cannadine, David. *Aspects of Aristocracy: Grandeur and Decline in Modern Britain.* New Haven, CT: Yale University Press, 1994.

————. *The Rise and Fall of Class in Britain.* New York: Columbia University Press, 1999.

Carlson, Julie. *In the Theatre of Romanticism: Coleridge, Nationalism, and Women.* Cambridge, England: Cambridge University Press, 1994.

Carlyle, Thomas. *On Heroes, Hero Worship, and the Heroic in History.* New York: Chelsea House, 1983.

————. *Past and Present.* Ed. Richard D. Altick. New York: New York University Press, 1965.

————. *Thomas Carlyle: Selected Writings.* Ed. Alan Shelston. London: Penguin, 1986.

Carretta, Vincent. *George III and the Satirists from Hogarth to Byron*. Athens : University of Georgia Press, 1990.

Carter, Philip. "Men about Town: Representation of Foppery and Masculinity in Early Eighteenth-Century Urban Society." In *Gender in Eighteenth-Century England: Roles, Representations, and Responsibilities*. Ed. H. Barker and E. Chalus. London: Longman, 1997.

————. *Men and the Emergence of Polite Society, Britain 1660–1800*. Harlow, England: Longman, 2001.

Castellanos, Gabriela. *Laughter, War and Feminism: Elements of Carnival in Three of Jane Austen's Novels*. New York: Lang, 1994.

Chandler, James K. *England in 1819: The Politics of Literary Culture and the Case of Romantic Historicism*. Chicago: University of Chicago Press, 1999.

Chew, Samuel C. *The Drama of Lord Byron: A Critical Study*. 1915. Reprint, New York: Russell and Russell, 1964.

Christensen, Jerome. *Lord Byron's Strength: Romantic Writing in Commercial Society*. Baltimore, MD: Johns Hopkins University Press, 1993.

Clemit, Pamela. *The Godwinian Novel: The Rational Fictions of Godwin, Brockden Brown, and Mary Shelley*. Oxford, England: Oxford University Press, 1993.

Cohen, Michele. *Fashioning Masculinity: National Identity and Language in the Eighteenth Century*. London: Routledge, 1996.

Coleridge, Samuel Taylor. *Essays on His Times, the Collected Works of Samuel Taylor Coleridge*. vol. 3. Ed. D. V. Erdman. Princeton, NJ: Princeton University Press, 1969.

————. *A Lay Sermon* (1817). *The Major Works*. Ed. H. J. Jackson. Oxford, England: Oxford University Press, 1985.

Colley, Linda. *Britons: Forging the Nation, 1707–1837*. New Haven, CT: Yale University Press, 1992.

Collings, David. "The Romance of the Impossible: William Godwin in the Empty Place of Reason." *English Literary History* 70.3 (2003): 847–74.

Collini, Stefan. *Public Moralists: Political Thought and Intellectual Life in Britain 1850–1930*. Oxford, England: Oxford University Press, 1991.

Constant, Benjamin. *Political Writings.* Trans. and ed. Biancamaria Fontana. Cambridge, England: Cambridge University Press, 1988.

Crompton, Louis. *Byron and Greek Love: Homophobia in Nineteenth-Century England.* Berkeley: University of California Press, 1985.

Cronin, Richard. *Romantic Victorians: English Literature, 1824–1840.* New York: Palgrave, 2002.

Davidoff, Leonore, and Catherine Hall. *Family Fortunes: Men, and Women of the English Middle Class, 1780–1850.* Chicago: University of Chicago Press, 1987.

Davidson, Jenny. *Hypocrisy and the Politics of Politeness: Manners and Morals from Locke to Austen.* Cambridge, England: Cambridge University Press, 2004.

DeLamotte, Eugenia C. *Perils of the Night: A Feminist Study of Nineteenth-Century Gothic.* New York: Oxford University Press, 1990.

De Man, Paul. "Shelley Disfigured." In *The Rhetoric of Romanticism.* New York: Columbia University Press, 1984.

———. "Sign and Symbol in Hegel's *Aesthetic.*" In *Aesthetic Ideology.* Ed. Andrzej Warminski. Minneapolis: University of Minnesota Press, 1996.

Desaulniers, Mary. *Carlyle and the Economics of Terror: A Study of Revisionary Gothicism in The French Revolution.* Montreal: McGill-Queen's University Press, 1995.

Diggins, John P. *The Lost Soul of American Politics: Virtue, Self-Interest, and the Foundations of Liberalism.* New York: Basic, 1984.

Donelan, Charles. *Romanticism and Male Fantasy in Byron's Don Juan: A Marketable Vice.* London: Macmillan, 2000.

Donovan, Robert A. "Carlyle and the Climate of Hero Worship." *University of Toronto Quarterly* 42 (1973): 122–41.

Dowling, Linda. *Hellenism and Homosexuality in Victorian Oxford.* Ithaca, NY: Cornell University Press, 1994.

Duckworth, Alistair M. *The Improvement of the Estate.* Baltimore, MD: Johns Hopkins University Press, 1971.

Dudink Stefan, Karen Hagemann, and John Tosh, ed. *Masculinities in Politics and War: Gendering Modern History.* Manchester, England: Manchester University Press.

Eagleton, Terry. *Myths of Power: A Marxist Study of the Brontës.* London: Macmillan, 1975.

Easthope, Antony. *Wordsworth Now and Then: Romanticism and Contemporary Culture.* Buckingham, England: Open University Press, 1993.

Elfenbein, Andrew. *Byron and the Victorians.* Cambridge, England: Cambridge University Press, 1995.

Elshtain, Jean Bethke. *Public Man, Private Woman: Women in Social and Political Thought.* Princeton, NJ: Princeton University Press, 1981.

Fafla, K., Joel and Julian Wright, ed. *Nervous Reactions: Victorian Recollections of Romanticism.* Albany: State University of New York Press, 2004.

Fay, Elizabeth. "Wordsworth's Balladry: Real Men Wanted." In *The 'Honourable Characteristics of Poetry'": Two Hundred Years of Lyrical Ballads. Romantic Circles.* http://www.rc.umd.edu/praxis/lyrical/fay/balladry.html.

Folker, Brian. "Wordsworth's Visionary Imagination: Democracy and War." *English Literary History* 69.1 (2002): 167–97.

Fludernik, Monika. "William Godwin's *Caleb Williams*: The Tarnishing of the Sublime." *English Literary History* 68.4 (2001): 857–96.

Francis, Mark, and John Morrow. *A History of English Political Thought in the Nineteenth Century.* New York: St. Martin's, 1994.

Fraser, Nancy. "Rethinking the Public Sphere: A Contribution to the Critique of Actually Existing Democracy. In *Habermas and the Public Sphere.* Ed. Craig Calhoun. Cambridge, MA: MIT Press, 1997.

Freud, Sigmund. *Totem and Taboo: Some Points of Agreement between the Mental Lives of Savages and Neurotics.* Trans. and ed. James Strachey. New York: Norton, 1989.

Fulford, Tim. *Romanticism and Masculinity: Gender, Politics and Poetics in the Writings of Burke, Coleridge, Cobbett, Wordsworth, De Quincey, and Hazlitt.* Hampshire, England: St. Martin's, 1999.

Galperin, William. *The Historical Austen.* Philadelphia: University of Pennsylvania Press, 2003.

———. "The Picturesque, the Real, and the Consumption of Jane Austen." *Wordsworth Circle* 28.1 (1997): 19–27.

Gilbert, Sandra M., and Susan Gubar. *The Madwoman in the Attic: The Woman Writer and the Nineteenth-Century Literary Imagination.* New Haven, CT: Yale University Press, 1979.

Girouard, Mark. *The Return to Camelot: Chivalry and the English Gentleman.* New Haven, CT: Yale University Press, 1981.

Gleckner, Robert F. *Byron and the Ruins of Paradise.* Baltimore, MD: Johns Hopkins University Press, 1967.

Godwin, William. *Caleb Williams.* Ed. David McCracken. New York: Norton, 1977.

Gold Jr., Alex. "It's Only Love: The Politics of Passion in Godwin's *Caleb Williams.*" *Texas Studies in Literature and Language* 19 (1977): 142–43.

Goode, Graham. *The Observing Self: Rediscovering the Essay.* London: Routledge, 1988.

Goodlad, Lauren M. E. *Victorian Literature and the Victorian State: Character and Governance in a Liberal Society.* Baltimore, MD: Johns Hopkins University Press, 2003.

Goux, Jean-Joseph. *Symbolic Economies: After Marx and Freud.* Trans. Jennifer Curtiss Gage. Ithaca, NY: Cornell University Press, 1990.

Grierson, Herbert. *Carlyle and Hitler.* Manchester, England: University of Manchester Press, 1930.

Habermas, Jürgen. *The Structural Transformation of the Public Sphere An Inquiry into a Category of Bourgeois Society.* Trans. by Thomas Burger. Cambridge, MA: MIT Press, 1991.

Handwerk, Gary. "Of Caleb's Guilt and Godwin's Truth: Ideology and Ethics in *Caleb Williams.*" *English Literary History* 60 (1993): 939–60.

Hall, Catherine. "Competing Masculinities: Thomas Carlyle, John Stuart Mill and the Case of Governor Eyre." In *White Male and Middle Class: Explorations in Feminism and History.* Ed. Catherine Hall. Cambridge, England: Polity Press, 1992.

———, Keith McClelland, and Jane Rendall. *Defining the Victorian Nation: Class, Race, Gender and the British Reform Act of 1867.* Cambridge, England: Cambridge University Press, 2000.

Hays, William Anthony. *The Whig Revival, 1808–1830.* New York: Palgrave, 2005.

Hazlitt, William. *Complete Works of William Hazlitt*. Ed. P. P. Howe. London: Dent, 1931.

———. *The Spirit of the Age* (1824, 1825). *English Romantic Writers*. Ed. David Perkins. Fort Worth, TX: Harcourt Brace Jovanovich, 1967.

Heilman, Robert B. "Charlotte Brontë's 'New Gothic'" (1958). In *Victorian Literature: Modern Essays in Criticism*. Ed. Austin Write. London: Oxford University Press, 1961.

Hendershot, Cyndy. *The Animal Within: Masculinity and the Gothic*. Ann Arbor: University of Michigan Press, 1998.

Herzog, Don. *Poisoning the Minds of the Lower Orders*. Princeton, NJ: Princeton University Press, 1998.

Heydt-Stevenson, Jill. "Liberty, Connection, and Tyranny: The Novels of Jane Austen and the Aesthetic Movement of the Picturesque." In *Lessons of Romanticism*. Ed. Thomas Pfau and Robert F. Gleckner. Durham, NC: Duke University Press, 1998.

Hilton, Boyd. *A Mad, Bad, and Dangerous People?: England 1783–1846*. Oxford, England: Oxford University Press, 2006.

Hoeveler, Diane. *Gothic Feminism: The Professionalization of Gender from Charlotte Smith to the Brontës*. University Park: University of Pennsylvania Press, 1998.

Hofkosh, Sonia. "The Writer's Ravishment: Women and the Romantic Author—The Example of Byron." In *Romanticism and Feminism*. Ed. Anne K. Mellor. Bloomington: Indiana University Press, 1988.

Homans, Margaret. "Dreaming of Children: Liberalization in *Jane Eyre*" (1986). In *The Brontë Sisters: Critical Assessments*, vol. III. Ed. Eleanor McNees. East Sussex, England: Routledge, 1997.

Houghton, Walter E. *The Victorian Frame of Mind 1830-1870*. New Haven, CT: Yale University Press, 1985.

Howe, P. P. *The Life of William Hazlitt*. Westport: Greenwood, 1972.

Howell, Margaret J. *Byron Tonight: A Poet's Plays on the Nineteenth Century Stage*. Surrey, England: Springwood, 1982.

Johnson, Claudia L. *Jane Austen: Women, Politics, and the Novel*. Chicago: University of Chicago Press, 1988.

Johnson, Nancy E. *The English Jacobin Novel on Rights, Property and the Law: Critiquing the Contract*. New York: Palgrave, 2004.

Jones, H. S. *Victorian Political Thought*. New York: St. Martin's, 2000.

Jones, Stanley. *Hazlitt: A Life from Winterslow to Frith Street*. Oxford, England: Oxford University Press, 1989.

Kant, Immanuel. *The Metaphysics of Morals*. Cambridge, England: Cambridge University Press, 1993.

Kaplan, Cora. "Pandora's Box: Subjectivity, Class and Sexuality in Socialist Feminist Criticism" (1985). *Feminisms: An Anthology of Literary Theory and Criticism*. Ed. Robyn R. Warhol and Diane Price Herndl. New Brunswick, NJ: Rutgers University Press, 1993.

Kaplan, Deborah. *Jane Austen among Women*. Baltimore, MD: Johns Hopkins University Press, 1992.

Kelley, Theresa M. "J. M. W. Turner, Napoleonic Caricature, and Romantic Allegory." *English Literary History* 58 (1991): 351–82.

Kelly, Gary. *English Fiction of the Romantic Period: 1789–1830*. London: Longman, 1989.

Kelsall, Malcolm. "The Slave-Woman in the Harem," *Studies in Romanticism*, 31 (Fall 1992): 315–31.

Kinnaird, John. *William Hazlitt: Critic of Power*. New York: Columbia University Press, 1978.

Kirkham, Margaret. *Jane Austen: Feminism and Fiction*. Totowa, NJ: Barnes & Noble, 1983.

Knight, G. Wilson. "'Simple and Bright': Sardanapalus" (1939). *The Plays of Lord Byron*. Ed. Robert Gleckner and Bernard Beatty. Liverpool, England: Liverpool University Press, 1997).

Knox-Shaw, Peter. *Jane Austen and the Enlightenment*. Cambridge, England: Cambridge University Press, 2004.

Landes, Joan B. *Women and the Public Sphere in the Age of the French Revolution*. Ithaca, NY: Cornell University Press, 1988.

———. "Further Thoughts on the Public/Private Distinction." *Journal of Women's History* 15.2 (2003): 28–39.

Langan, Celeste. *Romantic Vagrancy: Wordsworth and the Simulation of Freedom*. Cambridge, England: Cambridge University Press, 1995.

Lansdown, Richard. *Byron's Historical Dramas*. Oxford, England: Oxford University Press, 1992.

Lavalley, Albert J. *Carlyle and the Idea of the Modern: Studies in Carlyle's Prophetic Literature and Its Relation to Blake, Nietzsche, Marx, and Others.* New Haven, CT: Yale University Press, 1968.

Leavis, Q. D. *Collected Essays*, vol. 1. Ed. G. Singh. Cambridge, England: Cambridge University Press, 1983.

Lee, Yoon Sun. *Nationalism and Irony: Burke, Scott and Carlyle.* New York: Oxford University Press, 2004.

Lefort, Claude. "The Image of the Body and Totalitarianism." In *The Political Forms of Modern Society: Bureaucracy, Democracy, Totalitarianism.* Ed. John B. Thompson. Cambridge, MA: MIT Press, 1986.

Lehman, B. H. *Carlyle's Theory of the Hero: Its Sources, Development, History and Influence on Carlyle's Work.* Durham, NC: Duke University Press, 1928.

Lonsdale, Roger, ed. *Eighteenth-Century Women Poets: An Oxford Anthology.* Oxford, England: Oxford University Press, 1990.

Looser, Devon, ed. *Jane Austin and the Discourses of Feminism.* New York: St. Martins, 1995.

Lynch, Deidre. "Introduction: Sharing with Our Neighbors." In *Janeites: Austen's Disciples and Devotees.* Ed. Deidre Lynch. Princeton, NJ: Princeton University Press, 2000.

Macpherson, C. B. *The Political Theory of Possessive Individualism.* Oxford, England: Oxford University Press, 1962.

Maier, Charles S. "Democracy since the French Revolution." In *Democracy: The Unfinished Journey, 508 B.C. to A.D. 1993.* Ed. John Dunn. Oxford, England: Oxford University Press, 1992.

Makdisi, Saree. *Romantic Imperialism: Universal Empire and the Culture of Modernity.* Cambridge, England: Cambridge University Press, 1998.

Mandler, Peter. *Aristocratic Government in the Age of Reform: Whigs and Liberals, 1830–1852.* Oxford, England: Oxford University Press, 1990.

Martin, Phillip W. *Byron: A Poet before His Public.* Cambridge, England: Cambridge University Press, 1982.

Martin, R. B. *The Accents of Persuasion: Charlotte Brontë's Novels.* New York: Norton, 1966.

Marx, Karl. *The Marx-Engels Reader.* 2nd ed. Ed. Robert C. Tucker. New York: Norton & Company, 1978.

Mccann, Andrew. *Cultural Politics in the 1790's: Literature, Radicalism and the Public Sphere.* New York: St. Martin's, 1999.

McFarland, Thomas. *Romantic Cruxes: The English Essayists and the Spirit of the Age.* Oxford, England: Oxford University Press, 1987.

McGann, Jerome J. "Hero with a Thousand Faces: The Rhetoric of Byronism." *Studies in Romanticism* 31 (Fall 1992): 295–313.

———. *Fiery Dust: Byron's Poetic Development.* Chicago: University of Chicago Press, 1968.

———. *The Romantic Ideology: A Critical Investigation.* Chicago: University of Chicago Press, 1983.

McGowan, Todd. "Lost on *Mulholland Drive*: Navigating David Lynch's Panegyric to Hollywood." *Cinema Journal* 43.2 (2004): 67–89.

McMaster, Juliet and Bruce Stovel, ed. *Jane Austen's Business: Her World and her Profession.* New York: St. Martin's, 1996.

Mehta, Uday Singh. *Liberalism and Empire: A Study in Nineteenth-Century British Liberal Thought.* Chicago: University of Chicago Press, 1999.

Mellor, Anne K. *Romanticism and Gender.* New York: Routledge, 1993.

Meyer, Susan. "Colonialism and the Figurative Strategy of *Jane Eyre.*" In *New Casebooks: Jane Eyre.* Ed. Heather Glen. New York: St. Martin's, 1997.

Miles, Robert. *Gothic Writing 1750–1820: A Genealogy.* London: Routledge, 1993.

Miller, Andrew H. *Novels behind Glass: Commodity Culture and Victorian Narrative.* Cambridge, England: Cambridge University Press, 1995.

The Mind of Napoleon: A Selection from His Written and Spoken Words. Ed. and trans. J. Christopher Herold. New York: Columbia University Press, 1955.

Mitchell, W. J. T. *Iconology: Image, Text, Ideology.* Chicago: University of Chicago Press, 1986.

Morris, Marilyn. *The British Monarchy and the French Revolution.* New Haven, CT: Yale University Press, 1998.

Mouffe, Chantal. *The Democratic Paradox.* London: Verso, 2000.

Myerly, Scott Hughes. *British Military Spectacle from the Napoleonic Wars through the Crimea.* Cambridge, MA: Harvard University Press, 1996.

Myers, Mitzi. "Godwin's Changing Conception of *Caleb Williams.*" *Studies in English Literature 1500–1900* 12 (1972): 591–628.

Natarajan, Uttara. *Hazlitt and the Reach of Sense: Criticism, Morals, and the Metaphysics of Power.* Oxford, England: Oxford University Press, 1998.

Newfield, Christopher. *The Emerson Effect: Individualism and Submission in America.* Chicago: University of Chicago Press, 1996.

Nunokawa, Jeff. *The Afterlife of Property: Domestic Security and the Victorian Novel.* Princeton, NJ: Princeton University Press, 1994.

Page, Judith W. *Wordsworth and the Cultivation of Women.* Berkeley: University of California Press, 1994.

Parker, Andrew. "Unthinking Sex: Marx, Engels, and the Scene of Writing." In *Fear of a Queer Planet: Queer Politics and Social Theory.* Ed. Michael Warner. Minneapolis: University of Minnesota Press, 1993.

Pateman, Carole. *The Disorder of Women: Democracy, Feminism, and Political Theory.* Cambridge, England: Cambridge University Press, 1989.

Paulin, Tom. *The Day Star of Liberty: William Hazlitt's Radical Style.* London: Faber and Faber, 1998.

Perry, Jonathan. *The Rise and Fall of Liberal Government in Victorian Britain.* New Haven, CT: Yale University Press, 1993.

Pocock, J. G. A. *The Machiavellian Moment: Florentine Political Thought and the Atlantic Republican Tradition.* Princeton, NJ: Princeton University Press, 1975.

Politi, Jina. *"Jane Eyre* Class-ified." In *New Casebooks: Jane Eyre.* Ed. Heather Glen. New York: St. Martin's, 1997.

Poovey, Mary. "The Anathematized Race: The Governess and *Jane Eyre.*" In *New Casebooks: Jane Eyre.* Ed. Heather Glen. New York: St. Martin's, 1997.

Reid, Ian. *Wordsworth and the Formation of English Studies.* Burlington, VT: Ashgate, 2004.

Rich, Adrienne. "Jane Eyre: The Temptations of a Motherless Woman." In *On Lies, Secrets and Silence: Selected Prose 1966–1978.* New York: Norton, 1979.

Richardson, Alan. *A Mental Theater: Poetic Drama and Consciousness in the Romantic Age*. University Park: Pennsylvania State University Press, 1988.

———. "Romanticism and the Colonization of the Feminine." In *Romanticism and Feminism*. Ed. Anne K. Mellor. Bloomington: Indiana University Press, 1988.

Robertson, John. "The Legacy of Adam Smith": Government and Economic Development in the *Wealth of Nations*." In *Victorian Liberalism: Nineteenth-Century Political Thought and Practice*. Ed. Richard Bellamy. London: Routledge, 1990.

Roper, Michael, and John Tosh. *Manful Assertions: Masculinities in Britain since 1800*. London: Routledge, 1991.

Rose, Sonya O. *Limited Livelihoods: Gender and Class in Nineteenth-Century England*. Berkeley: University of California Press, 1992.

Rosenberg, Philip. *The Seventh Hero: Carlyle and the Theory of Radical Activism*. Cambridge, MA: Harvard University Press, 1975.

Ross, Marlon B. *The Contours of Masculine Desire: Romanticism and the Rise of Women's Poetry*. New York: Oxford University Press, 1989.

Rothstein, Eric, *Systems of Order and Inquiry in Later Eighteenth-Century Fiction*. Berkeley: University of California Press, 1975.

Roy, Parama. "Unaccommodated Woman and the Poetics of Property in *Jane Eyre*" (1989). In *The Brontë Sisters: Critical Assessments*. Vol. III. Ed. Eleanor McNees. East Sussex, England: Routledge, 1997.

Rule, Philip C. "The Function of Allusion in *Jane Eyre*" (1985). In *The Brontë Sisters: Critical Assessments*. Vol. III. Ed. Eleanor McNees. East Sussex, England: Routledge, 1997.

Russell, Gillian. *The Theaters of War: Performance, Politics, and Society, 1793–1815*. Oxford, England: Oxford University Press, 1995.

Scheuermann, Mona. "From Mind to Society: *Caleb Williams* as a Psychological Novel." *Dutch Quarterly Review* 7 (1977): 117

Schmitt, Carl. *The Concept of the Political*. Trans. George Schwab. Chicago: University of Chicago Press, 1996.

———. *The Crisis of Parliamentary Democracy*. Trans. Ellen Kennedy. Cambridge, MA: MIT Press, 1992.

Scott, Joan Wallach. "Gender: A Useful Category of Historical Analysis." In *Gender and the Politics of History.* Ed. Joan Scott. New York: Columbia University Press, 1988.

Searle, G. R. *Morality and the Market in Victorian Britain.* Oxford, England: Oxford University Press, 1998.

Sedgwick, Eve Kosofsky. *Between Men: English Literature and Male Homosocial Desire.* New York: Columbia University Press, 1985.

Seigel, Jules P. "Carlyle and Peel: The Prophet's Search for a Heroic Politician and an Unpublished Fragment." *Victorian Studies* 26 (1983): 181–95.

Semmel, Stuart. *Napoleon and the British.* New Haven, CT: Yale University Press, 2004.

Sharpe, Jenny. *Allegories of Empire: The Figure of Woman in the Colonial Text.* Minneapolis: University of Minnesota Press, 1993.

Shaw, Philip. *Waterloo and the Romantic Imagination.* New York: Palgrave, 2002.

Showalter, Elaine. "Charlotte Bronte: Feminine Heroine." In *New Casebooks: Jane Eyre.* Ed. Heather Glen. New York: St. Martin's, 1997.

Simpson, Michael. *Closet Performances: Political Exhibition and Prohibition in the Dramas of Byron and Shelley.* Stanford, CA: Stanford University Press, 1998.

Sinfield, Alan. *The Wilde Century: Effeminacy, Oscar Wilde and the Queer Moment.* New York: Columbia University Press, 1994.

Sinha, Mrinalini. *Colonial Masculinity: The "Manly Englishman" and the Effeminate Bengali in the Late Nineteenth Century.* Manchester, England: Manchester University Press, 1995.

Southam, B. C. *Jane Austen and the Navy.* New York: Hambledon and London, 2000.

Spivak, Gayatri C. "Three Women's Texts and Critique of Imperialism" (1985). *Feminisims: An Anthology of Literary Theory and Criticism.* Ed. Robyn R. Warhol and Diane Price Herndl. New Brunswick, NJ: Rutgers University Press, 1993.

Stedman, Jane W. "Charlotte Brontë and Bewick's *British Birds.*" *The Brontë Sisters: Critical Assessments.* Vol. III. Ed. Eleanor McNees. East Sussex, England: Routledge, 1997.

Stone, Lawrence. *The Family, Sex and Marriage in England, 1500–1800.* New York: Harper & Row, 1977.

Sullivan, Vickie B. *Machiavelli, Hobbes, and the Formation of Liberal Republicanism in England.* Cambridge, England: Cambridge University Press, 2004.

Sulloway, Alison G. *Jane Austen and the Province of Womanhood.* Philadelphia: University of Pennsylvania Press, 1989.

Sussman, Herbert. *Victorian Masculinities: Manhood and Masculine Poetics in Early Victorian Literature and Art.* Cambridge, England: Cambridge University Press, 1995.

Teichgraeber III, Richard F. "Adam Smith and Tradition: *The Wealth of Nations before Malthus*" In *Economy, Polity and Society: British Intellectual History, 1750–1950.* Ed. Stefan Collini, Richard Whatmore, and Brian Young. New York: Oxford University Press, 2000.

Thomas, Joyce. "Women and Capitalism: Oppression or Emancipation? A Review Article." *Comparative Studies in Society and History* 30 (1988): 534–49.

Thompson, James. "Surveillance in William Godwin's *Caleb Williams.*" In *Gothic Fictions: Prohibition/Transgression.* Ed. Kenneth W. Graham. New York: AMS Press, 1989.

Thormahlen, Marianne. *The Brontës and Religion.* Cambridge, England: Cambridge University Press, 1999.

Tosh, John. "What should Historians Do with Masculinity? Reflections on Nineteenth-Century Britain." *History Workshop Journal* 38 (1994): 179–202.

———. "The Old Adam and the New Man: Emerging Themes in the History of English Masculinities, 1750–1850." In *English Masculinities, 1660–1800.* Ed. Tim Hitchcock and Michele Cohen. London: Longman, 1999.

Traister, Bryce. "Academic Viagra: The Rise of American Masculinity Studies." *American Quarterly* 52.2 (2000): 274–304.

Trumpener, Katie. *Bardic Nationalism: The Romantic Novel and the British Empire.* Princeton, NJ: Princeton University Press, 1997.

Vernon, James. *Politics and the People: A Study in English Political Culture, c. 1815–1867.* Cambridge, England: Cambridge University Press, 1993.

Vickery, Amanda. "Historiographical Review: Golden Age to Separate Spheres? A Review of the Categories and Chronology of English Women's History." *Historical Journal* 36 (1993): 383–414.

Wahrman, Dror. *Imagining the Middle Class: The Political Representation of Class in Britain, c. 1780–1840.* Cambridge, England: Cambridge University Press, 1995.

Wang, Orrin. "Disfiguring Monuments: History in Paul de Man's 'Shelley Disfigured' and Percy Bysshe Shelley's 'The Triumph of Life.'" *English Literary History* 58 (1991): 633–55.

Wardle, Ralph M. *Hazlitt.* Lincoln: University of Nebraska Press, 1971.

Watkins, Daniel P. *A Materialist Critique of English Romantic Drama.* Gainesville: University Press of Florida, 1993.

Watson, Nicola J. "Trans-figuring Byronic Identity." *At the Limits of Romanticism: Essays in Cultural, Feminist, and Materialist Criticism.* Ed. Mary A. Favret and Nicola J. Watson. Bloomington: Indiana University Press, 1994.

Wehrs, Donald R. "Rhetoric, History, Rebellion: *Caleb Williams* and the Subversion of Eighteenth-Century Fiction." *Studies in English Literature* 28 (1988): 497–511.

Weintraub, Jeff. "The Theory and Politics of the Public/Private Distinction." In *Public and Private in Theory and Practice.* Ed. Weintraub and Krishan Kumar. Chicago: University of Chicago Press, 1997.

Williams, Carolyn. "Closing the Book: The Intertextual End of *Jane Eyre*" (1989). In *The Brontë Sisters: Critical Assessments.* Vol. III. Ed. Eleanor McNees. East Sussex, England: Routledge, 1997.

Wolfson, Susan. "'A Problem Few Dare Imitate': Sardanapalus and 'Effeminate Character,'" *English Literary History* 58 (1991): 867–902.

Wordsworth, William. "1801 (*I grieved for Buonaparte, with a vain*)." *English Romantic Writers.* Ed. David Perkins. Fort Worth, TX: Harcourt, 1967.

———. *The Convention of Cintra.* In *The Prose Works of William Wordsworth.* Ed. W. J. B. Owen and J. W. Smyser. Vol. III. Oxford England: Oxford University Press, 1974.

———. "Essay Supplementary to the Preface of 1815." In *The Prose Works of William Wordsworth.* Ed. W. J. B. Owen and J. W. Smyser. Vol. III. Oxford, England: Oxford University Press, 1974.

———. "On the Extinction of the Venetian Republic." In *English Romantic Writers.* Ed. David Perkins. New York: Harcourt Brace Jovanovich, 1967.

———. "Preface to *Lyrical Ballads,*" In *The Prose Works of William Wordsworth.* Ed. W. J. B. Owen and J. W. Smyser. Vol. III. Oxford, England: Oxford University Press, 1974.

Žižek, Slavoj. *Enjoy Your Symptom: Jacques Lacan in Hollywood and out.* New York: Routledge, 1992.

———. *The Metastases of Enjoyment: Six Essays on Woman and Enjoyment.* London: Verso, 1994.

———. *The Plague of Fantasies.* London: Verso Press, 1997.

———. *The Sublime Object of Ideology.* London: Verso, 1989.

———. *The Ticklish Subject: The Absent Center of Political Ontology.* London: Verso, 1999.

Zuckert, Michael P. *Natural Rights and the New Republicanism.* Princeton, NJ: Princeton University Press, 1994.

Zupancic, Alenka. *Ethics of the Real: Kant, Lacan.* London: Verso, 2000.

Index

Abrams, M.H. 22
Achilles, 1, 4
Adams, James Eli, 34, 103, 104
apostasy, 54
Armstrong, Nancy, 139, 145–6, 147, 148
aura, 87, 88–9, 105, 107, 109
Austen, Jane, 8, 9, 21, 22, 23, 25, 31, 32, 34–5, 113–36, 138, 148, 151; and the army, 132, 135–6; and commerce, 113; and Darcymania, 121–7, 131; and happiness, 115; and heroes, 121; and liberalism, 130; and male leadership, 113–5, 118, 122, 127–8, 129; and merit, 113, 120, 122–3, 126–7, 128, 130–1; and picturesque, 123–7, 128; and power, 113–6, 120–1, 122, 131; and politics, 114–5; and seductive leaders, 122–3, 131, 132; and uncalculatable desire, 132–5; Works, *Emma*, 136; *Pride and Prejudice*, 113, 114, 115, 116, 120–9, 13 1–6
authenticity, 75
authority, 22, 23, 24, 95, 96, 113, 115
authoritarianism, 7, 12, 14, 16, 18, 33, 34, 95
autonomy, 137

Bainbridge, Simon, 83, 84
Barrel, John, 45, 62–3
Bayly, C.A., 11
Bellamy, Richard, 17
benevolence, 8, 32, 54–6, 60, 63, 67, 70, 71, 146, 168n14

Benjamin, Walter, 105
Bewick, Thomas, 141, 150–1
Bickerstaff, Isaac, 128
Bray, Alan, 7
Britons, 2, 4, 5, 6, 9, 10, 11, 29, 54, 56, 117, 141
Brontë, Charlotte, 8, 9, 22, 25, 31–2, 34, 35, 137–53; and the domestic sphere, 138; and freedom, 137; and Gothic adventure, 137, 38, 141–3, 144–5, 148; and Gothic pleasure, 147–8; and hierarchy, 137; and imperialism, 139–41; and leadership, 137; and marriage, 144; and mastery, 139, 141, 143, 145, 147, 149, 150–1, 153; and politics, 137, 138, 141,143,144–5; and submission, 138, 148, 150; Works, *Jane Eyre*, 137–53; "Preface" to *Jane Eyre*, 151–2
Brougham, Henry, 16
Burke, Edmund, 5, 13, 22, 37, 42–6, 48, 73, 75, 82, 83, 90, 109, 118, 124; Works, *A Philosophical Enquiry into the Origin of Our Ideas of the Sublime and the Beautiful, 83; Reflections on the Revolution in France*, 42, 43, 90
Burrow, J.W., 55, 119, 120
Byron, Lord, 8, 9, 22, 31, 32, 33, 34, 53–70, 71, 77, 86, 93, 113, 148, 151, 169n19, 170n22, l70n25, 171n27, 171n30; as critic of nationalistic manhood, 53–70; and critique of liberal benevolence, 55–60, 61–2; and gender, 67–70; and hero

211